The Wenlock Branch

Wellington to Craven Arms

by
Ken Jones

THE OAKWOOD PRESS

© Ken Jones and Oakwood Press 1998

ISBN 0 85361 500 4

Typeset by Oakwood Graphics.
Repro by Ford Graphics, Ringwood, Hants.
Printed by Alpha Print (Oxford) Ltd, Witney, Oxon.

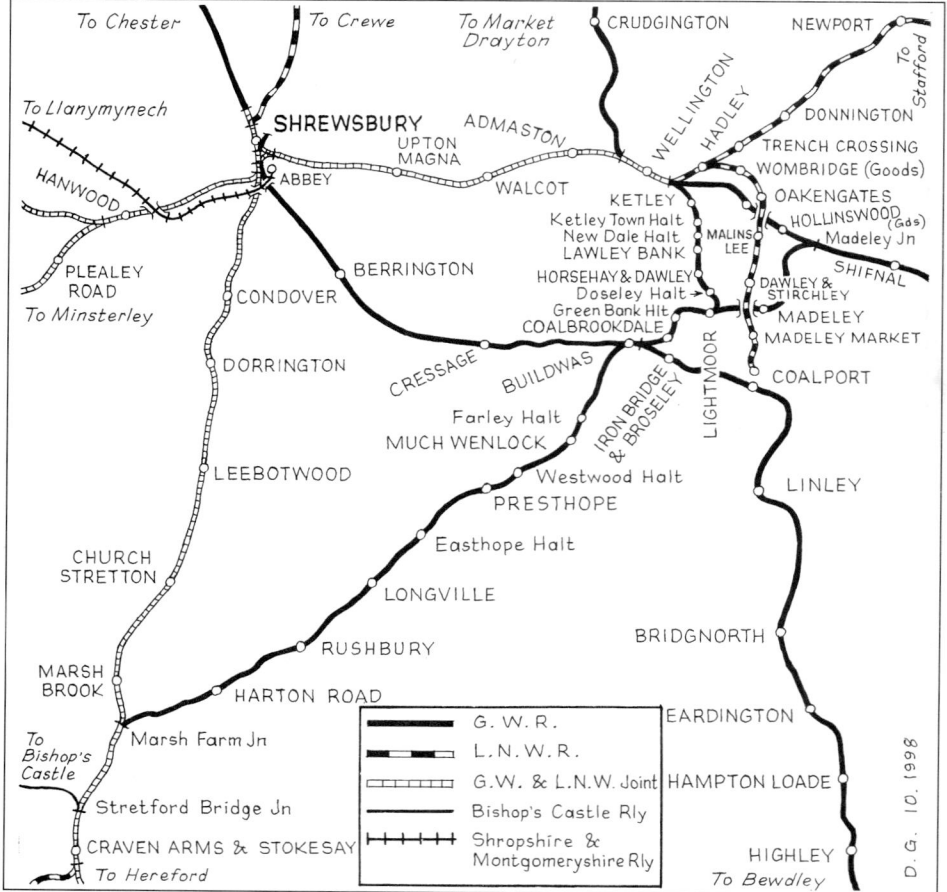

Title page: The 11.20 am Wellington to Much Wenlock train enters the leafy surrounds of Farley Halt headed by '57XX' class 0-6-0PT No. 9639 on 15th June, 1958. *Shropshire Museum Service*

Published by
The Oakwood Press
P.O. Box 13, Usk, Mon., NP5 1YS.

Contents

Alfred Darby (I) (1807-1852) joint manager of the Coalbrookdale Company together with his brother Abraham (IV) from 1827-1851. It was Alfred who walked the tramway route linking Ketley with Coalbrookdale in 1848 with his superintendent of mines Thomas Wilkes, and expressed a wish 'that one day passengers would travel over this route'.

Ironbridge Gorge Museum

Introduction

The Wenlock branch, with its four original constituent companies passed through areas as complex and diverse as its original organisation: from the slag tips and pennystone pit mounds of the East Shropshire coalfield to the wooded crest of Wenlock Edge and Ape Dale. The one central strand however on which the companies focused their attention was the ironworks nestling in the tree-lined Coalbrookdale valley, the success of their venture depending solely on the support which they would receive from the Coalbrookdale Company. It was in this valley in the first decade of the 18th century that the great pioneering discovery of smelting iron with coke, instead of the original charcoal method, took place. This tremendous innovation was brought about by the Quaker ironmaster, Abraham Darby (I), in 1709, who one year earlier took a lease of a derelict furnace at the head of the valley.

The close proximity of ample supplies of coal, ironstone, limestone, and water power, and at the bottom of the valley a navigable river, the Severn, all went to create this remarkable district. From these works there also emerged during the 18th century other great changes such as the first cast-iron wheels, and cast-iron rails, and the first cast-iron bridge which still spans the River Severn in the Ironbridge Gorge. In 1796 Richard Trevithick visited Coalbrookdale, and a number of his experiments in the use of steam power were carried out using castings made in the works.

The rural landscape of the Coalbrookdale valley, shattered by the noise of the furnace and forge, with their flames and smoke belching forth into the sky, attracted writers and artists to witness this great phenomenon.

Arthur Young in his *Tours of England*, writing in 1776, has the following to say of the valley.

> . . . the furnaces, forges, with their vast bellows that give those roaring blasts which makes the whole edifice horribly sublime . . . a winding glen between two immense hills which break into various forms . . . and all thickly covered with wood forming the most beautiful sheets of hanging wood . . . too beautiful to be much in unison with that variety of horrors art as spread at the bottom.

While Coalbrookdale was placed firmly in the industrial spotlight by the visits of various important persons who recorded their memories during the 18th and 19th centuries, other areas within the Coalbrookdale coalfield, later to be served by the Wenlock branch, also played an important role in the industrial development of this country. At Ketley large blast furnaces were opened in 1757 by Abraham Darby (II), and it was here that the first cast-iron aqueduct was made to carry Thomas Telford's Shrewsbury Canal over the River Tern at Longden in 1795. Ketley was also the site of the first inclined plane to be used successfully on a canal in Great Britain; this connected Ketley with the mines in the Oakengates area, and was opened in 1788.

It was at Horsehay in 1755 that Abraham Darby (II) blew in his coke blast furnace [commenced the smelting process], the experiments carried out by his father at Coalbrookdale having now come to a successful conclusion. The smelting of iron with coke had now become firmly established. A second furnace was also constructed on the site in May 1757. It was here that the iron plates for Brunel's SS *Great Britain* were made.

Leaving the Severn Valley the branch climbed through the wooded slopes of Farley Dingle to reach the town of Much Wenlock. This ancient Borough was granted its Charter by Edward IV in 1468, the Charter granting the Borough the right to send an MP to Parliament; in fact until 1885 two members were returned. The Charter also defined the area of jurisdiction of the Borough, this was delineated as the ancient parish of Wenlock which included the extensive estates held by the Cluniac Priory of Wenlock. Up to the Municipal Corporations Act of 1835 Wenlock in terms of acreage was the largest non-county borough in England. Agriculture dominated the economy of the town, but with the industrial activity taking place in the 18th and 19th centuries in the nearby parishes of Madeley and Broseley, the demand for Wenlock limestone increased for iron smelting, giving added impetus to Wenlock as a market town.

Whilst the Darby family dominated the industrial scene of the Coalbrookdale coalfield, one man dominated Victorian Wenlock, and that was the local GP. Dr William Penny Brookes was associated with many projects in Wenlock, but he is best remembered for being one of the founders of the Olympic movement. His dedication to athletics and gymnastics prompted him to form the Wenlock Olympian Society in 1850. In 1865 he was also responsible for founding the National Olympian Association. Baron Pierre de Coubertin visited the Olympic Games at Wenlock in 1890, and this visit no doubt influenced him when he set about the task of organising the modern Olympic Games in Athens in 1896.

Much Wenlock, the gateway to that great escarpment of limestone rock, Wenlock Edge, which the branch line traversed, opened up to the rail traveller a panoramic view of Ape Dale with its picturesque villages and hamlets, with its back drop of the Stretton Hills. This is the landscape which thrilled A.E. Housman, and inspired the verses relating to this area in *A Shropshire Lad*.

The landscape of the Wenlock branch from Ketley to Lightmoor was shaped by industry, the landscape also shaping the lives of the communities within it. The land in this area was owned mainly by absentee landlords, which gave the miners, furnace and brickyard workers in the 18th and 19th centuries the freedom to build their own cottages on the waste land of this loosely administered manorial area. In addition to these 'squatter' cottages, former industrial buildings were turned into domestic dwellings. Travelling along this section of the branch evidence could also be seen of the housing provided by the ironmasters for their work force, with the Coker's Row and Stable Row at Lightmoor and back-to-back houses in the mining community of New Dale.

This industrial framework created a culture dominated by the chapel and the pub. Behind virtually every pit bank was to be found a chapel of every Methodist persuasion, catering not only for the spiritual needs of the community, but also for their weekly leisure activities, such as the sisterhood, the men's own meeting, and the Wesley Guild social evening. In contrast the pub would provide for the pigeon flying club, the quoits alley team, also serving as the headquarters for the many Friendly Societies which operated in the coalfield.

On crossing the River Severn over the Albert Edward Bridge into Buildwas, the Wenlock branch between here and Craven Arms served the agricultural villages and scattered hamlets where the communities were subject to the 'closed village' administration dominated by the squire and the Church. This form of administration tended to give an architectural uniformity to the houses in the villages, which was not to be found in the haphazard house building of the coalfield area.

Until the mid-1890s the farm labourer would attend the annual May hiring fair at Much Wenlock where he would stand in the street waiting to be hired. Upon being hired by the farmer he would be paid his shilling 'honest money', which would bind him in the employ of the farmer for one year. The closed village system required the farmers to give one day's service to the squire, by providing the labour and horses for either timber-hauling on the estate, or the conveyance of coal from the station yard to the Hall. This service continued until the late 1920s.

The branch, in addition to serving the farmer and agricultural labourer, also served the quarry men of Farley and Wenlock Edge; also the men employed in the rural industries of the woodlands adjoining the line such as the charcoal burners, clog makers, and bark peelers.

The settlement of Coalbrookdale was however unique in that it did not fall into either the open or closed village pattern of life, but into a pattern created by Quaker philanthropy. Joseph Fogerty, the Assistant Engineer concerned with the building of the branch from Lightmoor Jn to Marsh Farm Jn, (writing in the late 1850s) states that 'the skilled workmen engaged in the Dale works were a superior class and as a rule were members of some dissenting body whose ministers looked pretty well after them'. This superiority was no doubt brought about by the Quaker ironmasters' concern for the education of their work force. As early as 1764 the Quaker Society allowed Mark Gilpin the use of the upper room over the Meeting House at Coalbrookdale as a school. Further impetus was added to this desire for self help and education in Coalbrookdale with the setting up in 1853 of The Literary and Scientific Institution. In 1859 the Scientific Institution was housed in a fine blue-brick building which also housed a school of art. This Institution was the training ground for the designers of the fine cast bronze work produced by the Coalbrookdale Company. It also produced men like Thomas Parker who founded the Electric Construction Company at Wolverhampton in 1891/1892, he was also responsible for the electrical work on the Liverpool Overhead Railway. Another designer for the Coalbrookdale Company was Cecil Fowler who designed the Coalbrookdale 'Serve All' fire grate which was used extensively by the London County Council.

In addition to the names of the men whose fame extended beyond the Coalbrookdale valley, there were the pattern filers, pattern makers, draftsmen, bronzers, and grate fitters, who, annually in the 1880s and 1890s, would produce some piece of art work and vie against each other for the coveted prize at the Dawley Craft Fair.

These, then, were the communities served by the Wenlock branch, which met their transport needs for both work and leisure from the opening ceremonies, with their parades headed by drum and fife bands, and the firing of cannon, until the dismal last day when locomotive No. 4178 (with wreath attached to its smokebox door) hauled the last train from Much Wenlock to Wellington on Saturday 21st July, 1962. It is the intervening 100 years that this book sets out to record.

The last passenger train, the 7.05 pm from Much Wenlock, on the evening of Saturday 21st July, 1962 hauled by '51XX' class 2-6-2T No. 4178. The notice on its smokebox door indicated that it was 'The Beeching Special' and the wreath below signifies that this was the end. Three locals have come out to pay their last respects. *M. Mensing*

Gother's boatyard on the River Severn at the Bower's Yard, Ironbridge *c.* 1870. It was here that the barges and trows that plied on the river between Ironbridge and Bristol were built and repaired. *Ironbridge Gorge Museum*

The Severn Warehouse on the wharfage at Ironbridge built by the Coalbrookdale Company in 1834 to house the products from its works before being transhipped down the River Severn to Worcester, Gloucester or Bristol. At the time the photograph was taken it was Long & Co.'s Crystal Mineral Water Works. The building today is the Ironbridge Gorge Museum's, Museum of the River. *Ironbridge Gorge Museum*

Chapter One

Early Transport

River

The River Severn was the main artery of the Coalbrookdale coalfield. Before the days of railways, coal from the mines, products from the furnaces and forges, and bricks and tiles made their way to the various wharves on the riverside between Buildwas and Coalport. The products of the coalfield were carried downstream to Worcester, Gloucester and Bristol, and upstream to Shrewsbury and Pool Quay for distribution to the towns of North and Mid-Wales.

Commercial traffic was using the river by the middle of the 13th century, the monks of Buildwas Abbey having obtained the right to load wool on to barges at Cressage, upstream from Buildwas. After the foundation of the Coalbrookdale Company in the early part of the 18th century, they depended on the river for the transportation of their products. From the Ford Goldney Letter Book, covering the period 1732-1736, an insight is given into the problems faced by the company concerning this mode of transport. Richard Ford, writing on 13th July, 1733 states, 'I am obliged to pay 10s. per ton to Gloucester the water being so very low the vessel could carry no more than 5 tons'. Not only was flood or drought on the river a problem facing the company, as we glean from the letter written by Ford to Goldney on 1st July, 1734:

Frank Owen's usage is intolerable and not to be borne with, but his play in excuses that they durst not come in to Bristol for fear of the men on the barge being taken from them by a Man of War lying in the Kings Road in which there may be something, but this can be no excuse for his former neglect. I hope for the future we shall be served better by sending them direct into Bristol.

An article in the *Gentleman's Magazine* in 1756 states:

This river, being justly esteemed the second in Britain, is of great importance on account of its trade, being navigated by vessels of large burden, more than 160 miles from the sea without the assistance of any lock: upwards of 100,000 tons of coals are annually shipped from the collieries about Broseley and Madeley to the towns and cities situate on its banks: also great quantities of grain, pig and bar iron, and earthenwares are constantly exported to Bristol and other places. This traffic is carried on with vessels of two sorts: the lesser kinds are called barges and frigates, being from 40 to 60 feet in length: the trows are larger vessels are from 40 to 80 tons burthen, these have a main and top mast, about 80 feet high, with square sails and mizen masts, and when new and completely rigged are worth about £300.

The barges and trows went downstream with the current, using their sails when possible. In the upstream direction, until the end of the 18th century, they were hauled by gangs of men called 'bow hauliers'. The Revd John Fletcher, who was Vicar of Madeley at this time, describes the work of these men as follows:

How they are bathed in sweat and rain. Fastened to their lines as horses to their traces, wherein do they differ from the laborious brutes? Not in any erect posture of the body, for in the intenseness of their toil, they bend forward, their head is foremost, and their hand upon the ground. If there is any difference it consists in this: horses are indulged with a collar to save their breasts; and these, as if theirs was not worth saving draw without one; the beasts tug in patient silence and mutual harmony; but the men with loud contention and horrible imprecations.

Richard Reynolds of Ketley considered that bow-hauling was not only degrading, but 'a means of harbouring and collecting men of bad character and facilitating a system of plunder injurious to the trade and destructive of the morals of the people engaged in it'. It would appear that at his own expense Reynolds built a horse towing path two miles long between

A Francois Vivares (1709-1780) engraving showing a team of pack-horses carrying coal or ironstone down Lawton's Lane into the wooded valley of Coalbrookdale. Plumes of smoke can be seen rising from the coke hearth and furnaces in the floor of the valley.

Ironbridge Gorge Museum

A James Fittler (1758-1835) engraving of Lincoln Hill and the Coalbrookdale Company's Lode Croft wharf on the River Severn at Ironbridge. Pack-horses are being unloaded with coal which is being stacked, and then loaded into trows prior to transport down river.

Ironbridge Gorge Museum

Coalport and Ironbridge. However, under an Act of 1799, a towing path was authorised between the Meadow Wharf, Coalbrookdale and Bewdley Bridge. In 1809 another Act was passed enabling a further towing path to be laid between the Meadow Wharf, Coalbrookdale, and Mardol and Frankwell Quays at Shrewsbury. By this time the river between Shrewsbury and Gloucester had been linked with a horse towing path, thereby bringing to an end the laborious task of bow-hauling trows and barges on the River Severn.

With the opening of the Severn Valley Railway between Shrewsbury and Worcester in 1862, the demise of river traffic was inevitable. In consequence the last barge left the Severn Warehouse at Ironbridge in the early 1880s for Bristol. Today reminders may still be seen in the Severn Gorge of the economic importance of the river to the industries of the Coalbrookdale coalfield in the 18th and 19th centuries; the remains of the old quay wall and its steps leading down to the river on the wharfage at Ironbridge, the Severn Warehouse built by the Coalbrookdale Company, the Hay inclined plane (1,050 ft long) at Coalport once linking the Shropshire Canal with the river. These industrial monuments are now in the ownership of the Ironbridge Gorge Museum, who are interpreting to the thousands of visitors to this fascinating area the importance the River Severn once held to the coalfield.

Pack-Horse

When Abraham Darby (I) came into the Coalbrookdale Valley in 1708, the coal ironstone and limestone for his furnace would have been brought in by pack-horses with panniers strapped to their backs. Adam Lucock, the Coalbrookdale centenarian talking to John Randall in the early part of the 19th century, tells how teams of pack-horses brought the coal down to the Dale: 'These strings of horses, the first having a bell to tell of their coming, they called the bells "crickers", and it was a pretty sight to see them winding through the upland wood and meadow. Pedlars and pack-horses were the means of locomotion, and the means of news in my day'.

Through the upland wood and meadow to which Lucock refers would have been the 'pack and prime ways' which the strings of pack-horses would have traversed. The responsibility for the maintenance for these prime ways was the Parish; in certain instances, however, an individual landowner could be responsible. This is evidenced by the fact that the Shropshire Quarter Sessions in January 1760 found a person not guilty on indictment for failing to maintain 'a pack and prime way'. Writing of the early 18th century Brian Hindle, in his book *Roads, Tracks and their Interpretation*, states 'that these prime ways were the norm throughout Britain, and were obviously cheaper to maintain than a full width wagon or cart road'. In view of the state of the roads, with the upsurge of industry in the East Shropshire coalfield at the beginning of the 18th century, the use of pack-horses on these prime ways would have been far more efficient than the use of wheeled vehicles on the deep rutted tracks of the so-called roads.

These prime ways were often referred to as 'hollows', tracks with high embankments worn down over the years by continued use of man and animals. One such route, to the north of the Coalbrookdale valley, was the track used in the early days of the iron industry by the smallholders or 'ground colliers' as they were called, who from the drifts or adits in their holding would be supplying the early ironmasters with coal and ironstone. The ore extracted by these smallholders from the Stocking, Burroughs Bank, and Stoney Hill areas, would doubtless have been transported by pack-horse along the well-worn track still known today as the 'Hollow', down the White Hill and Lawton's Lane which led directly on to the Coke Hearth at Coalbrookdale. Each pack-horse bringing coal and ironstone into the furnace at Coalbrookdale would carry in its panniers a load of 3 to 3½ cwt, at a cost of 3s. 6d. per ton.

Whilst the ore was brought into Coalbrookdale by pack-horses owned by the Coalbrookdale Company, there were also private individuals that operated these pack-horse teams. One such individual was William Smith, of Watling Street, Wellington, whose inventory of goods and chattels taken at the time of his death on 4th October, 1659 shows that he had 'nine nags and mares, with packsadles, packcloathes, girths, wonteys, and cords'.

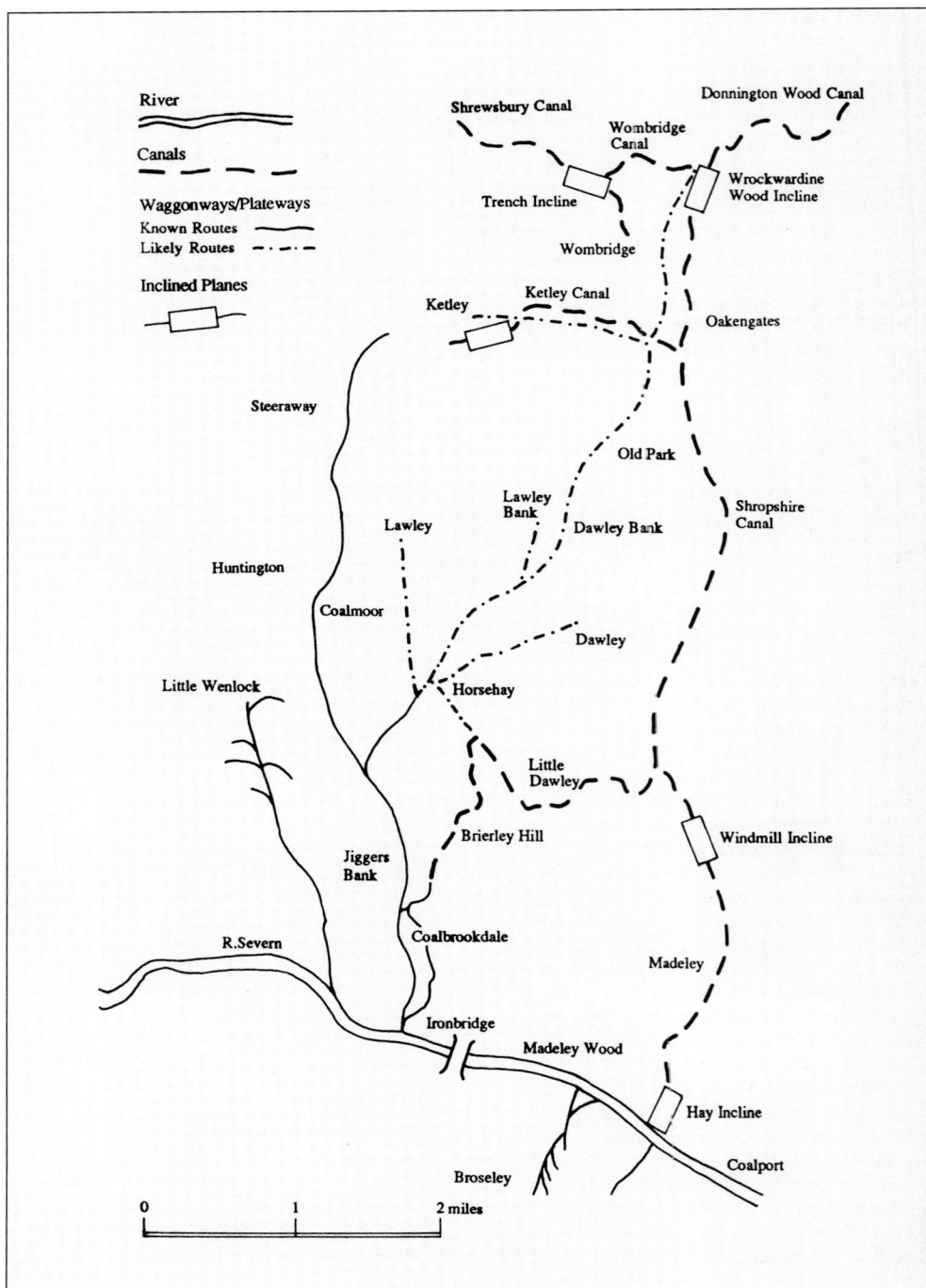

River

Canals

Waggonways/Plateways
Known Routes
Likely Routes

Inclined Planes

Shrewsbury Canal

Donnington Wood Canal

Wombridge Canal

Trench Incline

Wrockwardine Wood Incline

Wombridge

Ketley

Ketley Canal

Oakengates

Steeraway

Old Park

Lawley Bank

Dawley Bank

Shropshire Canal

Lawley

Huntington

Coalmoor

Dawley

Little Wenlock

Horsehay

Little Dawley

Brierley Hill

Windmill Incline

Jiggers Bank

Coalbrookdale

Madeley

R.Severn

Ironbridge

Madeley Wood

Hay Incline

Coalport

Broseley

0   1   2 miles

The Horsehay Company's account book makes a clear distinction between 'wagon loads' and 'horse loads', for the following entry appears for 11th May, 1760: '35 horse loads of bricks from Lightmoor to Horsehay'. These 'horse loads' undoubtedly refer to pack-horses; if this be the case this mode of transport was still being used at this late date despite the introduction of tramways into the area.

Tramways

The Coalbrookdale coalfield was renowned for its great innovations, no more so than in the field of rail transport. A wooden railway is recorded as early as 1605 between the River Severn at the Calcutts, Jackfield and a pit in the Birch Leasow. Dr Barrie Trinder, author of *The Industrial Revolution in Shropshire*, states, 'The existence of a railway at such an early date evidences the advanced technology of the Shropshire coal industry at this time, and one of the first railways for which records survive in Great Britain'. Most of these early wooden railways linked the mines with the wharves on the River Severn. The Coalbrookdale Company's rails in the 1750s would have been wide gauge for wagons holding 50 cwt of coal or more, in accordance with the well established practice of the Tyne-Wear coalfield, the company having dealings with several coal owners in the Tyne-Wear area. In 1780, Abiah Darby, writing about her husband Abraham (II) said, 'He got roads made with sleepers and rails, as they have them in the North of England, that of iron wheels and axle trees for these wagons was I believe my husband's invention'.

In 1749 William Forester began to construct a line about two miles in length from mines in the Coalmoor area in the parish of Little Wenlock to Coalbrookdale, using wooden rails 3½ in. x 4½ in. laid transversely. With the opening up of the Horsehay furnaces by Abraham Darby (II) in 1755 the transport system within the coalfield was to change dramatically. No longer was the area dominated by wagonways linking the mines to the wharves on the river side, but now furnace was linked to furnace, furnace to limestone quarries, and furnace direct to the mines. The main reason which prompted Darby to erect his furnace at Horsehay was to be near the source of coal and ironstone in the Dawley area. Numerous leases were entered into with Robert Aglionby Slaney, the Lord of the Manor of Dawley, for the extraction of coal and ironstone within the Manor. Many of the leases gave Darby the right 'to lay rails and make a railway'.

One of the leases entered into on 20th May, 1756 gave Darby the right to lay a railway from the Lordships of Ketley and Lawley, 16 ft in breadth. The route of this line was later to be followed very closely by the Wellington and Severn Jn Railway, except that, just beyond what was later to be Lawley Bank station, it veered to the west over what was then called Dawley Haye (later known as Heath Hill) into the Frame Rough Leasow, across the Furnace Pool Dam, and Clover Leasow, to a railway already made by the Coalbrookdale Company leading from Horsehay Farm to Coalbrookdale. The lease for the railway from Ketley to Horsehay was for 19 years at a yearly rent of £12 10s. Abraham Darby (II) was to put up fences, wickets and gates between the several pieces of land through which the line would pass. Probably soon after 1759, a branch from the mines in the Lawley and New Works area linked into the Ketley to Horsehay line at New Dale, this link crossing over a two-arch masonry bridge which still survives today at New Dale. The first direct waggonway link between Ketley and Coalbrookdale had been completed.

Returning to the tramway linking Horsehay with Coalbrookdale, this was laid down in 1755 following an agreement between Brooke Forester of Willey, the owner of the land, and Abraham Darby (II) in August of that year, at an annual rental of £4 4s. The agreement set out the goods and minerals which were to be transported. The tramway ran from Horsehay Farm through the Moreton Coppice, on through what was then known as the Spring Field which was at the rear of the present 'Forester's Arms' public house. The bed of the tramway could still be clearly seen in this field until 1989 when the new road works linking Horsehay

A chaldron wagon being lowered down the incline on Jiggers Bank, Coalbrookdale. This was part of the tramway built in 1749-1750 by William Forester linking his mines in little Wenlock with the furnaces at Coalbrookdale. A line was later built by Abraham Darby (II) in 1756 linking his furnaces at Horsehay into Forester's line at Cox's Wood just to the north of the incline shown. The scene depicted is from a print of William Williams' 'Morning view of Coalbrookdale', 1777.

Forester's Waggonway

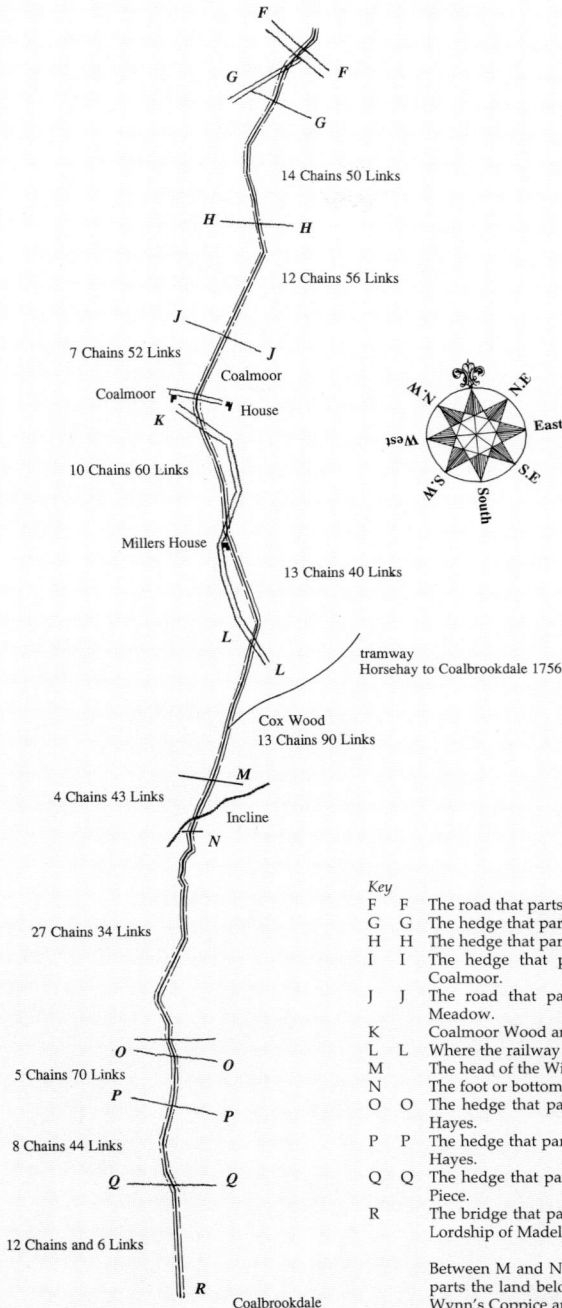

F — F

G — G

14 Chains 50 Links

H — H

12 Chains 56 Links

J — J

7 Chains 52 Links

Coalmoor

Coalmoor — House

K

10 Chains 60 Links

Millers House

13 Chains 40 Links

L

L

tramway
Horsehay to Coalbrookdale 1756

Cox Wood
13 Chains 90 Links

M

4 Chains 43 Links

Incline

N

27 Chains 34 Links

O — O

5 Chains 70 Links

P

P

8 Chains 44 Links

Q — Q

12 Chains and 6 Links

R

Coalbrookdale

Compass directions: N, N.E, East, S.E, South, S.W, West, M.W

Key

F	F	The road that parts the Coalpit Leasow and Coalmoor Wood.
G	G	The hedge that parts Coalmoor Wood and Coalmoor Hay.
H	H	The hedge that parts Coalmoor Hay and Wykes Leasow.
I	I	The hedge that parts Wykes Leasow and Ann Dorrals Coalmoor.
J	J	The road that parts George Garbet's Yard and Miller's Meadow.
K		Coalmoor Wood and Miller's House.
L	L	Where the railway enters Cox's Wood.
M		The head of the Wind.
N		The foot or bottom of the Wind.
O	O	The hedge that parts Wynn's Coppice and the Upper Bald Hayes.
P	P	The hedge that parts the Upper Bald Hayes and Lower Bald Hayes.
Q	Q	The hedge that parts the Lower Bald Hayes and the Clover Piece.
R		The bridge that parts the Lordship of Little Dawley and the Lordship of Madeley

Between M and N a small stream or rivulet of water which parts the land belonging to the Rt Hon. Lord Craven called Wynn's Coppice and the land belonging to the Hon. William Forester Esq. called Cox's Wood.
The railway is 2 miles 2 furlongs and 154 yards in length.

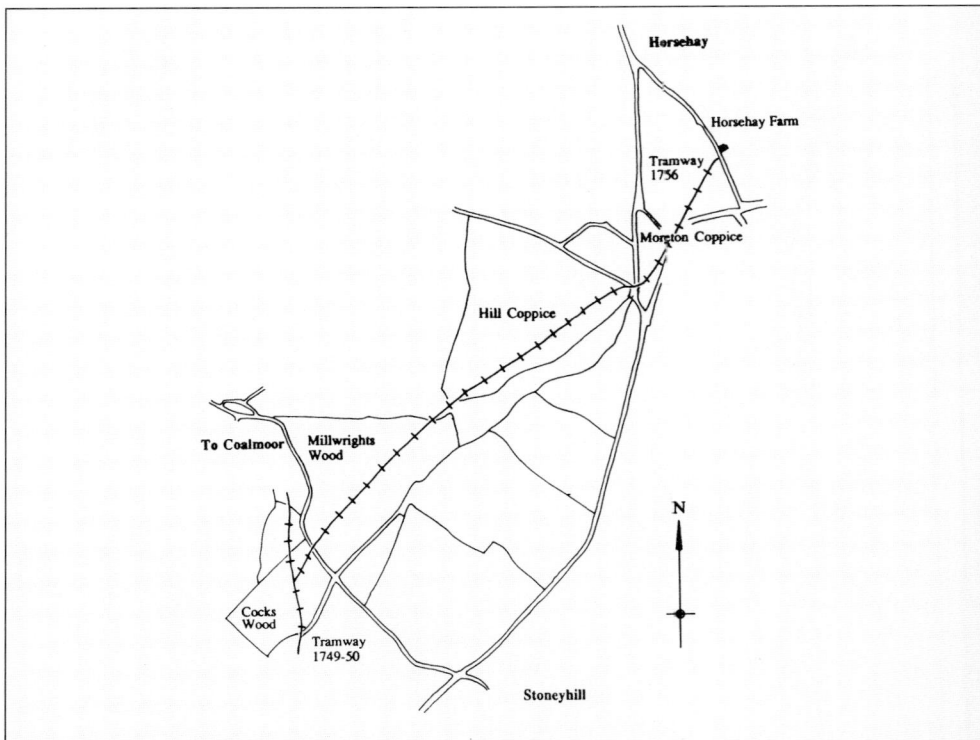

The route of the tramway from Horsehay Farm to Cock's Wood as referred to in the lease of 7th August, 1755 between William Forester and Abraham Darby (II).

The site of the former Deepfield incline which linked the Deepfield Colliery at Little Dawley with the Doseley Wharf on the Coalbrookdale arm of the Shropshire Canal. *Author's Collection*

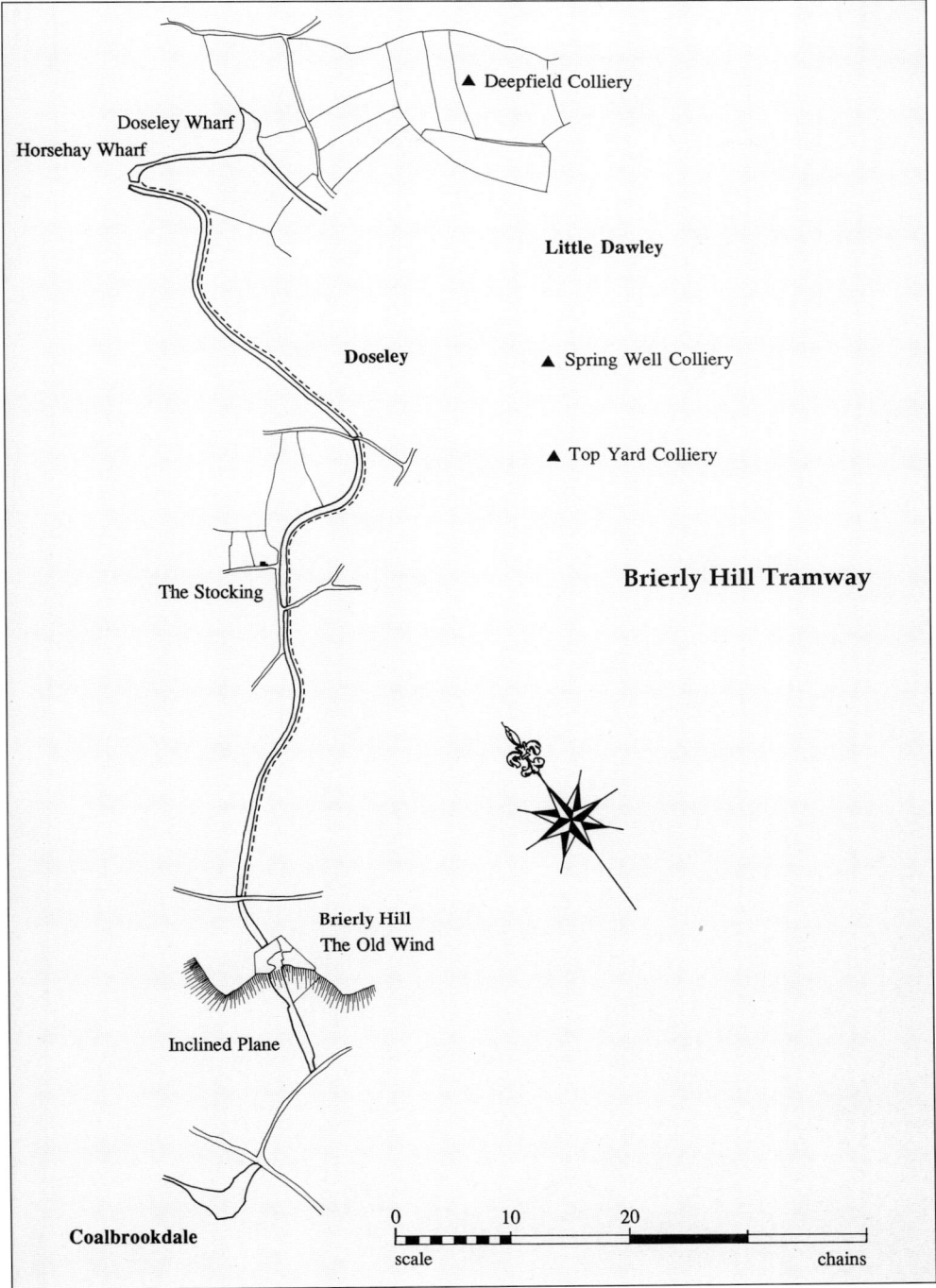

▲ Deepfield Colliery

Doseley Wharf

Horsehay Wharf

Little Dawley

Doseley

▲ Spring Well Colliery

▲ Top Yard Colliery

The Stocking

Brierly Hill Tramway

Brierly Hill
The Old Wind

Inclined Plane

Coalbrookdale

0   10   20

scale   chains

An engraving by W.W. Law *c.* 1850 showing the tramway built in 1756 linking the Coalbrookdale works with the River Severn. In the foreground can be seen the Upper Forge pool, and the lower works. In the centre is the Great Warehouse built in 1839 with its clock tower of 1843.   *Ironbridge Gorge Museum*

Another view of the Coalbrookdale valley showing the jinney rails, part of the lower works and the group of dwellings in the forge. Dominating the scene is Holy Trinity Church built in 1854 and the Coalbrookdale's Company's Literary & Scientific Institute built in 1859. In the foreground is the timber-framed building of 1636 'Rose Cottage', together with the wooden bridge crossing the Coal Brook as it makes its way to the River Severn.

Ironbridge Gorge Museum

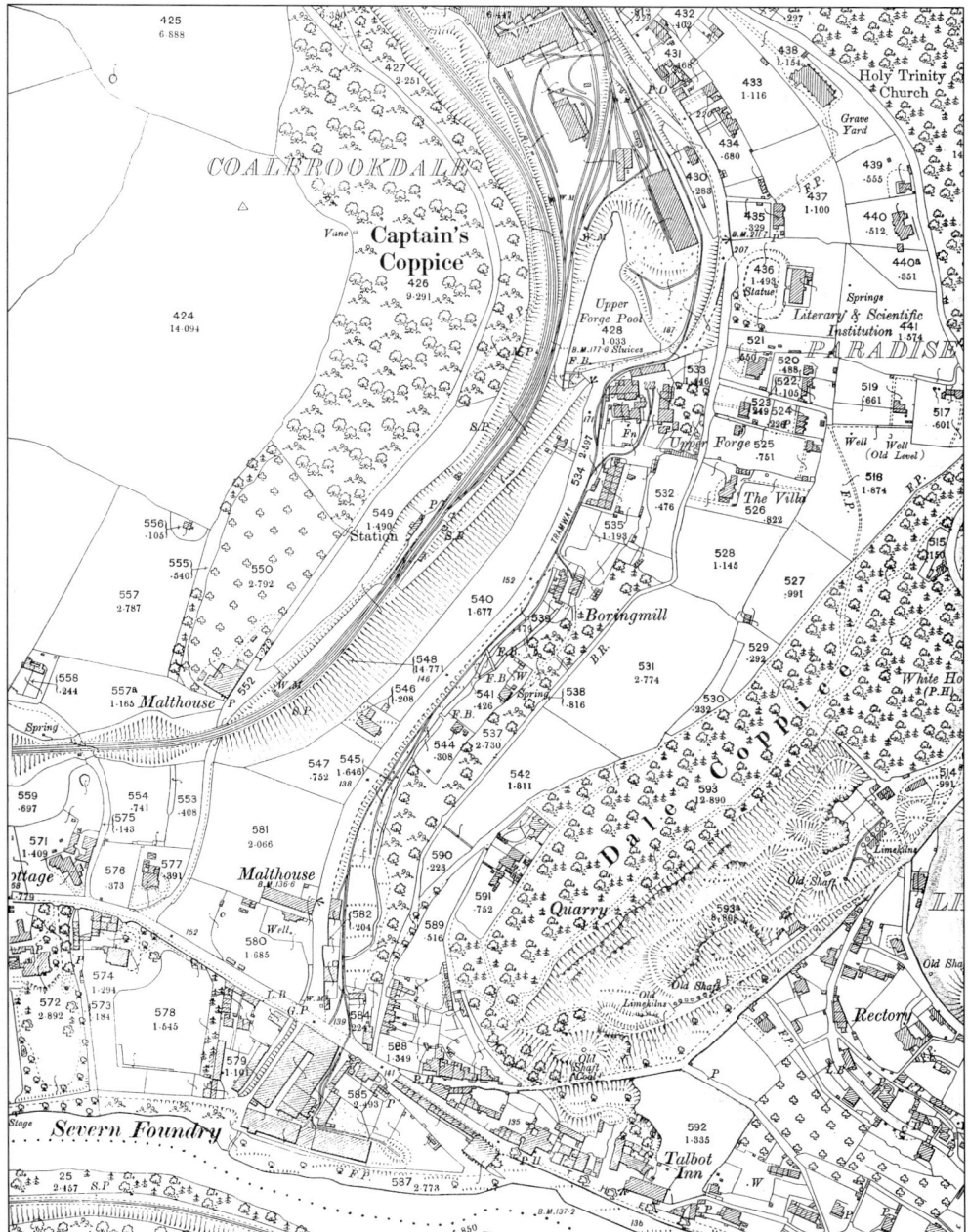

Coalbrookdale showing the tramway system laid in 1756 down the valley from the works to the Severn Warehouse on the riverside. Note also the standard gauge sidings extending from Coalbrookdale station into the Coalbrookdale works.

Reproduced from the 25″, 1882 Ordnance Survey Map

Wellington and Severn Junction Railway

Estimated internal Traffic of the Coalbrookdale Company, between Wellington and the River Severn at Ironbridge

	From Coalbrookdale To				From Horsehay To				From Lightmoor To				From Lawley To			From Dawley To			Totals
	Lawley Tons	Lightmoor Tons	Horsehay Tons	Dawley Tons	Coalbrookdale Tons	Lawley Tons	Lightmoor Tons	Dawley Tons	Coalbrookdale Tons	Horsehay Tons	Lawley Tons	Dawley Tons	Horsehay Tons	Coalbrookdale Tons	Dawley Tons	Lightmoor Tons	Horsehay Tons	Coalbrookdale Tons	Tons
Pig Iron / Raw Iron					500			4500	5000		4000		9500		21500
Castings	10	350	25		500	220							500
Sundries						60							385
Ironstone			5760	5760	4300			2700				3402 23000	280
Limestone &c		5120					250	50				28402
Coal & Coke					50			200	2100	6500	9700 60000	16570
Bricks	112				150			626				11500
Sundries &c	752	1954	46	679								400
Sand	32											230
Clay & Fire Bricks												3635
Timber												1444
												1500
Total	112	7628	5831	6009	5480	60	370	180	7650	5455		676	10500	13752 124500	

£10060 · | £6010 · | £6010 · | £4457 · | £11050 · | £191652 · | £188908 ·

Terminal Traffic ———— 28773
Total Traffic of Coalbrookdale Co. £211652

An estimate compiled by the Wellington & Severn Junction Railway of the internal traffic of the Coalbrookdale Company between its various furnaces, this estimate was compiled in 1856.

Author's Collection

with the Ironbridge by-pass cut through it. The tramway continued on over the Coalmoor Road through Cox's Wood, at which point it joined an exisiting tramway laid in 1749 linking the Forester mines in the Coalmoor area with the furnaces at Coalbrookdale (the route of this 1749 tramway is shown on p. 15). After leaving Cox's Wood, the tramway descended by an inclined plane into the Loamhole Dingle, through the Bald Hayes and Clover Piece Fields, and on to the bridge at the bottom of the Jiggers Bank. This bridge was over a stream which flowed from the New pool at Coalbrookdale into the Upper Furnace pool. This then brought the line directly on to the Coke Hearth at Coalbrookdale.

A map of 1786 shows the course of an old tramway running down the eastern side of the Dale Valley which branched off the main tramway of 1756 at the pool tail of the Lower Forge pool, running to the east of the Boring Mill pool and the old Forge buildings to an old pit shaft.

A further major step forward was achieved by the Coalbrookdale Company in 1767 when it produced the first cast-iron rail, and by 1785 Richard Reynolds and his partners claimed that the company had over 20 miles of iron railway.

Hannah Mary Rathbone the granddaughter of Richard Reynolds writing in 1852 said:

> For the conveyance of iron to different parts of the works, and to the River Severn, wooden rails had been in use, which from the great weight carried upon them, were not only soon worn out, but were liable to give way and break occasioning loss of time and interruption to business, and great expense in repairing them. It occurred to him that the inconveniences would be obviated by the use of cast iron. He tried it at first with great caution, but found it to answer well, that soon all their railways were made with iron. He did not attempt to secure by patent the advantage of this invention, and the use of cast iron in the construction of railways was afterwards generally adopted.

Various horse-drawn tramway links were made from the Coalbrookdale branch of the Shropshire Canal to the nearby mines and iron works. The canal branch ran from Southall Bank, just south of Dawley and ended at Brierly Hill, above Coalbrookdale. The Coalbrookdale Company built two vertical shafts in the hill 120 ft deep and 10 ft wide, down which coal and ironstone, two tons at a time, was lowered in crates from the canal boats to waggons standing on a tram road in the tunnel below. In the reverse direction limestone was brought up from the Severn Wharf for use in the Horsehay furnaces. The branch canal was opened by 4th October, 1792, for it was minuted by the Shropshire Canal Company that 'they were unwilling to take over the shafts and tunnel from the Coalbrookdale Company, but they agreed to the company charging them a toll'. The original intention was to continue the canal along the Coalbrookdale valley, and to end with an incline on Lincoln Hill above the river at Ironbridge; this, however, did not materialise, and along the proposed line of the canal a tramway was laid which was known as the Lincoln Hill rails.

Following the opening of the canal a tramway was built down the Horsehay Dingle linking the Horsehay furnaces with the canal at Horsehay Wharf. The *Coalbrookdale Settling Journal* of 1798 shows that the cost of carrying coals from Horsehay Wharf to the Severn for four months during that year amounted to £41 10s. 11d., and for the same period the cost of carrying limestone from the Severn to Horsehay Wharf amounted to £15 2s. 0d. For 10 months during that year the Shropshire Canal Company was paid a tonnage toll of £2 13s. 6d.

The tunnel and shaft system at Brierly Hill did not operate for long, for Telford writing in Plymley's *Agriculture of Shropshire* in 1803, states:

> This method not having found to answer so well as the inclined planes, it has been left off for some time, and there is now a small inclined plane erected in its place. On this inclined plane (there being no steam engine attached to it) the descending crate does not bring up a crate with so large a quantity as when the perpendicular machine was employed, but there is more business done in the same time, by means of the inclined plane, and with a smaller proportion of manual labour.

The Coalbrookdale branch of the Shropshire Canal had only a relatively short life. In 1796 the Coalbrookdale Company purchased additional land at Brierly Hill, and in October 1800 it

The Coalbrookdale Company's locomotive No. 5 built by the company in 1865, it continued to work as a shunting engine around the works up to 1930 when it was sold to the Victoria Coal Co. at Wellington. It was then sold to the Netherseal Colliery, Derbyshire in 1934. Later that year it was sold to Bardon Hill Quarry in Leicestershire. It finally returned to Coalbrookdale in 1959 after being purchased by the then Allied Ironfounders as an exhibit in their new museum at Coalbrookdale. This posed photograph shows both Coalbrookdale Co. and GWR staff, the railway goods checker and shunter being easily identifiable by their uniform caps and brass-buttoned waistcoats.   *Ironbridge Gorge Museum*

A variety of tramway or jinny trucks used by the Coalbrookdale Company to convey coal, ironstone, limestone bricks and tiles between its mines, brickyards and furnaces.
                                        Ironbridge Gorge Museum

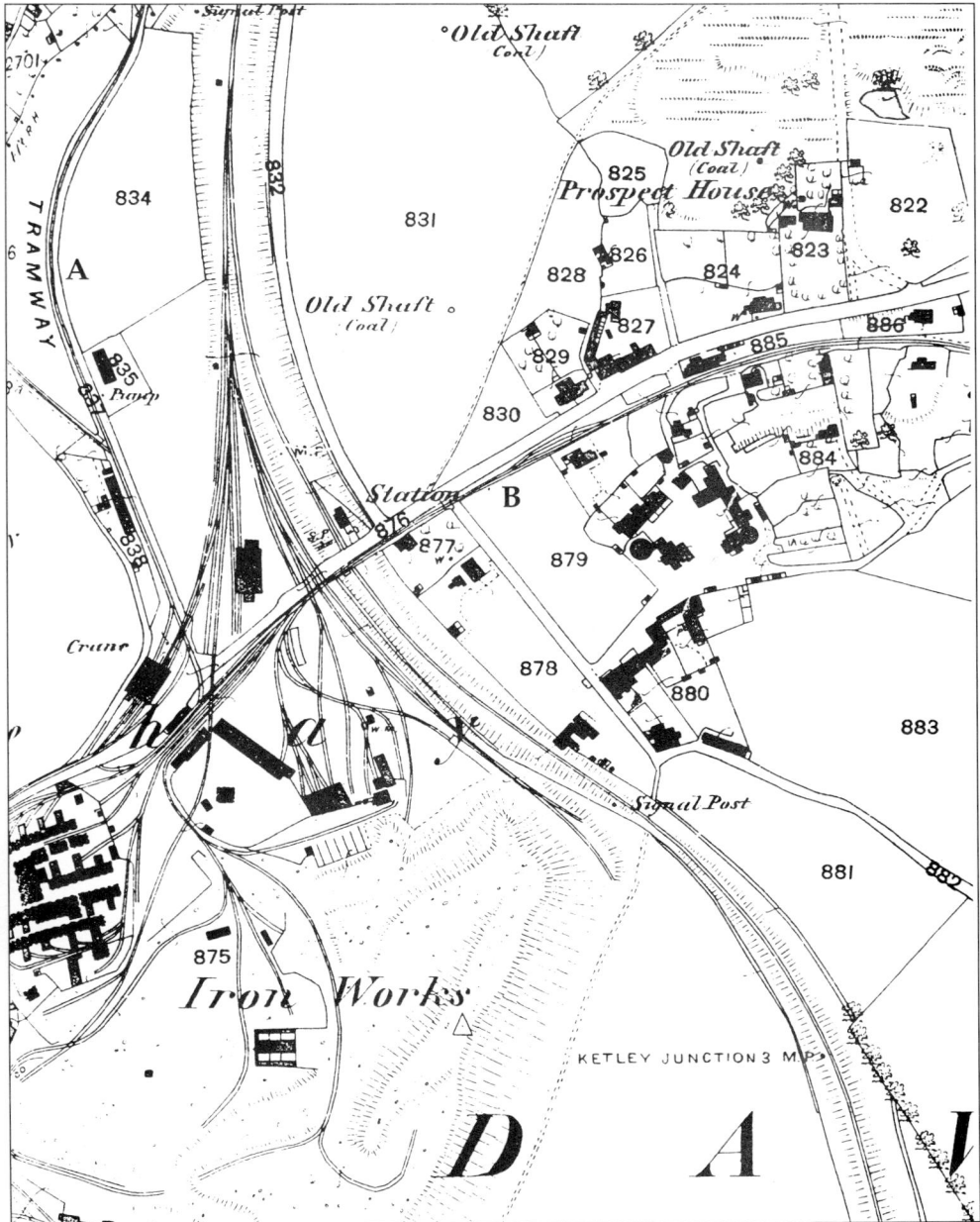

The tramway system around Horsehay. The point marked 'A' is part of the tramway which linked Ketley and mines in the Lawley area with the former Horsehay furnaces, and 'B' is the tramway which once linked the furnaces at Horsehay with the Dawley Castle furnaces. Horsehay & Dawley station on the Wenlock branch can also be clearly seen.

Reproduced from the 25", 1882 Ordnance Survey Map

A tramway bridge at New Dale between Ketley and Lawley Bank used to convey coal and ironstone from mines in the Lawley area to the Ketley furnaces.   *Author's Collection*

Bed of the tramway at Woodside Coalbrookdale, built by the Coalbrookdale Co. This was the horse-drawn tramway built in 1810 to link the Coalbrookdale's Co.'s works with the Lightmoor and Dawley Castle furnaces.   *Author's Collection*

The trackbed on a high embankment between Lightmoor and Dawley Castle furnaces just south of Dawley Parva Crossing. This track was used prior to the opening of the Wellington & Severn Junction Railway in May 1859; following the opening the route of the tramway was diverted, due to the fact that it crossed the branch line on the level, it was re-routed under the line between this spot and Lightmoor Junction. *Author's Collection*

An early photograph showing limestone being transported on the jinney trucks on the tramway at the passing point by the side of the New pool at Coalbrookdale. The limestone was being transported to either Lightmoor or Dawley Castle furnaces. *Ironbridge Gorge Museum*

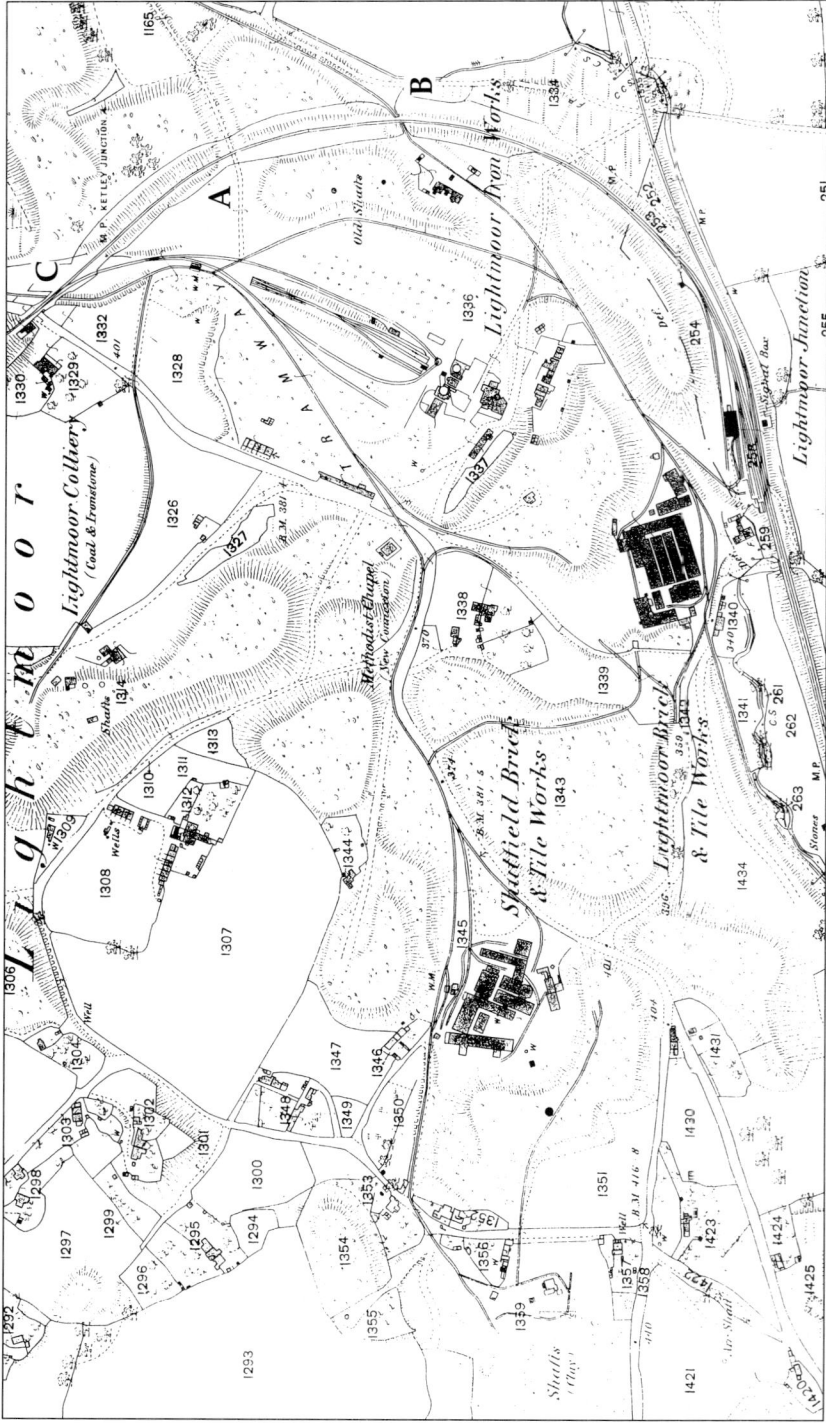

The tramway system around Lightmoor linking the ironworks with the Lightmoor and Shutfield brick and tile works, and the various mines in the area. 'A' denotes the point at which the tramway linking Dawley Castle furnaces crossed the Wellington & Severn Junction Railway on the level. This was later diverted (see 'B') following the report of the Board of Trade Inspector. The point marked 'C' was the former Lightmoor Road sidings operated by Dawley Parva Crossing ground frame. The Madeley branch converged from the east to make a junction with the Wenlock branch at Lightmoor Junction. A station, Lightmoor Platform was sited just to the west of the junction in 1907. Note also that Lightmoor signal box was at this time situated on the Madeley branch.

Reproduced from the 25", 1883 Ordnance Survey Map

was permitted by the canal company to construct a railway along the towing path from Horsehay Wharf to Brierly Hill, on condition that it would pay a toll of 1*d*. per ton for goods carried along the railway. By August 1801 the railway had been completed at a total cost of £1,496 16*s*. 5*d*. This new line of railway along the canal towing path undoubtedly replaced the Horsehay to Coalbrookdale railway opened in 1756. Also by August 1801, the rails along Lincoln Hill were being removed; doubtless the Coalbrookdale Company, on the opening of the Brierly Hill inclined plane, linked the rails at the bottom of the incline with the existing tramway system down the Coalbrookdale valley to the Load Croft Wharf on the side of the river.

The first waggoner to bring coal down the Horsehay rails (or Jinney) was Jonah Jones in August 1801, for which he was paid the sum of £1 18*s*. 0*d*. From the Horsehay Wharf to Brierly Hill the coal was being 'jinneyed' by Francis Green. The Coalbrookdale Company's teams of horses for the period 12th November, 1801 to 10th December 1801 had drawn 1,198 tons of coal down the Horsehay Jinney to the wharf on the canal. These teams were stabled at the company's Horsehay farm. The tub boats were still being used on the canal in 1802, for we find that coal from Dawley was being loaded on to the boats at Horsehay Wharf for Severn sale.

In 1803 there is first mention of the Doseley Wharf on the canal. This wharf was put in to serve the newly opened Coalbrookdale Company's Deepfield Colliery which had been sunk to the south of the canal on the boundary between the Manor of Dawley and the Manor of Dawley Parva. The Coalbrookdale Company in this same year supplied two chains for use on the Deepfield incline at a cost of £22 14*s*. 2*d*., from the colliery the line of the tramway came across the Pool fields down the Deepfield incline, the remains of which may still be seen today, across Sandy Bank to the wharf at Doseley.

The tramway along the canal was fully operational by 1803 for the Coalbrookdale Company's *Settling Journal* shows that John Hamlett was paid £50 for overlooking the railwaymen. The distance from Doseley Wharf to Brierly Hill was slightly longer than from the Horsehay Wharf, for the tonnage paid to the Shropshire Canal Company from the Doseley Wharf was 1¼*d*., while from the Horsehay Wharf it was only 1*d*.

In 1804 the Coalbrookdale Company charged the Horsehay Company the sum of £1,806 18*s*. 7*d*. for laying rails from the Castle pit, which had recently been sunk, to Horsehay. This was the line which came across the Park Fields in the Manor of Dawley, across the top of Pool Hill road and the Lower Brandlee, on to the Horsehay to Dawley road, and into the furnaces. Included in the cost of building this line was the cost of laying a branch line to connect with the existing Deepfield Colliery line, thereby giving the Castle mine direct access to the Doseley Wharf. The great mound of pennystone clay which today dominates the area to the south of Dawley Church was the site of the Castle pit.

For the period July 1806 to July 1807 the tonnage of goods carried from the Doseley Wharf to Brierly Hill amounted to 35,742 tons. For the same period only 4,801 tons was carried from Horsehay Wharf, the reason for this difference no doubt being the amount of coal that was being carried along the tramway from the Castle and Deepfield pits to Doseley Wharf. The rails from the bottom of the incline at Brierly Hill along Lincoln Hill to the incline above the Severn had been removed by 1806, and were consigned to the Horsehay furnaces.

In addition to the Coalbrookdale Company's team of horses hauling along the tramway from Doseley and Horsehay Wharves, teams were also operated by Mary Maching of Horsehay Farm, and George Fletcher of the Croppins Farm, Stoney Hill.

In June 1810 the Coalbrookdale Company agreed that due to the increase in demand for its goods, the Upper Furnace, which had ceased to operate in 1806, should be brought into blast again. It was also agreed that it should ascertain the least expensive mode of conveying coal from Dawley to the Dale. On 10th July, 1810 the furnace had been in blast for two weeks, and it was agreed by the company that a railway linking the mines and the newly opened Castle furnaces with the Dale should be made, as soon as agreement could be reached with the owners of the land over which the proposed railway would pass. The railway would be laid up the south side of the Lightmoor valley, past the New pool through the coppices belonging

The narrow gauge tramway or 'jinney rails' which linked the Lightmoor tileworks with the Shutfield tileworks on the Ridges at Lightmoor. *Author's Collection*

The Coalbrookdale Company's tramway system at Lightmoor with its brick and tile works in the background. The line veering to the left is to the tile shed at Lightmoor Junction. From the state of the rails it would appear that derailments were not uncommon.

Ironbridge Gorge Museum

The tile shed at Lightmoor Junction sidings *c.* 1928, showing the jinney trucks alongside the loading bay with the Coalbrookdale Company's workmen and the GWR yard shunter taking their ease, with two company horses which were stabled at Lightmoor. The straw in the cart was not for stable use, but for packing tiles in the railway wagons. *Ironbridge Gorge Museum*

The Coalbrookdale Company's stables at Lightmoor. Horses stabled here hauled the jinney trucks between Lightmoor and Coalbrookdale. To the left of the stables is Lightmoor Methodist New Connexion Chapel. In the foreground is the Lightmoor furnace pool.

Ironbridge Gorge Museum

William Boycott and his wife Sarah seen outside their cottage at the Dell Hole, Lightmoor. William was the last waggoner to work on the tramway down the Lightmoor Dingle linking the Lightmoor and Shutfield brick and tile works with the foundry in Coalbrookdale. *Fred Briscoe*

to Richard Reynolds, and over land in Lightmoor belonging to the Earl of Craven, in the occupation of the Lightmoor Furnace Company. The railway then continued on through the Brick Kiln Leasow, the Five Butts, and The Yards to Wheatcroft Leasow. At this point it joined the tow path of the Coalbrookdale arm of the Shropshire Canal, near a wooden bridge over which the lane from Little Dawley to the Aqueduct ran. The line then continued along the tow path to the recently opened Castle furnaces. In addition to the line linking Coalbrookdale with the Castle furnaces, the line was also extended into land near the canal side between the Castle wharf and the Aqueduct where the Coalbrookdale Company was sinking a shaft for the extraction of clod coal. The line was completed and opened for traffic by 22nd April, 1811.

The later Wellington & Severn Jn Railway (Wgton & SJR) crossed the tramway on the level, just below the Dawley Parva crossing. The Board of Trade Inspector would not allow a passenger-carrying line to be crossed on the level by a tramway, in consequence, before giving his consent for the opening of the Wgton & SJR in May 1859, an embankment and a bridge had to be constructed 300 yards south of the crossing point, thereby diverting the tramway in front of the old Coker's Row in Lightmoor.

Following the closure of the Dawley Castle and Lightmoor furnaces in 1883, the tramway between these furnaces also closed. The section between Lightmoor and Coalbrookdale continued to operate until the late 1920s. By 1930 the only part of the tramway still operating was between the Lightmoor and Shutfield tile works. The stabling at Lightmoor built by the Coalbrookdale Company in 1811 was by then reduced to two shire horses, and a pit pony which was used in the drift mine on the Ridges.

The scene at the Lightmoor stables one Saturday morning in October 1932 was one of great sadness, for William Boycott, the last waggoner for the Coalbrookdale Company, was feeding his grey shire horse 'Prince' for the last time. Not only was 'Prince' retiring but so was William, after spending over 60 years in the employ of the Coalbrookdale Company, most of which had been spent working on the jinney rails between Lightmoor and Coalbrookdale. That morning in October 1932 there came to an end an era of a transport system which had been the life blood of the Coalbrookdale coalfield.

Former trackbed of the tramway from Lightmoor to Dawley Castle showing the point at which it crossed the trackbed of the Wellington & Severn Junction Railway on the level just south of Dawley Parva Crossing. *Author's Collection*

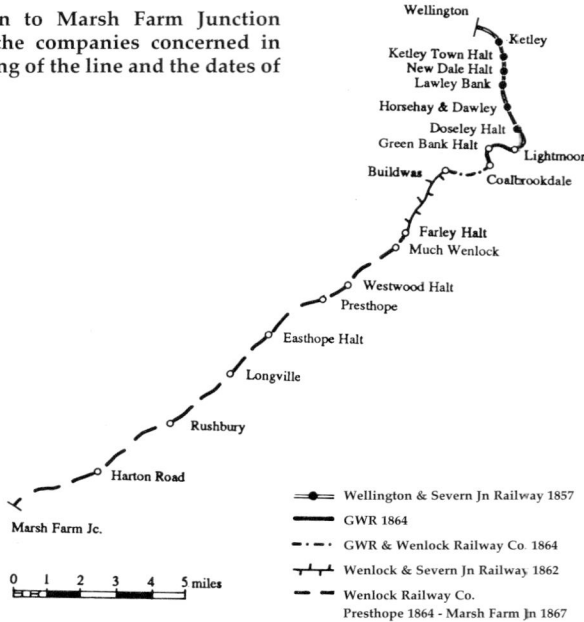

Wellington to Marsh Farm Junction showing the companies concerned in the building of the line and the dates of opening.

Wellington
Ketley
Ketley Town Halt
New Dale Halt
Lawley Bank
Horsehay & Dawley
Doseley Halt
Green Bank Halt
Lightmoor
Buildwas
Coalbrookdale
Farley Halt
Much Wenlock
Westwood Halt
Presthope
Easthope Halt
Longville
Rushbury
Harton Road
Marsh Farm Jc.

	Wellington & Severn Jn Railway 1857
	GWR 1864
	GWR & Wenlock Railway Co. 1864
	Wenlock & Severn Jn Railway 1862
	Wenlock Railway Co. Presthope 1864 - Marsh Farm Jn 1867

0 1 2 3 4 5 miles

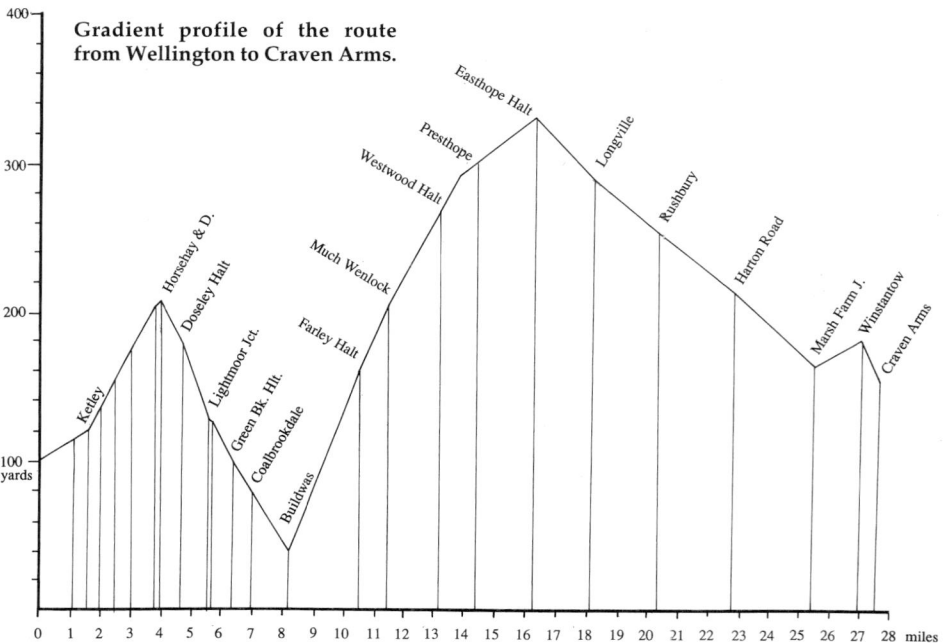

Gradient profile of the route from Wellington to Craven Arms.

400
300
200
100 yards

Ketley
Horsehay & D.
Doseley Halt
Lightmoor Jct.
Green Bk. Hlt.
Coalbrookdale
Buildwas
Farley Halt
Much Wenlock
Westwood Halt
Presthope
Easthope Halt
Longville
Rushbury
Harton Road
Marsh Farm J.
Winstanstow
Craven Arms

0 1 2 3 4 5 6 7 8 9 10 11 12 13 14 15 16 17 18 19 20 21 22 23 24 25 26 27 28 miles

Chapter Two

Building the Line

Wellington & Severn Jn Railway (Ketley Jn to Lightmoor)

Despite the fact that the Coalbrookdale Company introduced the cast-iron rail into the Coalbrookdale Valley in 1767, it was to be nearly 100 years before the company was to experience the benefit of the standard gauge railway. The Railway Mania had very little impact on the Coalbrookdale Company, evidenced by the fact that it built the Severn Warehouse on the side of the river at Ironbridge in the early 1830s still considering the river as its main means of transportation. Linking Shrewsbury to the Midlands by railway was very much in the minds of many business people over the ensuing years. A railway had been projected in the 1830s from Birmingham, through Dudley and Wolverhampton, to Shrewsbury, but this never materialised. There is no evidence to suggest that the Coalbrookdale Company expressed any interest in seeing such a rail link established.

It was not until 1848 that Alfred Darby (I), no doubt influenced by the Shrewsbury & Birmingham Railway (S&B) project then coming into fruition (from Shrewsbury to Wolverhampton, with a branch to Coalbrookdale), walked over a route connecting Ketley with Coalbrookdale. He was accompanied by his superintendent of mines, Thomas Wilkes, and they followed the lines of the existing tramways that linked Ketley, Horsehay, and Lightmoor with Coalbrookdale. As they did so Darby expressed a wish that one day passengers would also be conveyed over this route. Alfred Darby (I) died in 1852, and following his death the Coalbrookdale Company entered into an agreement with John Dickson, of the Shropshire Works, Wellington, to construct a line from Ketley to the turnpike road at Coalbrookdale (to the bottom of Jiggers Bank at the north end of the Coalbrookdale valley) at a cost of £30,000. This was to be an extension of an existing branch built by John Dickson as a private venture, linking the Shrewsbury & Birmingham Railway, at its Waterloo Sidings (Wellington), with Ketley furnaces. The branch's sidings were 250 yds north of what was later to become Ketley Junction. This branch opened for traffic in February 1851.

Following the agreement with Dickson in October 1852, the Coalbrookdale Company requested running powers from Waterloo Sidings into Wellington. This was promptly rejected by the Shrewsbury & Birmingham Directors, but within three weeks they changed their minds, upon learning that the Shropshire Union Railway (SUR) had given notice of its intention to apply for powers to build a railway from Wellington to Coalbrookdale. In all probability the Shrewsbury & Birmingham's Directors suspected the Coalbrookdale Company would abandon its scheme and support the Shropshire Union.

As events turned out the Coalbrookdale Company did not support the Shropshire Union scheme, neither did it proceed with the agreement entered into with John Dickson for building the line from Ketley to Coalbrookdale. It was quite evident that it was not prepared to commit itself to the capital outlay of £30,000, even though it was still anxious that a rail link should be made with Coalbrookdale and the S&B line.

Following the likely intervention of the Shropshire Union Railway into the East Shropshire coalfield, the relationship between the Coalbrookdale Company and the S&B greatly improved, even to the extent of the latter offering technical assistance to the Coalbrookdale Company for the laying of its proposed line.

In order to get around the problem of having to commit itself to heavy capital outlay for the building of the line, the Coalbrookdale Company was instrumental in setting up the Wgton&SJR. On 30th November, 1852 maps and plans were deposited with the Clerk of the Peace at the Shirehall, Shrewsbury for the making of a railway from Wellington to Coalbrookdale, with an extension to Broseley, and for running powers over the S&B. The line was to commence with a double junction with the S&B near Ketley in the parish of

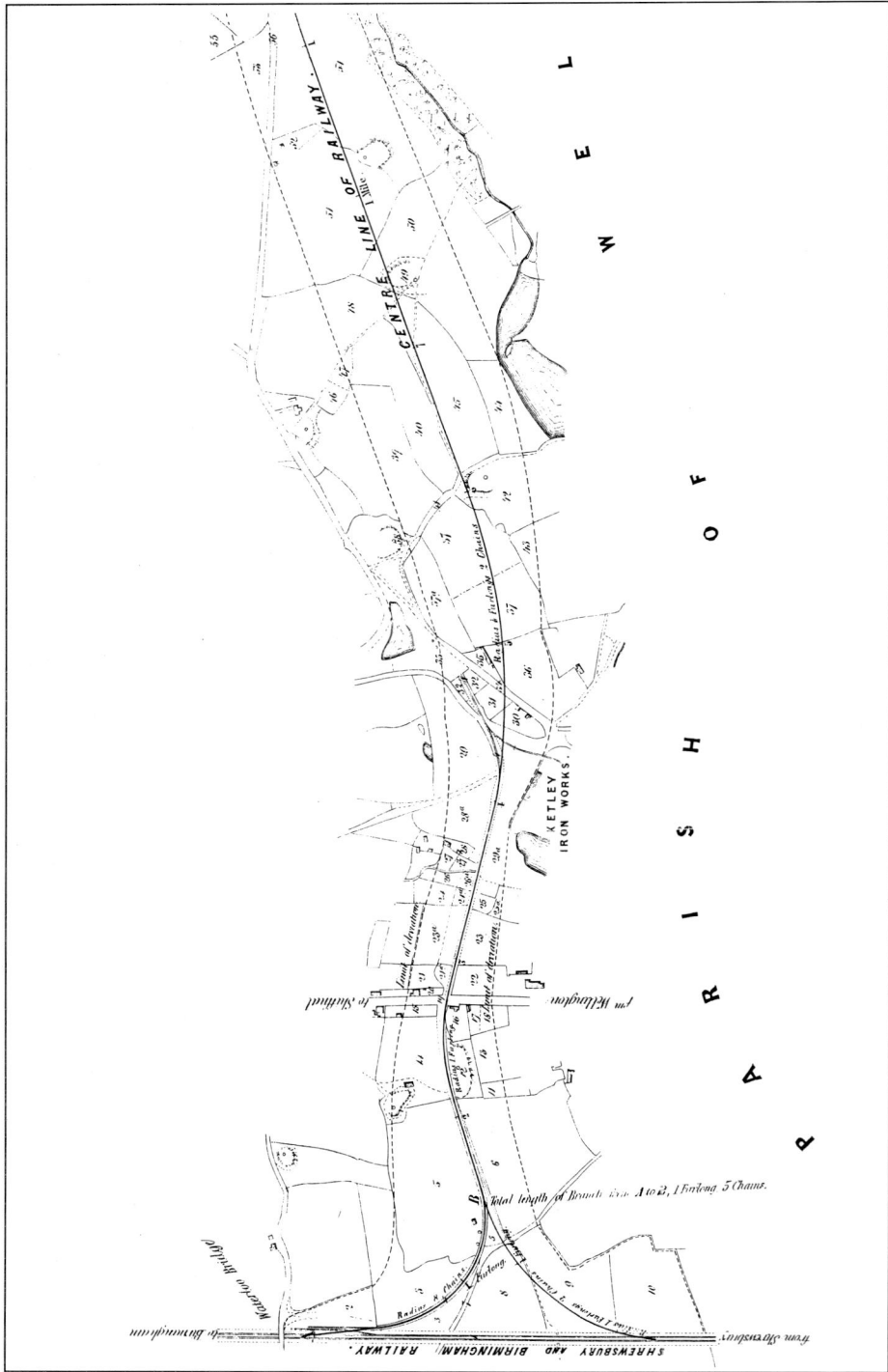

Map showing the route of John Dickson's private railway of 1851 linking the Shrewsbury & Birmingham Railway's Waterloo Sidings with the Ketley ironworks. Just south of the line can be seen the route of the branch as built by the Wellington & Severn Junction Railway.

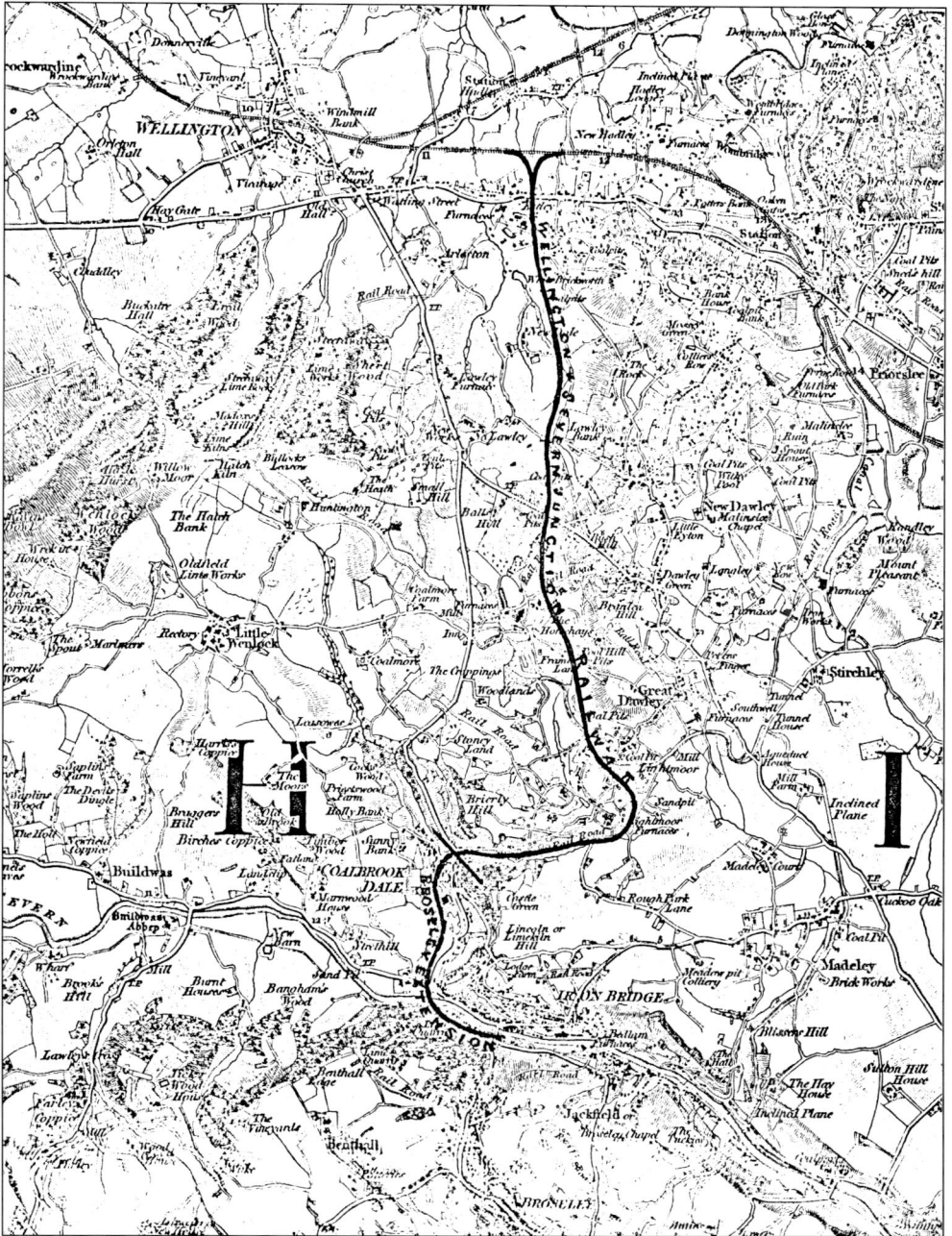

Ordnance Survey map of 1833 with the route of the Wellington & Severn Junction Railway superimposed, as submitted by John Barber of Wellington to the Clerk of the Peace at the Shirehall, Shrewsbury on 30th November, 1852.

Wellington station shortly after opening in 1849. Note the Shrewsbury & Birmingham Railway goods shed on the left, this shed was purchased in 1867 by the GWR from the LNWR&GW Joint Committee and was utilised as its engine shed. Note also to the right of the shed the pump house and water tank which remained in that position until the demise of steam on the line.

Ironbridge Gorge Museum

Wellington, terminating near the ironworks of the Coalbrookdale Company. A second line was to commence with a junction near the Coalbrookdale Ironworks, pass over the River Severn into the parish of Benthall, and terminate near to the tollgate on the south side of the Iron Bridge. The plans were submitted by Robert D. Newill, solicitor, of Wellington, who eventually was to become the first Secretary of the company. In June 1853, a Bill was submitted to Parliament for the building of the line, but this was immediately opposed by the Shropshire Union Railways & Canal Company (SUR&CC), and the Shropshire Canal Company (SCC) who had already made known their intention of building a line from Wellington to Coalbrookdale.

Evidence was taken before a House of Lords' Select Committee on 5th August, 1853. The Parliamentary Agents, Cameron and Martin, appeared as agents for the Bill, neither agents nor solicitors appearing in support of the petition submitted by the SUR&CC or the SCC. Evidence in support of the Bill was given by Charles Crookes, who was at this time the manager of the Coalbrookdale Company; John Dickson, a railway engineer who was in the process of building the Madeley branch for the S&BR, and Thomas Wilkes of Dawley, superintendent of the Coalbrookdale Company's mines.

Dickson, in his evidence to the Committee, stated that the main object in building the line 'was to link the ironworks and mines with S&BR at the Waterloo Sidings'. As most of the land between Ketley and Coalbrookdale was in the hands of the Coalbrookdale Company at this time, little difficulty would be experienced with regards to land purchase.

The branch from Waterloo Sidings to the Ketley Works had been constructed by John Dickson at his own expense; in the Parliamentary Bill it was proposed that this branch should be incorporated with the plans for the line to Coalbrookdale. Dickson had secured an agreement with the Ketley Iron Company under which he was paid for all traffic conveyed either by rail or road from the Ketley Works. In evidence given to support the Bill, Dickson stated that the Waterloo Sidings-Ketley Works branch was at times worked by a steam locomotive, and when the traffic was not so heavy it was worked by horses.

With the opening of the S&B from Shrewsbury to Wellington on 1st June, 1849, John Dickson who was also a Wellington businessman as well as an engineer, and a friend of Alfred Darby (I), the then manager of the Coalbrookdale Company, saw the great advantages to be gained by linking the heart of the Coalbrookdale coalfield by rail with the S&B line. Consequently, in 1852 he established his Shropshire Works, adjoining the main line of the S&B at Wellington. The *Wellington Journal* reported the following relating to the Shropshire Works in August 1855:

> We are certainly no little astonished at the establishment which has here sprung up by the side of the railway line in the short space of three years. Extending over eight acres of land, are the appliances for making and constructing almost every article connected with a railway, from the simple block of wood that secure the rail to the sleepers, to the carriages which roll over them. Machinery of the most improved character is dispensed over the place, which will execute anything from the making of a brick to the planeing of a piece of iron. In another place the visitor could walk through a large tube for burnetising wood etc. by which process a certain fluid is forced into the material by high pressure, thus rendering it almost imperishable. A vast amount of what is commonly done by hand is done by steam, and in carrying out the various operations about half a mile of shafting is set in motion by a compact high pressure engine, the furnace of which is fed at very little cost, the fuel being used being the refuse, saw dust and tar. To show the capabilities of this establishment, it may be stated that in a short space of two months 170 wagons were turned out for the Newport & Abergavenny Railway Company. A large number of passenger carriages are now on the stocks, in various stages, for the Great Western Company. It is whispered that no less a sum than £30,000 has here been sunk, and that the wages paid amount to £100 per day. The benefit thus accruing to Wellington may be easily imagined.

By 1882 John Dickson's railway engineering works had been taken over by the brothers Richard and Thomas Groom, timber merchants.

The Wgton&SJR plans submitted to the House of Lords' Committee had been drawn up by Dickson, and the questions put to him by the members of the Committee, and the answers given, throw an interesting light on the industrial activity of the Horsehay, Lightmoor, and Coalbrookdale areas of the coalfield in the late 1840s and early 1850s. For instance these show that the proposed line was to deviate slightly from the existing tramway which operated between the Ketley and Horsehay works. The line would approach Lightmoor on a level with the top of the furnaces, and coke house, and would be on a level with the yards in front of the brickworks. Dickson also stated that the Coalbrookdale arm of the Shropshire Canal, which ran from Southall Bank near Dawley to the incline plane at Brierly Hill above Coalbrookdale, had now been stopped up and planted over in certain places, and that parts of the canal were being used as ponds to serve the Coalbrookdale Company's pumping and pit winding engines.

Certain local inhabitants of Coalbrookdale had expressed concern about the fact that, if the line went down the centre of Coalbrookdale, this would endanger the church, which was then being built. However, Dickson stated that the line would be 15 yards from the church, on an embankment 30 to 38 feet above the church yard.

In 1853, the Coalbrookdale Company was sending very little pig-iron down the Severn, most of it was being sent by horse and waggon from its works to Wellington for transportation by rail to Liverpool, Manchester and other parts of the country.

With the opening of the S&BR Coalbrookdale (or Madeley) branch in November 1854, from Madeley Junction (between Oakengates and Shifnal) as far as Lightmoor, a direct link was afforded with the Coalbrookdale Company's tramways, one going south down Lightmoor Dingle into the works at Coalbrookdale, the other going north, skirting the boundary of the Manor of Dawley Parva into the Dawley Castle furnaces. The branch also gave a direct link to the Lightmoor furnaces. The Shrewsbury & Birmingham Railway became part of the GWR on 1st September, 1854.

The focal point for all the proposed railways into the coalfield was Coalbrookdale, and each proposed scheme had looked to the Coalbrookdale Company for financial help for the final thrust into the Dale. This help was not forthcoming from the company, due no doubt to the fact that it had its tramway links with Lightmoor and the standard gauge rail link thence, thereby satisfying all its transport needs.

Despite early opposition from the London & North Western Railway (LNWR) which had plans for the laying of a railway from Wellington to Coalbrookdale, the Wellington & Severn Junction Railway Act was given the Royal Assent on 20th August, 1853. The company was given powers to build a railway from a junction with the Shrewsbury & Birmingham Railway near Ketley, to Coalbrookdale, near to the Coalbrookdale Company's ironworks. The Act also gave powers for an extension from the ironworks to terminate at a piece of land on the north side of the River Severn, opposite limekilns belonging to John Patten, in the parish of Benthall. The Severn Valley Railway Company was authorised by its Act to construct a branch from its main line near these same limekilns and, at this point, to cross the River Severn, to connect with the Coalbrookdale extension of the Wellington & Severn Junction line. Had the latter extension been built it would have followed the line of the Coalbrookdale Company's tramroad from the bottom of the incline of the Old Wynde on Cherry Tree Hill, skirting the north-east side of the Coalbrookdale valley, and terminating below limekilns on Lincoln Hill, above the Coalbrookdale Company's riverside warehouse on the wharfage at Ironbridge.

The first meeting of the Wellington & Severn Junction Company was held at the Bull's Head Hotel, Wellington on 5th September, 1853, when again the involvement of the Coalbrookdale Company in its affairs was in evidence. Henry Dickinson was elected as the company's first Chairman. A Director of the Coalbrookdale Company, the Dickinson family had been associated with the Darbys over many years. Dickinson would remain Chairman of the Wgton&SJR throughout most of its working life. Charles Crookes and William Norris were also elected Directors, as was John Williams of the Ketley Iron Company. Crookes was then manager of the Coalbrookdale Company. (On the day that he had been due to give evidence to the House of Lords' Committee dealing with the Wgton&SJR Bill, he fell in his hotel and broke his leg. During most of the hearing he was confined to his hotel bedroom.)

The Shrewsbury & Birmingham Railway was ever mindful of the likelihood of the LNWR endeavouring to extend its influence over the newly formed Wgton&SJR. To counter this it was ready to look with favour upon most of the requests for assistance from the company. In fact one of its staff, a Mr F. Gibbon, was loaned to give technical assistance to the Wgton&SJR, plus the sum of £4,500, the amount required for the deposit with the Court of Chancery for the Railway Bill.

It was estimated that the cost of building the railway from Ketley to Coalbrookdale would be £60,000, and that the number of shares into which the capital should be divided should be 6,000, each share being £10.

On 21st September, 1853 the Directors appointed Henry Robertson as Engineer. Robertson had been Engineer to the Shrewsbury & Chester Railway, and to him is ascribed those two great viaducts on that line, over the valleys of the Dee at Cefn, and the Ceiriog at Chirk. It was agreed that Robertson should be paid £1,050, and it was reported that he was prepared to take £700 on account in shares. At their meeting on the 27th February, 1854, the Directors agreed that a call of £2 per share should be made' when the 2,347 shares already taken up were fully paid up, this would give an amount of £23,470, sufficient to build the line between Ketley and Horsehay. On 25th April, 1854 the Directors agreed that they should purchase John Dickson's interest in his Ketley branch; the purchase price to be £3,000.

With the purchase of the Ketley branch successfully negotiated, Robertson was instructed to obtain tenders for building the line from Ketley to Horsehay. Tenders were obtained from Messrs Field & Teasline, a Mr Frost and a Mr Clinic, and also from John Dickson. Subsequently, Robertson reported to the Directors on 24th July, 1855 in favour of Dickson's tender for building the line from Ketley to Horsehay for under £10,000. He did not state if in fact this was the cheapest tender, but he was possibly influenced by Dickson's involvement in the early stages of planning the line, and also the close proximity of his engineering works in Wellington.

Whilst the Wgton&SJR had entered into a contract for the building of the line from Ketley to Lightmoor, its sights were still firmly set on an extension into Coalbrookdale. This is evidenced by the fact that on 16th April, 1855 it approached Mr Newcombe, the manager of the Northern division of the GWR, requesting him to inspect the area, and to obtain his opinion with regards to making a line from Lightmoor to Coalbrookdale. This decision was possibly influenced by the Coalbrookdale Company's dominance on the Board of the Wgton&SJR.

The cutting of the first sod of any railway line was usually an occasion for great celebration, and the Wgton&SJR, not to be outdone by any of its rivals, organised an event that would have been long remembered by the inhabitants of Ketley and the surrounding area. The *Wellington Journal* of 25th August, 1855 carried the following report:

At an early hour in the morning of Tuesday last the inhabitants of Wellington were awakened by the firing of cannon from the Shropshire Works, this works usually a busy hive of industry, was however materially changed in its general aspect. The place was decorated in a most pleasing manner. Over the entrance gate (to the contractors works) was a triumphal arch, with a design for illumination at night of a star and the name of the works. At 10 o'clock a procession was formed:

Marshall on horse back - Eight horses in trappings
Twelve 'navvies' in white smocks carrying picks and shovels
Band
Banner - 'Success to the Wellington and Severn Junction Railway'
Barrow, with spade and pick carried by two 'navvies' in smocks
Shropshire Works officials.

The cortege passed through Market Square, New Street, along Watling Street to Ketley. The party on arrival at Ketley were received with a salute from two large pieces of artillery.

The first sod was turned in a field adjoining the Shrewsbury and Birmingham Railway. The route commences with the Shrewsbury and Birmingham Railway about a mile east of Wellington. A portion of the line from the junction to Ketley Works has been made some years ago as a private enterprise of Messrs Dickson and Company and now forms part of the scheme.

Passing from Ketley over Lawley Common it will arrive at Horsehay Works which is the limit to which the line is at present confined. From Horsehay the project extends to Lightmoor where a junction is to be formed with the Shrewsbury Railway. The neat oak barrow and spade, having been placed on the appointed spot, J. Williams ironmaster Ketley, cut the first sod. Several bottles of champagne were un-corked. The cortege then returned to Wellington, where lunch was served to one hundred and fifty guests.

In October 1855 it was reported that the works between Ketley and Horsehay were in active progress, and that the cost of building the line would be about £4,000 to £5,000 per mile, exclusive of stations. At this stage the Directors were still appealing for increased support to enable the line to be extended from Lightmoor to Coalbrookdale.

By September 1856 the line was nearing completion between Ketley and Horsehay, 13,300 cubic feet of shale and sandstone having been cut through at the summit of the line to form the Horsehay tunnel. The shareholders were also informed that the building of Horsehay station was progressing, and that the sidings and goods shed there were nearing completion. The amount expended on the building of the line from August 1853 was £17,268, and the amount received from shareholders by way of deposits and calls was £25,346.

The purchase of land between Ketley and Lightmoor had not posed any problems for the Wgton&SJR due, no doubt, to the co-operation of the main landholders, the Duke of Sutherland, the Earl of Craven, and the Coalbrookdale Company.

On the 21st February, 1857 the *Wellington Journal* reported that a trial run had been made from Ketley to Horsehay, when a number of shareholders proceeded along the line in coaches provided by the GWR and propelled by a new tank engine provided for the line by Beyer, Peacock. On leaving Ketley fog signals were placed on the line, and this great occasion was witnessed by large crowds gathered on the pit mounds alongside the line. Fog signals were also heard to explode in Horsehay tunnel. The *Wellington Journal* reported that, on arrival at Horsehay, the shareholders celebrated by drinking champagne, and that they 'viewed from an eminence the progress of the works from Horsehay to Lightmoor'. When viewed from the vantage point at Horsehay station the problems facing the engineers in constructing the line down the valley between Horsehay and Pool Hill towards Doseley can be readily appreciated; the whole of this section had to be built on an embankment constructed on the spoil extracted from the cutting made from Horsehay tunnel to the station, and from slag taken from the Horsehay furnaces tip.

At their meeting on 27th March, 1857 the Directors reported to the shareholders that the expenses of working the line by the company would be costly for so short a distance, and that negotiations had been entered into with the GWR for providing stock and locomotives. It was also reported that services on the line would be confined to goods and mineral traffic for the time being, and that the stations at Horsehay, Lawley Bank and Ketley would be ready for this traffic from the 1st May.

On 20th April, 1857 a fatality occurred at Ketley, when John McWiggin, who was employed on the tip, was knocked down by a waggon which passed over him. He died later in the Shrewsbury Infirmary.

The building of the line from Horsehay to Lightmoor proved to be costly, due to the terrain over which it passed. It involved the construction of the embankment across the Frame Fields between Horsehay and Doseley, the cutting through, and draining of, the Coalbrookdale arm of the Shropshire Canal, and the provision of culverts for the draining of water pumped from the Coalbrookdale Company's Springwell and Top Yard collieries into the stream flowing into Lightmoor furnace pool, and on down the Lightmoor valley into the Coalbrookdale pools. Before approaching Lightmoor, a further obstacle had to be overcome: the cutting through of the Bandridge Leasow pit mound, spoil from a colliery once operated by the Coalbrookdale Company.

By 25th March, 1858 the line was nearly completed into Lightmoor, where a junction was to be formed with the Coalbrookdale (Madeley) branch of the GWR (only completed as far as Lightmoor) near to the Lightmoor furnaces. Subject to agreed tolls, the GWR would have running powers from its junction with the Wgton&SJR, into Lightmoor station. The *Railway Times* reported on 27th March, 1858 that the GWR was working the Wgton&SJR and that the goods of the Coalbrookdale Company were being carried at 6*d*. per ton, this was considered by the Directors of the Wgton&SJR to be far too low. However, no action seems to have been taken by the Directors to increase this charge.

The finances of the Wgton&SJR would not allow the extension of the line from Lightmoor into Coalbrookdale. At this time the Coalbrookdale Company held three-quarters of the allotted shares, and it was willing to make up the dividend at the rate of £5 per cent. However, despite its heavy involvement in the Wgton&SJR it was not prepared to inject further capital into the project for the purpose of extending the line into Coalbrookdale, no doubt considering that the standard gauge railway into Lightmoor was sufficient to meet its transport needs.

In September 1858 the accounts showed that Stevens & Co. had been paid £239 3*s*. 8*d*. for signals, and Thomas Brassey £68 for points and crossings. The Coalbrookdale Company had supplied the chairs and keys, no details of the charge being given against this item.

The section from Ketley to Horsehay was inspected by Capt. Tyler for the Board of Trade on the 3rd March, 1859, his report outlining certain problems which he considered had to be rectified before he could give his approval to the opening of this section to passenger traffic. Firstly, he stipulated that catch points had to be provided at Ketley Jn leading into a blind siding, and that all trains off the branch must be brought to a stand on approaching the main line, as at this point the branch runs on to the main line on a falling gradient of 1 in 50. Secondly, he stated that he was not satisfied with the short tunnel at Horsehay which had been built of brick 2 ft 3 in. thick, of defective construction, and very much out of shape at the Horsehay end. He also suggested that the private line built by John Dickson, from the Waterloo Sidings on the former S&BR into the Ketley Ironworks should be taken out of use. The minute book of the Wgton&SJR is silent with regard to what action it took following Capt. Tyler's report.

Capt. Tyler was not impressed with the tank engine on which he rode to make his inspection, for in his report he had the following to say:

> I may add that the four-wheeled tank engine on which I inspected the line, and which was pointed out to me to be the one for working the line, does not appear to be suited for passenger traffic on account of its small wheel base, and overhanging weight, it gives a jumping and rolling action which may cause excess damage to the permanent way.

At the shareholders' meeting on 28th March, 1859, the Directors reported that they had hoped to announce the opening of the line, however Captain Ross of the Board of Trade had indicated that a safer junction should be made at Lightmoor with the GWR and that certain alterations should be made to the signals. He had also stated that he could not allow the tramway which ran from the Dawley Castle furnaces into the Lightmoor furnaces to pass on the level the Wgton&SJR line between Dawley Parva level crossing and Lightmoor Junction. This alteration necessitated the construction of an embankment and a bridge 300 yards south of the existing crossing point, to carry the diverted tramway. Despite this delay the line was opened for passenger traffic on Monday 2nd May, 1859. The *Wellington Journal* reported 'that at 10 am the first passenger train left Wellington for Lightmoor Junction [reversing here], and on to Shifnal via Madeley over the GWR branch line arriving at its destination at about 11 o'clock. The party of railway officials and passengers returning by the GWR line direct to

Wellington'. The Wgton&SJR officials celebrated the occasion on a grand scale. The *Wellington Journal* reported: 'At 3 o'clock in the afternoon a party of gentlemen together with a number of shareholders sat down to a sumptuous repast at the Bull's Head Hotel in this town'. The unusual Wellington-Lightmoor (reverse)-Shifnal passenger service was maintained from 2nd May.

From the speeches made at the celebratory opening dinner it was evident that the company had not reached its eventual goal, that being its link up with the Coalbrookdale ironworks, and the Severn Valley district. This was a problem that would remain with the company until the extension was finally built by the GWR in 1864 (see page 61).

From the opening of the line discussions had been taking place with the GWR with regard to leasing the line to that company, although negotiations between the two companies were far from amicable at times. At the shareholders' meeting held on 30th March, 1860, William Trevor proposed that negotiations with the GWR should cease, and that they should consider joining with another company. At the same meeting it was reported that the GWR receipts for passenger traffic in the first six months of the line's existence were £429 16s. 2d. The Coalbrookdale Company had passed over the line 11,581 tons of goods traffic, and the Ketley Company 6,219 tons. The capital account showed receipts of £52,366 3s. 9d., and expenditure to date was £51,939 7s. 9d. The Chairman also reported that the construction of the line from Ketley Junction to Lightmoor had cost less than £13,000 per mile.

The local inhabitants made good use of the new mode of transport, from the opening of the line in May 1859 to 30th June 1860, 33,335 passengers had been carried over the line. No doubt the easy access afforded into the market town of Wellington from Horsehay, Lawley Bank and Ketley accounted for a good number of these passengers. To 31st December, 1860, 39,975 passengers had been carried, of which 34,676 were third class.

Concern was still being expressed in many quarters to the ending of the Wgton&SJR line at Lightmoor. This is recorded in an undated note in a letter book in the Darby family papers as follows:

The very unsatisfactory state of the terminus of the Wellington & Severn Jn Railway at Lightmoor, has induced some parties to consider whether it would not be desirable and practicable to get the railway extended to the upper part of Coalbrookdale, where there would be a much more convenient station, better access, better roads, and better neighbourhood, than at present. It appears that the present shareholders decline making further advances, and that therefore there is no immediate prospect of the line being extended beyond its present limits. It is stated by the Chairman and Managing Director that it will require from five to six thousand pounds to complete the line to Coalbrookdale with a convenient station, and he pledges himself that if this sum is subscribed for in shares (which are at £10) the work will be immediately put in hand; and it is thought would be completed by the ensuing autumn. It is therefore earnestly hoped that parties interested in the neighbourhood will take the matter up and by a moderate subscription enable the Directors to complete the railway as described to Coalbrookdale.

The subscription list was set out below this appeal. However, it would appear that the residents of Coalbrookdale were not sufficiently interested in extending the railway to Coalbrookdale, as none of their names appear on the list despite the fact that their area had been described as a better neighbourhood than Lightmoor. It was evident that the Coalbrookdale Company was not prepared to head this list, due to the fact that it had already achieved a direct rail link into its Horsehay and Lightmoor furnaces, and this direct rail link connected by tramway to its Dawley Castle furnaces, and the Coalbrookdale foundry.

The Wenlock & Severn Junction Railway (Much Wenlock to Buildwas)

With the incorporation of the Severn Valley Railway in August 1852, together with the proposals submitted by the Wgton&SJR to link the Shrewsbury and Birmingham Railway with the Coalbrookdale valley, the influential citizens of the ancient Borough of Wenlock saw the potential of linking their town with these two schemes and the world beyond the Dale. In consequence, the Mayor of Much Wenlock, George Adney, called a meeting in the library attached to the Corn Market on 5th September, 1853 to consider 'railway communication between the proposed Wellington & Severn Jn, and the Severn Valley railways at or near Coalbrookdale'. Among those present was George Benson of Lutwyche Hall, an extensive land owner in the Easthope and Presthope areas, who was destined to play an important role in the future Wenlock Railway Company between Much Wenlock and Craven Arms. Also present was Dr William Penny Brookes, who founded the Wenlock Olympian Society in 1850. By 1860 the games were open to the whole country, Dr Brookes later playing an important part in the foundation of the modern Olympic movement.

From the tone of others present at the meeting, it was evident that they were not just looking at rail communication with the Coalbrookdale coalfield, for many of them spoke with enthusiasm of eventual links with London, Liverpool, and South Wales. R.C. Blakeway, the Town Clerk, pointed out that many tons of limestone were at present conveyed by horse and wagon down the tortuous route of Farley Dingle to the coalfield furnaces; Evan Davies, a farmer, spoke of the importance of a railway to the town if it was to survive as a Corn Market. George Chune reported that the timber taken from the woodlands around Much Wenlock to his timber yard at Dale End, Coalbrookdale amounted to 400 tons per annum, and had to be transported down the Farley Road at a cost of 9*d*. per mile; and Beriah Botfield of the Stirchley furnaces stated that the cost of transporting the limestone precluded them from using it, and he expressed a hope that a railway would soon be laid connecting the Wenlock lime rocks with the coalfield.

Agriculture, timber and limestone were the cornerstones of Much Wenlock's economy and that of the surrounding area. The main route from the woodlands and lime quarries was the tortuous one down Farley Dingle to Buildwas, and on into the Coalbrookdale coalfield. Tom Hughes, who spent the greater part of his life in Farley, recalled as a boy seeing waggoners placing iron shoes under the wheels of the waggons carrying the stone and timber down the Farley Dingle, and that when the wagons reached the Dingle bottom the braking shoes would be wafer thin. In many cases the limestone would be handled twice from the quarries; it would first have been taken to the wharf near the Buildwas Bridge and then loaded into barges for transhipment down the River Severn to the Coalbrookdale Company's Loadcroft Wharf at Ironbridge, or at the Madeley Wood Company's Stone Wharf a little lower down the river.

Over a period of four years the Guildhall and Corn Exchange witnessed many meetings to discuss linking the town with Buildwas and Coalbrookdale, and many suggestions were put forward regarding the route of the line. Many of the public figures suggested a route from Much Wenlock through the Wyke to link up with the Severn Valley Railway at the foot of Benthall Hedge, near the Meadow Ferry river crossing, whilst others supported plans submitted by a Mr Taylor showing the route of the line down Farley Dingle to link with the Severn Valley Railway (SVR) at a point near the Abbey Farm at Buildwas. With a ruling gradient of 1 in 45, climbing to a height of 352 feet in 3 miles, this latter scheme was the one finally decided upon.

At a public meeting called at the Corn Market on 1st January, 1859, with George Benson of Lutwyche Hall in the chair, it was reported that Thomas Brassey, the contractor, and John Fowler, the Engineer, had viewed with favour the line between Much Wenlock and Buildwas down Farley Dingle, providing land could be purchased for £100 per acre. At this same meeting Dr Andrew Goode Brookes, of Cressage, the brother of William Penny Brookes, was appointed Chairman of the company, and Roger Blakeway, the Wenlock Town Clerk, was appointed Secretary. It was also agreed that the station should be sited in the Cinqueion field near the Wynstay Arms (now called the Gaskell Arms.)

The Wenlock & Severn Jn Railway (Wen&SJR) planned an extension from its proposed terminus at the Abbey Grange Farm at Buildwas, by way of a spur to the River Severn, but this was strongly objected to by the SVR. To counteract this objection the Wen&SJR applied to Parliament for running powers over the SVR's line to Ironbridge. This application met with a swift response from the Directors of the Severn Valley, who immediately agreed that the Wen&SJR should be allowed to lay a spur to the river.

The two main land owners from Much Wenlock to Farley were Lord Forester of Willey Park, and the Gaskell family, of Much Wenlock, both of whom were enthusiastic about the projected railway. The Forester family dominated the political scene in the Borough of Wenlock from 1529, when John Foster (or Forester) first represented the Borough, and from 1785 to 1885 the local MP was always a Forester. The family had also played an important role in the industrial development of the Ironbridge and Broseley areas. The Gaskells also played a prominent part in the administration of the Borough of Wenlock, being the owners of the Abbey Estate, which covered the greater part of Much Wenlock town. Both families were aware of the potential benefits to be achieved from linking the limestone quarries (or lime rocks as they were known locally) on their land into the proposed line down the Farley Dingle.

From Farley into Buildwas the route of the line entered the Buildwas estate of the Moseley family of Buildwas Park. Unfortunately William Moseley was not at all happy about the line proceeding through his lands. The advantages to be gained by Forester and Gaskell from the route of the line, were not available to him, for he had no direct access to the line from his stone quarries and woodlands. The line's promoters began negotiations with Moseley on 4th May, 1859. For the first 15 acres of land he was offered £2,250, which he would not accept, also making demands for three road bridges and two level crossings, to which the promoters would not agree. At each meeting with Moseley's Agent no agreement was reached on any matter raised. On 6th January, 1860 the Directors reported, 'No agreement yet with Mr Moseley his claims are so excessive we find it impossible to settle amicably'; and so protracted negotiations continued, until a final settlement was eventually reached in June 1860.

On 21st July, 1859 Royal Assent was given 'for the making of a Railway from Much Wenlock in the County of Salop to communicate with the Severn Valley Railway and the River Severn in the same County'. The first Directors were named as George Adney, Joseph Amphlett, Robert Horton, William Penny Brookes, Andrew Goode Brookes, and Ralph Augustus Benson. The authorised capital of the company was £24,000, the number of shares was 2,400 at £10 per share, the company was also authorised to borrow on mortgage the sum of £8,000. The amount of £2 was to be the amount of any one call which the company could make on the shareholders; the first of these calls was made on 1st August, 1859.

On 25th August, 1859 it was agreed that the Directors should walk the route of the proposed line from Much Wenlock to Buildwas. An entirely new vista would have been opened up to them as they followed the route of the Farley Brook, and above Lawley's Cross the Severn valley would open out before them with the Wrekin in the background. No doubt they would have examined the proposed diversion of the Benthall and Buildwas public road past the New Barn at Buildwas, which was another aspect of the railway to which William Moseley strongly objected.

Lord Forester, anxious to take advantage of the route of the line through his property, applied for sidings to be built at the Tickwood Road, where line crossed the road from Lawley's Cross to Posenhall. He also made a similar application for sidings to join the line at Norrey's Rock, which is situated in a deep valley extending into the Acland's Coppice through which flows a fast-flowing stream linking into the Farley Brook. (Sadly, on the closure of the line, this enchanting view was lost to the general public, but with the recent diversion of the Farley road the view can be seen once again.) Neither of the sidings proposed by Lord Forester was ever built.

The first ordinary meeting of the shareholders was held on 19th January, 1860, when it was agreed that Mr Blakeway, the Secretary of the company should have his salary fixed at £100 per annum.

At a meeting of the Directors held on the 2nd March, 1860 it was agreed to accept Mr Brassey's tender for £21,000 for building the line. At this same meeting it was reported that Mr Caleb Harper, the owner of the Farley Corn Mill, had accepted the sum of £174 for his land in Farley, and for other properties owned by him in the same area he agreed to take up shares by way of compensation. Mr Fowler also assured the Directors that the line would be completed within nine months, and that the cost of building the station and sidings at Much Wenlock would be £2,000.

Construction of the railway began on Monday 26th March, 1860, and it is evident from the following extract from the *Shrewsbury Chronicle* of 30th March, that the townspeople of Wenlock intended this to be an occasion to call for a great celebration:

The first sod of the line was cut on Monday last, a glorious sunny day, it being Market day the town was thronged with people. There were between two and three peals of bells to announce the proceedings. At 3 o'clock the procession started from the Wynstay Arms Hotel in the following order:

Herald - Drum Major with staff
Seven Flags - Juvenile Drum and Fife Band
Four little boys bearing spriggs of holly
Band - 36 Drums and Fifes led by G. Moreton
Chairman and Directors
Friends
Members of the Olympian Cricket Club
Flags and Banners of the Friendship Society
Provident Society (Raven Inn)
School Children

The procession passed down High Street, along Barrow Street, and into Cutlers Yard. Here an immense concourse of people had assembled. A neat wheel-barrow and spade had been prepared for the opening. The Rev. W.H. Wayne addressed the younger portion of the gathering, and hoped they would remember this occasion in later life. He went on to say that the wonders of the steam age would bring prosperity to the town and surrounding area, and it will enable friends and relatives to visit each other more often. Miss Mary Brookes (Daughter of Wm Penny Brookes) then lifted the first sod, placed it in a barrow, and ran it along a plank.

The lifting of the first sod, in the field between the Wenlock Priory and what was later to be the station, was a landmark in the history of the ancient town of Wenlock, for no longer would the inhabitants be dependant on John Roberts setting out from the 'Stork' on Tuesday morning at 8.0 am for Shrewsbury, or Thomas Davies setting out from the 'Falcon' on Wednesday morning at 9.0 am for Bridgnorth, for the transport of their goods. No longer too would the limestone and timber have to be conveyed down the perilous route of the Farley Dingle to the Severn valley and beyond.

Returning to the progress of building the line the Directors at their meeting on 1st May, 1860 discussed the proposals with regards to the building of a railway from Much Wenlock to Craven Arms, by the Corvedale route. This would be via the Five Chimneys on Wenlock Edge, Bourton, and Shipton, linking in with the Shrewsbury & Hereford line below Craven Arms. This was to prove a contentious subject, and one which would occupy the time of the Directors of the Wen&SJR and the Wenlock Railway Company (WenRC) for many months to come, but more of this later.

The Wen&SJR Directors instructed their solicitors to prepare an agreement with the provisional Directors of the WenRC, by which all traffic over any part of the proposed new

Above: The wheelbarrow used by Miss Mary Brookes, the elder daughter of William Penny Brookes, to wheel the first sod cut for the Wenlock & Severn Junction Railway on 26th March, 1860.

Author's Collection

Right: Walter Moseley of Buildwas Park. The Wenlock & Severn Junction Railway experienced considerable difficulty with Moseley in regards to the purchase of land through his estate over which the railway had to pass.

Shropshire Records & Research

railway, the Coalbrookdale extension (*see page 57*) or the Wen&SJR should be charged at equal mileage rates, to be mutually agreed.

At a shareholders' meeting held on 20th October, 1860 it was reported: '. . . that the line was progressing satisfactorily and that all earthworks and permanent way would be completed by the agreed time, and also that to date the following expenses had been incurred: Parliamentary Bill £1,371, Land and compensation £4,604, Surveying and Engineering £500'. Like so many smaller railway undertakings at this time the Directors saw that the future of the company lay with a larger company operating the line, it was therefore agreed that an early meeting should be agreed with the GWR Directors to discuss this.

The townspeople of Wenlock knew that the future of their town lay in the linking of the town to the outside world by rail, but they must have had some misgivings at times when the peace and tranquillity of the town was disturbed. The *Wellington Journal* of the 27th October, 1860 reported, 'that on Saturday evening last, four Irish navvies were arrested for causing an affray in Much Wenlock, incidences of this seem to have been all too frequent of late by labourers involved in building the railway from Much Wenlock to Buildwas'.

Despite the disruption to the peace of the ancient Borough, the Directors pressed on with the line, finally agreeing with Mr Moseley's agent to pay £200 for land at the New Barn at Buildwas (later to be the site of the station). This was on the understanding that Mr Moseley would give up the two level crossings that he had requested east and west of the New Barn, and also diversion of the road to Benthall.

The coping stone of the Sheinton Street bridge at Much Wenlock was laid by Lt Col Benjamin Edwards on 4th November, 1860. In his speech he had the following to say about the railway that was to pass over it, which the stone mason sought fit to inscribe on the stone:

> Success to the railroad,
> And strength to this bridge,
> May money pass over it heavily,
> Time lightly, and men and women safely.

The coping stone remains *in situ*, but, sadly, due to passage of time, the words are hardly legible.

The Directors were also anxious to exploit the economic necessity of transporting limestone to the various furnaces in the coalfield and beyond, and agreed that sidings should be connected into the line at Standhill and Shadwell quarries on land owned by Mr Gaskell, and operated by the South Wales & Cannock Chase Coal & Coke Co. These sidings were to be just south of Much Wenlock station. It was also agreed to lay sidings into the Bradley and Norrey's Rock quarries, both on land owned by Lord Forester.

The Bradley quarries were operated by the Botfields of the Old Park and Stirchley furnaces, and were on the opposite side of the Farley Road to the quarries operated by the Coalbrookdale Company. It was agreed by the Wen&SJR to expend £100 on each siding, but after lengthy discussion with Lord Forester the sidings were never laid into the quarries worked by the Botfields, or the Norrey's Rock quarries.

From the census for Much Wenlock of 1861 it records that there were 49 navvies involved in the construction of the Wen&SJR. Of these 11 were from Much Wenlock, 12 were from elsewhere in Shropshire, 20 were from elsewhere in England, 3 were from Ireland, whilst the origins of the remaining three were not shown. The census recorded that 21 of these men were residing in the common lodging house at Much Wenlock.

It was hoped that the opening of the line would coincide with the 12th annual meeting of the Wenlock Olympian Society and notices were posted both at Shrewsbury and Hartlebury to the effect that cheap fares would operate on 23rd October, 1861 to Much Wenlock. Unfortunately, these arrangements had to be cancelled owing to the fact that the Board of Trade Inspector had not yet travelled over the line. The citizens of Wenlock were nevertheless determined that a train should arrive in the town on that day.

The *Shrewsbury Chronicle* of 25th October, 1861 reported as follows:

Captain Field to avoid disappointment was determined that a special train should run from Shrewsbury taking such ladies and gentlemen as had confidence in the security of the line; from the steadiness of the train, and the care taken by the staff concerned the possibility of an accident was very remote. The train left Coleham at 10.0 am with the Shropshire Artillery band occupying one of the coaches. On entering the Wenlock Branch at Buildwas crowds thronged the route through the Farley Dingle. On the platform at Wenlock the train was greeted by the Wenlock Juvenile band playing 'See the Conquering Hero Comes'. The town of Wenlock was decorated with floral arches, each arch bearing the inscription 'Success to the Railway'.

The arrival of the train safely at Wenlock must have given Ralph Benson, one of the Directors of the Wen&SJR, a great sense of relief, for in his welcoming address from a railway wagon he stated that: 'The first train had brought Directors and shareholders, who had risked life and limb upon the iron way first, and they had made the journey without accident'.

A Board of Trade inspection of the line was carried out by Col William Yolland on 31st December, 1861. He made certain observations with regards to the siting of the engine turntable at Wenlock, and said that the line between the engine shed and the carriage sidings should be at a greater distance to enable a clearer view to be given during shunting operations. At Buildwas a blind siding should be provided in the yard at the foot of the Wenlock branch so that any vehicle that might break away on the steep gradient would pass into this siding. These observations were acted upon, and on 30th January, 1862 Col Yolland stated that he was prepared to sanction the opening of the line.

The line between Much Wenlock and Buildwas was opened on 1st February, 1862, for both passenger and goods traffic, the opening being timed to coincide with the opening of the Severn Valley Railway between Shrewsbury and Hartlebury. Following an agreement with the West Midland Railway Company (WMR) the Wen&SJR was operated by them until the WMR amalgamated with the GWR on 1st August, 1863. The GWR then took over fully the obligations of the agreement entered into between the WMR and the Wen&SJR.

Returning to the first day of the official opening to passenger traffic the *Wellington Journal* carried the following brief report:

The first market day after the opening of the line gave evidence of the valuable addition the line will be to the town and trade of Much Wenlock, there being many strange faces observable in the throng of people who frequented the market.

The published timetable shows that at the opening of the line there were three up trains from Wenlock to Shrewsbury, via the Severn Valley line from Buildwas, and four in the opposite direction.

From its Shadwell quarry the Cannock Coal & Coke Company was supplying the Madeley Wood Company with limestone for use at its Blists Hill furnaces, and both companies applied to Wen&SJR to lay sidings to the river wharf, near the engine house at Buildwas. This would enable limestone to be conveyed down river in the Madeley Wood Company's boats. The engine house referred to was built by the Wen&SJR to enable water to be pumped from the river to a tank at the north end of the Wenlock branch line at Buildwas station; this in turn supplied two water columns there. After the cessation of the barge traffic on the River Severn, the sidings were used for taking coal to the engine house to fire the stationary boiler.

At their meeting on 20th August, 1862 the Directors were informed that an agreement had been reached between the GWR and the West Midland Railway Company for the joint working of the line. At this same meeting it was also announced that passenger receipts from the date of opening to the 30th June, 1862 were £166, and that receipts for the transport of coal, limestone etc. were £272.

Following the approval of the Wenlock Railway Co.'s Bill for the building of a line from Much Wenlock to the Shrewsbury & Hereford line at Marsh Farm Jn, and for an extension commencing with a junction with the Wen&SJR at Buildwas to Coalbrookdale Ironworks, it was agreed that a joint committee should be set up between the two companies to oversee the building of the extension from Buildwas to Coalbrookdale. The two representatives from the Wen&SJR were Alfred Goode Brookes, and his brother William Penny Brookes. It was also agreed that the Wen&SJR should recommend to its shareholders that £10,000 should be subscribed to the Wenlock Railway Co., thereby enabling them to become shareholders in that company.

The landscape of the northern end of the town of Much Wenlock was to change dramatically with the coming of the railway. An approach road had to made from Sheinton Street to the station, the cost of which was £150, £80 to be paid by the Directors, £50 by the Smithfield company, and £20 by the Borough of Wenlock Council. To enable a better approach to the goods station to be made, £2 was given to a Mrs Edwards for giving up her cottage in Pouk Lane, Mrs Gaskell was paid £18 for Mrs Evan's brewhouse in Pouk Lane, which had to be demolished, also a road had to be made from Pouk Lane into Fox Lane to prevent trespass on the goods station.

The Directors, at their meeting on 28th October, 1863, expressed concern that both the Coalbrookdale Company and the Madeley Wood Company were not making use of the line for transporting limestone to their furnaces. It was stressed that the profit of the line was based on the transportation of this traffic. They hoped that the opening of the WenRC line to the Presthope Rocks, and their own extension from Buildwas to Coalbrookdale, would help to increase the lime traffic.

It was evident that the Madeley Wood Company was not prepared to make use of the line until the spur to the river near the Meadow Ferry had been completed. This is made clear in the large amount of correspondence that passed between the Wen&SJR and the Madeley Wood Company.

Joint meetings were held between the Directors of the Wen&SJR and the Wenlock Railway Company with the view to amalgamation of the two companies. The outcome of these meetings was that a Bill* was placed before Parliament. The Bill received the Royal Assent on the 29th July, 1864, but did not authorise the amalgamation of the two concerns and their separate titles and Boards of Directors were maintained until both companies were absorbed by the GWR in 1896. This Act also gave the Wen&SJR additional powers to issue shares and borrow money for the purpose of building the Coalbrookdale extension, and extended the time for purchase of land by the WenRC for the building of the line from Much Wenlock to Craven Arms.

Under the terms of the agreement entered into with the GWR, the Wen&SJR shareholders were entitled to 57½ per cent of the gross receipts, and the GWR 42½ per cent for working the traffic and maintenance. The gross receipts from passenger traffic to 31st December, 1863 were £544 9s. 7d.

Returning now to the building of the Wen&SJR, on the night of 8th January, 1864 a disastrous fire took place, which destroyed the goods station and office at Much Wenlock. This prompted the Directors to urge the contractor to complete Wenlock station, and station house which was in the course of erection, 'to ensure the constant presence of the station master'. The cost of building the station, with its free stone quoins, and the approaches, was £2,500. The Directors also thought that it would be desirable to construct a refreshment room at Buildwas, but this latter suggestion never came to fruition.

When the Directors held a meeting on 30th September, 1864 it was reported that work on the passenger station had commenced, thereby relieving the goods station and wharf from being used as a passenger station. At this meeting it was reported that the Board of Trade

* The preamble to the Bill was as follows: 'And whereas the railway of the two Companies are so situated relatively to each other, that it would be advantageous to the said Companies, and to the public, if the said undertakings were united and placed under the management and control of one Company, and it is expedient that the said Companies be amalgamated into one Company, as in this Act provided.'

An early photograph of Much Wenlock station shortly after opening showing an unidentified locomotive and carriages. To the left of the train can be seen a platelayers' trolley.

Shropshire Records & Research

A view of the newly-built station at Much Wenlock taken from the Abbey Fields, showing West Midland Railway coaches standing in the platform, also the West Midland ground frame cabin and to the right an early semaphore signal.   *Ben Stone Collection/Birmingham City Library*

Inspector required a portion of the line between Buildwas station and the junction with the Severn Valley Railway to be a double instead of a single line junction; the estimated cost of this alteration was £1,100. The Directors still expressed concern that the ironmasters were not making full use of the line. From its opening on 1st February, 1862 to date only 23,000 tons of limestone had been sent down the line.

The influence of the Forester family was added to the Board by the appointment of the Rt Hon. George Weld Forester. In January 1871, shortly after his appointment to the Board, a further application was made by Lord Forester for a siding to be placed into his quarry at 'Norrey's Rocks' situated in Farley Dingle, but no siding was put in at this spot.

The remaining years of the lives of the Wenlock railways were spent in litigation with the GWR. Working arrangements between the companies never worked smoothly, from the opening of the line to the final takeover by the GWR. As each half-yearly payment became due to the Wenlock companies, arguments ensued as to the correct amounts due to them from the GWR. In fact the Directors, at their meeting on 27th March, 1871, agreed that legal action should be taken against the GWR if it went ahead and deducted the costs incurred in erecting the signal box and gear at Much Wenlock from the traffic receipts. The amount was still outstanding in May 1871, the outcome being that the Wenlock companies issued a writ for the recovery of the sum due. After protracted legal arguments this was eventually paid.

R.C. Blakeway, the Town Clerk of the Borough of Wenlock, who had been Secretary to both the Wen&SJR and the Wenlock Railway Company since their inception, died in August 1875. He was succeeded by another solicitor, Mr C.J. Cooper of Bridgnorth, at a salary of £75 per annum.

The GWR made the following proposals to the Wenlock companies in December 1887. With regards to traffic carried over the line, on all minerals carried it would be prepared to pay ¼ of the tonnage, on goods traffic ½ of the tonnage. On passenger traffic it would pay ¼ of the receipts for 3rd class passengers, ⅜ on 2nd class passengers and ½ on 1st class passengers. By the end of 1888 still no agreement had been reached between the GWR and the Wenlock companies.

The working agreement with the GWR expired at the end of June 1893, but by the end of December 1893 agreement had still not been reached, and the GWR stated that it was not prepared to continue to work the line on the present terms. In the event of a sale it would be prepared to take over the stock at par, in exchange for the preference shares of the Wenlock companies, and allow 1 per cent on the ordinary shares. This offer the Wenlock companies would not accept. Whilst these negotiations were continuing, with no apparent hope of agreement, the financial problems facing the companies were getting more serious daily.

In November 1895 Andrew Goode Brooks died. He had been Chairman of the Wen&SJR since its inception in 1859, a period of 36 years. His restraining hand had helped to keep the balance between the more radical shareholders and members of the Board who wished to make the break with the GWR and control the line themselves, and the long and, at times, frustrating negotiations with the GWR.

Following the death of Andrew Goode Brookes, Charles Milnes Gaskell was appointed Chairman of the company. The finances of the company were now in a desperate state, the lease with the GWR having expired in 1893, and since then the Ordinary shareholders had received no dividend. With no apparent working agreement in sight, the GWR threatened to cease working the line. With this threat hanging over them the Directors had no alternative but to propose to the shareholders that the GWR's terms should be accepted. These were that the GWR would take over the £11,000 debentures, for the £20,000 guaranteed on the Coalbrookdale extension it would give 90 per cent of 5 per cent GWR stock, and for the Preference and Ordinary shares in the Wen&SJR it would pay £25,000 within seven days of the appointment of an official liquidator.

A special meeting of the shareholders was held at the Corn Exchange, Much Wenlock on 13th June, 1896, when the GWR offer was put to them. The real threat of the closure of the

Dr William Penny Brookes, Director of the Wenlock & Severn Junction Railway and Chairman of the Wenlock & Craven Arms Railway and founder of the Wenlock Olympian Society.
Shropshire Records & Research

line, and the consequence this would have for the Town and surrounding countryside, left the shareholders with no alternative but to accept its offer. Godfrey Cooper of Much Wenlock was appointed official liquidator in accordance with the GWR (Additional Powers Act 1896) for which he was paid the sum of £50.

The last meeting of the company was held on 12th October, 1896, when 'it was ordered that the seal of the Company be affixed to the conveyance of the Company's undertaking to the GWR'. The trials and tribulations of the Wen&SJR at last came to an end, a line built by local business men, a line that had transformed the lives of the citizens of the ancient Borough of Wenlock, yet a line that had never paid, and like so many branch lines of the period, one completely at the mercy of the larger company which had been chosen to operate it.

The Wenlock Railway Company (Much Wenlock to Craven Arms)

From the commencement of the building of the line from Much Wenlock to Buildwas it was the wish of the Directors of the Wen&SJR that a rail link would eventually be made with Presthope on Wenlock Edge, to link in with the limestone works there, and continue on to Craven Arms. Here a connection would be made with the Central Wales line, then under construction (in 1860) between Craven Arms and Knighton, and eventually on to the industrial heartland of South Wales. However, the Directors' commitment to building the line from Wenlock to Buildwas precluded them from financial involvement in extending the line to Craven Arms.

A public meeting was held in the Corn Exchange, Much Wenlock on 1st March, 1860 to discuss the proposed extension of the line to Craven Arms and also the extension of the railway from Buildwas to Coalbrookdale; Ralph Augustus Benson was in the chair. The object of the meeting was to enlist the support of landowners in the area to be served by the proposed railway. From the list submitted to the meeting it would appear that there was no lack of support for the project, with names like Sir George Harnage, of Belswardine Hall, Moses Benson, of Lutwyche Hall, and the rectors of the parishes through which the line was to pass, who were also considerable landowners. It was also stated that the Coalbrookdale Company, the Old Park Company, the Madeley Wood Company, and the Lilleshall Company had expressed an interest in the proposed extension.

At this meeting a provisional committee was set up, consisting of Ralph Augustus Benson, William Penny Brookes, and Robert Horton, who were also Directors of the Wen&SJR and T. Campbell Eyton who was a Director of the Wellington & Severn Jn Railway. John Fowler, was appointed Engineer, George Potts, of Broseley, Solicitor, and Roger Blakeway, Town Clerk of Wenlock, Secretary.

The proposed extension was to commence with an end on junction with the Wen&SJR at Much Wenlock and pass over Wenlock Edge, between the Five Chimneys at Presthope, into Ape Dale, through Easthope, Longville, Rushbury, Eaton and Wolverton. At Marsh Farm it would join the Shrewsbury & Hereford Railway (S&HR) and continue with running powers over that line into Craven Arms. It was also announced at this meeting that Messrs Brassey & Field had consented to construct the line under similar arrangements to those under which they were at present constructing the Wen&SJR. It was also agreed that arrangements should be made with the Wen&SJR by which all traffic conveyed over any part of the proposed new railway should be charged at equal rates.

The Coalbrookdale extension was to commence with a junction with the Wen&SJR and the Severn Valley Railway at Buildwas and cross the River Severn into Coalbrookdale, thereby affording direct access into Coalbrookdale Ironworks, something which all the proposed local railway schemes had endeavoured to do.

At a meeting of the Wenlock Borough Council held on 18th February, 1861 it was proposed by the Mayor, George Adney, and seconded by Joseph Amphlett, that a petition in favour of the Bill in respect of the Wenlock & Craven Arms and Coalbrookdale Extension Railway should be sent to Parliament, the one dissenting voice against the petition being Henry Dickinson, a Director of the Coalbrookdale Company, and Chairman of the Wgton&SJR. Doubtless Dickinson saw the encroachment of the Wenlock company into Coalbrookdale as a direct threat to his plans to take the Wgton&SJR into that place.

The petition was set out as follows:

That in the opinion of your Petitioners the construction of the said Railways will be of great public advantage to the Borough of Wenlock by bringing distant parishes forming part of the said Borough into communication by Railway with each other and with the town of Much Wenlock where the public business is transacted. The Borough contains a population of 20,000 and extends over 30,214 acres divided into 18 parishes. The parish of Madeley in the northern part of the Borough is distant 18 miles from the parish of Eaton-under-Heywood in the southern part, and that both parishes will be intersected by the said Railways. The Quarter Sessions, Corporation Meetings, and other public meetings are held in the Town of Much Wenlock, and the petty sessions alternatively at Much Wenlock, Broseley, and Ironbridge.

A large portion of the population of the Northern Parishes of the Borough is employed in manufacture of iron, bricks, and other articles, and in the south it is entirely dependent upon agriculture.

From the outset the new Wenlock company was faced with a dilemma. A rival scheme had been put forward by Henry Robertson, the Engineer of the South Staffs and Central Wales Railway, who proposed a line from the Dudley district to Bridgnorth, and via the Corvedale to Craven Arms to connect with the Central Wales line and link into the South Wales coalfield at Llanelly, and on to Carmarthen, Milford and Pembroke.

On 28th July, 1860 a meeting was held in the Corn Exchange, Much Wenlock, to consider if a union could be effected between the parties for promoting railways from Much Wenlock, Bridgnorth and Craven Arms. Henry Robertson brought along to the meeting a strong contingent of gentry from Bridgnorth to support his Corvedale scheme. The Much Wenlock gentlemen were ably assisted by the Assistant Engineer of the Wenlock & Craven Arms Railway, Joseph Fogerty, who favoured the Ape Dale scheme.

The chairman of the meeting was Lord Forester, who began by asking the Bridgnorth gentry if they had considered linking their proposed line from Bridgnorth into the Wenlock line at the Five Chimneys at Presthope, to which Mr Robertson replied: '. . . that he considered the interests of Much Wenlock and the Shropshire district could best be served by constructing a short line of about three miles from Much Wenlock to Acton Round, or by constructing a line through Bourton down the Corvedale to connect with Herefordshire and South Wales'.

After at times acrimonious argument and counter-argument for both schemes, between Moses Benson for the Ape Dale scheme and Henry Robertson, William Penny Brookes summed up for the new Wenlock company by saying: 'It was impossible for them without sacrificing the interests of the town of Wenlock and neighbourhood to join in any scheme propounded by the Bridgnorth people. They had therefore come to a determination not to sanction any union in the scheme proposed. It was their intention to do all they could to make a line from Wenlock to Craven Arms by Wenlock Edge and Ape Dale'.

For the Bridgnorth gentlemen, and the proposed South Staffs Railway, Henry Robertson replied: 'The general interests ought to be considered as well as the particular locality of Wenlock, and I hope the Wenlock gentlemen will bear in mind that if they ever come to Parliament with the Ape Dale scheme they will be met with a competing general scheme through Corvedale which can in my opinion can be made to suit local interests better than the Five Chimneys scheme'.

The arguments for and against the two rival schemes continued on for some considerable time, as is evidenced by letters in the local press. However, despite the threat of Henry Robertson to oppose the scheme, the Wenlock company went ahead with its planned line down the Ape Dale. The Much Wenlock & Craven Arms & Coalbrookdale Extension Bill passed through its various stages without opposition, and received the Royal Assent on 22nd July, 1861. The company authorised to build these lines was called the Wenlock Railway Company (WenRC).

John Fowler was appointed Engineer, with Joseph Fogerty as his assistant. Fogerty was resident in the area during the building of the Wenlock railways, and the Coalbrookdale extension, residing for a while in Coalbrookdale, and later in Shrewsbury. Fogerty's influence can be seen in the design of the stations from Coalbrookdale to Harton Road, likewise in other buildings and bridges on the line. Messrs Brassey & Field were, as expected, appointed contractors; as they were engaged in the construction of the Wen&SJR line the Directors felt it would be beneficial to the WenRC if Brassey & Field built the line from Wenlock to Craven Arms.

The cutting of the first sod of the WenRC was arranged to coincide with a special train which ran from Shrewsbury to Wenlock on 23rd October, 1861 for the 12th Annual Meeting of the Wenlock Olympian Society. It was reported in the local press that on arrival of the train in the yard at Wenlock, the ladies and gentlemen alighted and moved over to the north-west corner of the yard, where the ceremony of the cutting of the first sod was performed by Mr C.J. Ferriday, the Mayor of Wenlock. Mrs Blakeway, the wife of the Secretary of the company, wheeled the first barrowload of earth a little distance off.

The Wenlock companies, not content with the first sod-cutting ceremony, sought fit to hold another ceremony, as the line progressed for the laying of the corner stone on the Shrewsbury to Much Wenlock Turnpike road bridge. *Eddowes Journal* of 15th October, 1862 carried the following report:

Thursday last was a great day in Wenlock. Wenlock was a deserted village, but now it is being connected with the outside world, from which it has been shut off by reason of its difficulty of access, a condition from which it could hardly have emerged but for the energy and perseverance of its citizens, headed by the zeal and patriotism of Mr W.P. Brookes. Once impressed with and convinced of the advantages of railway communication by the opening of the branch line to Buildwas, the inhabitants began to look for fresh extensions of those advantages, and a line was projected and commenced more immediately to connect the town with a wider range of country by means of the line to Craven Arms, the construction of which is being undertaken by those eminent contractors Messrs Brassey and Field. A portion of the line is now completed, and it was at a bridge crossing the Shrewsbury and Wenlock turnpike road that the ceremony took place.

It was fixed to take place at 1 o'clock, at this hour Mr W.P. Brookes the Vice Chairman of the company, and several other Directors assembled at the Library, and preceded by the drum and fife band, with a number of small flags and banners proceeded to the spot. Arches of evergreens and flowers had been strewn across the road. Presently the preparation for laying the corner stone being complete, it was lowered into its place, Mr Brookes wielding the trowel and mallet. Mr Brunker, the principal stone mason, then mounted the stone, and proclaimed it to be well and truly laid. Mr Brookes then addressed the assembly.

'I have several reasons for laying this stone to-day, first because I have in common great respect for the builder Mr Brunker. I am a great admirer of his work, they are solid, massive in detail, effective in appearance, and so durable. Secondly over this bridge will pass in immense quantities for the use of the Lilleshall Company, and other companies, the best limestone for smelting and building, the best that this kingdom produces. The access therefore which this railway and the Coalbrookdale extensions will give next summer to these important products will lead to the employment of many labourers, and will be a source of great wealth to the district. I cannot allow you to depart without adverting to the very important services the Chairman of the Directors - Lord Wenlock - has given throughout every stage of our proceedings, preliminary, Parliamentary and financially. He became our surety for the building of the line, thereby releasing the deposit required by the Court of Chancery, and enabling us to devote it to the construction of the works.'
Cheers were then given for Lord Wenlock and Mr Brookes.

In the Parliamentary session of 1862 the Shrewsbury & Hereford and the LNWR had jointly promoted a Bill to lease the former to the latter alone, but reserving powers to admit the GWR on terms to be agreed. Despite this offer the GWR fiercely fought this Bill over a period of six days before a Commons Committee, but without success. In the end the GWR withdrew its opposition to the lease and agreed to share the lease equally with the LNWR. In the six days prior to the passing of the Leasing Bill the WenRC also mounted considerable opposition to the Bill, which the company saw as a means by which its traffic could be diverted at Craven Arms, and they were also disturbed by the prospect of being hemmed in both at Craven Arms and Wellington by the LNWR. Opposition to the Bill on behalf of the WenRC was submitted by Thomas Horton of the Lilleshall Company, and by Charles Crookes of the Coalbrookdale Company (best known for his design of a set of cast-iron gates for the Great Exhibition of 1851 which were later erected in Hyde Park).

Another voice in opposition was no less a personage than John Leman, Deputy Chairman of the North Eastern Railway Company. Leman was a partner in a firm of solicitors who had been legal advisers to Lord Wenlock and his family for many years. Lord Wenlock and Moses George Benson of Lutwyche Hall also spoke in opposition to the Shrewsbury & Hereford Leasing Bill. The main thrust of the opposition was that the Shrewsbury & Hereford was a local company, and should be prepared to serve local interests. In the event of the LNWR taking over the line the WenRC's traffic both going to, and coming from, the South-West would be obstructed by the LNWR at Craven Arms.

The line from Much Wenlock to Presthope was built on gradients of 1 in 45 and 1 in 48 up to the summit at Presthope (635 ft), thence through a 198 yds-long tunnel opening out into Ape Dale.

Much of the land required for the building of the railway between Much Wenlock and Presthope was owned by Moses Benson, whose family had purchased the Lutwyche Estate in the early part of the 19th century and over the years had acquired considerable sums of money by way of royalties on the limestone extracted from their estate. Therefore an early rail link to Presthope, and the limestone quarries, would be of considerable financial advantage to Benson, who was ever willing to lend his considerable influence in promoting the line. This is evidenced by the Wenlock Railway Act (1861): 'The Company at their own expense shall make a proper and convenient siding at Presthope at the eastern end of the proposed tunnel, and at their own expense, maintain this siding for the exclusive use of Benson'. This same clause also states that the Wenlock company 'shall at all times keep a sufficient number of trucks for the removal of lime and stone from the land of Moses George Benson'. (The siding to be laid by the company was to be 50 yards in length, and to be continued further if necessary, which, in the event, it was.)

Clause 32 of the Act also stated that 'Benson may at his own expense make and maintain any other siding in addition to the siding provided by the Wenlock Company'. This he duly did, for in 1862 he had leased a parcel of land to Earl Granville, of the Lilleshall Company, for the purpose of extracting limestone from his estate. Into the Lilleshall Company's quarry he laid a standard gauge track, which linked into the WenRC's sidings at Presthope station, the opening of which coincided with the opening of the line to Presthope.

The Directors, at their meeting held on 24th March, 1864, were informed by Joseph Fogerty, the Assistant Engineer, that the Westwood and Presthope sidings were completed for the conveyance of limestone. Colonel Yolland, the Board of Trade Inspector, had informed the Directors that there was no need to inspect the line from Wenlock to Presthope in view of the fact that it was only intended to carry mineral traffic.

Without any great ceremony at Much Wenlock the line to Presthope was opened for mineral traffic only on 5th December, 1864, thereby opening up the 'lime rocks' of Wenlock Edge to the iron industries of the Coalbrookdale coalfield and beyond. Moses Benson claimed that no longer would the tenants of his limestone quarries have to send their stone by horse and waggon into South Wales to compete with the Welsh. It would appear that the goal of the Wenlock companies had been reached by the opening up of the line to Presthope and the adjacent limestone quarries, it having been agreed at a joint meeting held on 4th December, 1863: 'not to proceed with the line from Presthope to Craven Arms for the time being'. The conveyance of limestone had been their priority, and the interests of the agricultural districts between Presthope and Craven Arms could wait a little longer to experience the benefits of rail transport. At the same time, the companies proposed that the scheme submitted by the South Staffs Co. for a line down the Corvedale should be opposed.

It was to be three years before the rest of the line between Presthope and Marsh Farm Jn on the S&HR line was completed (and, in fact, the section to Presthope opened to passengers). This delay was brought about by the lack of capital available to the WenRC. To enable the latter to complete this section of the line the GWR, under an Agreement dated 17th April, 1865, agreed to make an annual payment of £5,000 to the WenRC. This was in lieu of the half-yearly payments, based on traffic receipts, made by the GWR in accordance with an agreement of the 24th March, 1864 for the working of the line between Wenlock and Presthope. One provision in the agreement was to the effect that the expenditure on stations, sidings, and signals should not exceed the sum of £5,000. The expenditure on the construction of the stations was exceeded by an amount of £4,175, and the installation of the signalling and locking gear was overspent by an amount of £860.

This section of the line was completed by the end of September 1867, but a serious blow was to befall the WenRC following the inspection by Col Rich for the Board of Trade, who reported that the rail chairs of 21 lb. and 22 lb. were too light and had to be replaced by 30 lb. chairs. This decision meant that the whole of the track between Presthope and Marsh Farm Jn had to be taken up and relaid at an extra cost of £2,244. The company felt that they had been harshly treated in view of the fact that the 22 and 23 lb. chairs were the same as those laid on many of the Shropshire railways at this time.

Mr Brassey, the WenRC contractor, maintained that the additional cost of this work should be borne by the GWR, who immediately declined to make any additional contribution to the cost of constructing the line. However, after numerous meetings and considerable correspondence between Mr Brassey and the consulting engineer for the GWR, the latter agreed to make a contribution of £3,500 towards the additional overspend. The WenRC owed Thomas Brassey the sum of £12,932 for which he was given an acknowledgement note, which was duly surrendered in exchange for Preference shares in the company. In addition he was given authority to elect two members to the WenRC Board, one of which was his son.

On the 9th December, 1867 Colonel Rich travelled over the line with the Directors of the WenRC, and expressed his satisfaction with the state of the line. This final section of the branch between Presthope and Marsh Farm Jn was finally opened for passenger traffic on 16th December, 1867.

The Coalbrookdale Extension (Buildwas Jn to Coalbrookdale)

The Wenlock Railway Company saw the necessity of linking its line to Craven Arms with Coalbrookdale, through the line that was already under construction by the Wen&SJR from Wenlock to Buildwas. The company was aware that the West Midland and Severn Valley railways* had deposited plans with the Clerk of the Peace on 30th November, 1860 for a branch from their line at Bower Yard, near Benthall Edge, across the Severn through Coalbrookdale, to join the Wgton&SJR at Lightmoor. The WenRC saw this as an attempt to divert the Wenlock limestone traffic into Coalbrookdale, and beyond, by a rival company.

The WenRC sought the help of the GWR, who had already submitted plans for a 1½ mile extension, from its Madeley branch at Lightmoor, to Coalbrookdale. The GWR agreed to provide financial assistance with the building of the Buildwas-Coalbrookdale extension. The original plan by the WenRC in linking Buildwas with Coalbrookdale was for the line to cross the Severn by the Meadow Ferry, and for a tunnel to be constructed under Sheep Walk Meadow and Captain's Coppice, and to emerge near the Top Works of the Coalbrookdale Company. However, this plan was abandoned when the GWR agreed to build the extension from Lightmoor into Coalbrookdale.

* The Severn Valley Railway was leased to the West Midland Railway from 1st July, 1860.

Testing the ribs of the Albert Edward Bridge at the Coalbrookdale Company's works in 1863. The gentlemen in the top hat holding the testing equipment on the right of the photograph is Joseph Fogerty the Assistant Engineer to the Wenlock railway companies.

Ironbridge Gorge Museum

The Albert Edward Bridge over the River Severn at Buildwas under construction in 1864. Under the second arch from the right can be seen the newly-constructed Severn Valley Railway under Benthall Edge between Buildwas and Ironbridge.   *Ironbridge Gorge Museum*

The plans submitted by the West Midland and Severn Valley railways, for an extension of the SVR line from Benthall Edge through Coalbrookdale to Lightmoor, were thrown-out in Parliament in June 1861 in favour of the WenRC's scheme. The Wenlock Company's Act 1861 gave the company powers to build 'an extension commencing by a junction with the Wenlock & Severn Jn Railway at Buildwas thence across the River Severn to a wood and cinder bank (the property of the Coalbrookdale Company) adjoining the lower works of the Coalbrookdale Company'. The wood referred to was the Captain's Coppice, and the cinder bank was adjoining the Coalbrookdale Company's Upper Forge pool. Powers were also given to enlarge the size of the station at Buildwas.

The schedule to the Wenlock Railway Companies Act of 29th July, 1864 set out the terms and conditions under which the GWR would operate the Coalbrookdale extension. The estimated cost of building the extension was to be £40,000, of which the Wen&SJR would subscribe £10,000, the WenRC £10,000, and the GWR £20,000. The Wenlock companies to be responsible for the building of the station, sidings, sheds and conveniences at Coalbrookdale.

The major engineering work on the extension was the Albert Edward Bridge over the River Severn by the Meadow Ferry linking Buildwas with Coalbrookdale. This massive structure, like the Victoria Bridge at Arley on the Severn Valley line was cast by the Coalbrookdale Company.

Following the completion of the bridge the *Illustrated London News* of 5th November, 1864 carried the following report:

> One of the most remarkable of those great engineering works that attend the construction of railways throughout this country is the new bridge represented in our illustration. It is, we believe the largest cast-iron arch carrying a double line of railway that has yet been erected anywhere in the world with a rise of $\frac{1}{10}$th, and the height 60 feet at the centre. The engineer is Mr Fowler. The bridge is situated in a commanding position, with a magnificent landscape in the background, it will be sure to attract much of the attention of all travellers and visitors to the neighbourhood. The Albert Edward Bridge is composed of four cast-iron ribs, stiffened and connected with struts and ties of cast and wrought iron. These at the springing of the arch, rest in hollow shoes, which are sunk into large blocks of Derby stone and are bolted down through the masonry; thus forming an immovable abutment on which the stability of the structure mainly depends, whilst at the same time the arch is free to rise and fall under the effect of change of temperature or load. When recently inspected by the Government Inspector Capt Tyler, the deflection under a load of 400 tons was only half an inch; and on removal of the weight the bridge resumed its original level. After long and repeated experiments with severe rolling loads, which showed that no perceptible vibration existed, Capt Tyler expressed himself fully satisfied with the structure in all respects. We are informed that about 450 tons of cast and wrought iron were used in the structure. The bridge was constructed and erected by the well known ironmasters the Coalbrookdale Company, for the contractors of the line Messrs Brassey and Field. The work was executed under the immediate superintendence of Mr Joseph Fogerty, member of the Institute of Civil Engineers, in whose charge as resident engineer the works both of this line and the Severn Valley and Wenlock Railways have been carried on during these past five years.

From the Albert Edward Bridge the line was cut through the steep-sided slopes of Sheep Walk Meadow over a foot road that had once carried a plateway, from Little Wenlock to Strethill and on to the Meadow Wharf, on the side of the River Severn. The level crossing at this point was named 'Chunes' after the name of the family who farmed the land in this area, and who supplied the Coalbrookdale Company with sand from their sand holes a little to the north of the crossing.

Under the Wenlock Railway Companies Act of 1864 the GWR was given powers to operate the Coalbrookdale extension. The Act also set out that: 'The Great Western Company shall pay in perpetuity to the Wenlock Companies, in lieu of their share in the said net receipts and earnings of the Coalbrookdale Extension, and in lieu of any dividend on their subscription of £20,000, a fixed annual payment of £1,000'.

The scene was at last set for the railway to enter Coalbrookdale, a goal that had been set by so many but never achieved.

The New pool, Coalbrookdale, before the Lightmoor extension was cut through in 1863. The area covered by the pool gives some indication of the engineering work involved firstly building the large retaining wall, and secondly cutting through the pool dam. *Ironbridge Gorge Museum*

The Lightmoor extension under construction in 1863 at Cherry Tree Hill, Coalbrookdale, showing the newly constructed retaining wall. To the left can be seen the beam engine house and stack, in the distance to the right can be seen the stacks of the Cherry Tree Hill brickworks.
Ironbridge Gorge Museum

The Lightmoor Extension (Lightmoor to Coalbrookdale)

Following the joint venture of the GWR and the Wenlock companies to link Buildwas with Coalbrookdale, the GWR saw the necessity of completing the last link in the chain by continuing the line from Lightmoor to Coalbrookdale. The connection would then give it complete operating control from Wellington to Craven Arms.

Both the Wgton&SJR and the Shrewsbury & Birmingham Railway had seen the necessity of reaching Coalbrookdale. However, due to financial constraints, this goal was never achieved by them. In the case of the Shrewsbury & Birmingham nearly a decade was to pass before the GWR submitted plans for a line commencing near the goods shed of the Wgton&SJR at Lightmoor, and terminating in a field, the property of Abraham Darby (IV) in the occupation of George Chune. This field was just a little way south of what was later to become the site of Coalbrookdale station; a total distance of 1 mile 5 furlongs 1 chain was involved. It was seen earlier that the link with the Coalbrookdale extension was eventually made a little to the north of this spot at the Cinder Hill, near the Upper Forge pool. In 1860 Lightmoor was a scene of great industrial activity, with its furnaces, and the Shutfield and Lightmoor Tile Works operated by the Coalbrookdale Company. There were also the maze of horse-drawn tramways linking into the Dawley Castle furnaces, the local mines, and down the Lightmoor valley into Coalbrookdale.

The Act, authorising the construction of the extension, was passed on 1st August, 1861 and was known as the GWR (Lightmoor & Coalbrookdale) Act. The first sod was cut at Lightmoor on 12th March, 1862. The author's great-grandfather, Thomas Davies, worked as a navvy on the building of this line, and would often refer to it as 'The Golden Mile', no doubt due to the cost of building the extension. Firstly it was double track, cutting through the Coalbrookdale Company's reserve pool known as the 'New pool'; to do this necessitated the building of a large stone retaining wall, the stone probably being extracted from the Black Rock quarry situated in the Lightmoor Dingle. South of the New pool the railway severed the bottom of the Brierly Hill incline plane. In addition to cutting through the site of the incline they had to demolish six cottages at the bottom of Cherry Tree Hill. To compensate the Coalbrookdale Company for the demolition of these cottages, they had to erect six cottages on Woodside, Coalbrookdale. These cottages are often referred to locally as 'The Railway Cottages'.

Another costly piece of railway architecture is the 26-arch curved viaduct, carrying the line into the Dale valley over the Coalbrookdale Company's Upper Furnace pool, and a portion of their ironworks known as the 'Upper Works'. At this point the viaducts were built into part of the older ironworks' buildings, and also over the pig styes and earthen toilets at the bottom of the gardens of the cottages facing on to the works. The line was then trenched out of the steep-sided slope of the Captain's Coppice, and continued on this valley platform to link into the Coalbrookdale extension of the WenRC line, known as the Wenlock No. 2 Railway, opposite the Upper Forge pool.

The Board of Trade Inspector Capt H.W. Tyler, RE inspected the line on 30th September, 1864 and reported as follows:

> Whilst I am aware that the GWR are undecided about retaining Lightmoor as a passenger station, should they decide to retain it, it should be greatly improved and a second platform added. If not the present platform should be removed. Also the facing points off the Horsehay Branch should be made to interlock with the signal controlling the Madeley Branch.

Captain Tyler also drew attention to the unfinished waiting rooms at Coalbrookdale, and for the need for 'speaking telegraphs' at the stations. He also pointed out that the carriages that they proposed to use on this line had not yet been fitted with continuous brakes.

Captain Tyler's recommendations were met, for on 1st November, 1864 the first train entered the Coalbrookdale valley (the Coalbrookdale extension opening on the same day). There were no bands playing, no floral archways, no flag waving, and no long speeches. Just one single entry in the log book of the Coalbrookdale Girls' and Infants' School to the effect that, 'Today 1st November, 1864 the children were given a day's holiday to witness the coming of the railway into Coalbrookdale'. One wonders what the thoughts of the children were as the train entered the Dale valley from the tree-lined Lightmoor Dingle, and curved its way over the viaducts. No doubt as the years rolled on they would relate to their children and grandchildren their emotions at seeing the first train entering Coalbrookdale.

Whilst there were no reported celebrations on the opening day of the line, there was a celebratory dinner at the Bull's Head Hotel, Wellington, on the evening of 5th November, 1864, when representatives were present from the various industrial interests of the district. Mr J. Fox, the manager of the Coalbrookdale Company's Bradley limestone quarries at Farley, stated that he was one of the first passengers to set foot on the station at Coalbrookdale on the day of its opening. Mr Rimmer, the GWR divisional superintendent at Chester, said that he saw the line becoming the great highway of traffic between Manchester and the West of England. Sadly history never bore out this prediction.

John Randall, painter, antiquarian, and a man of many parts who contributed regularly to the *Wellington Journal* and wrote under the pseudonym 'Son of the Vale' had the following to say when writing in the 'Journal' following the opening of the Coalbrookdale extension:

What shall we say of this modern innovation - the railway. Those who were born, have laboured, and grown grey within the valley, can scarcely believe the evidence of their own eyesight when they look around and see the rapid strides which their native place has taken in the march of civilisation. The railway, far from detracting from its picturesqueness, only adds new charms to the scene, forming as it does a bold and striking background to a spot already beautifully fashioned.

The Lightmoor to Coalbrookdale extension had been 2 years and 7 months in the making, at a total cost of just over £70,000. At last the Coalbrookdale Company had direct access to the outside world by standard gauge railway. Fourteen years had elapsed since Alfred Darby (I) had a vision that one day a railway would carry passengers into the Coalbrookdale valley. The company that had produced the first cast-iron rails, and the first cast-iron wheels, was one of the last places to benefit from its inventiveness.

A view from Woodside, Coalbrookdale, showing a contractor's wagon poised on the newly-built embankment at the north end of the Coalbrookdale valley during the construction of the Lightmoor extension in 1863. Note just below the embankment the wooden bridge over the Upper Furnace pool, linking Darby Road with the Green Bank farm.   *Ironbridge Gorge Museum*

Chapter Three

The Madeley Branch

While this book is mainly concerned with the branch line from Wellington to Craven Arms, it is not possible to look solely at this without taking into account an integral part of this line, the Madeley branch, the 3 miles 76 chains from Madeley Junction to Lightmoor Junction.

The Madeley branch was built by the Shrewsbury & Birmingham Railway before it amalgamated with the GWR in 1854. The Engineers were Robert Stephenson and William Baker, the contractors being Messrs Dickson and McKensie of the Shropshire Railway Works, Wellington, the contractors who built the Wgton&SJR from Ketley to Lightmoor.

The main aim of the S&B was to connect its main line from Shrewsbury to Wolverhampton completed in November 1849, with the ironworks and mines of East Shropshire. Its rivals, the LNWR, also had had plans for constructing a line from Wellington to Coalbrookdale. It was no doubt this rivalry that brought about the delay in the building of the Madeley branch. The branch had to cross the Shropshire Canal at the Windmill Farm incline, the canal being owned by the Shropshire Union Railway & Canal Company. The latter company was under the influence of the LNWR, consequently every legal obstacle was placed in the way of the S&B in its endeavour to complete its branch to Lightmoor.

The problems facing the S&B can be seen from the following report of the *Wellington Journal* of 8th July, 1854:

For some time now a branch of the Shrewsbury and Birmingham Railway has been under construction from Madeley Jct. to Lightmoor. Owing to some informality or neglect of some essential clause, the contractors have for a long time been prevented from completing the junction across the incline which communicated with the Stirchley and Madeley Canals. These form part of the Shropshire Union Canals in the hands of the Shropshire Union Railway and Canal Company, and of course are under the influence of the London and North Western Railway. Buttress walls had been erected on either side of the canal incline at the extreme boundary of the new line of rails, but possessing no right to erect any works, temporary or otherwise between these points, some little engineering skill was needed in order to bridge across the span of 95 feet. This was accomplished on Saturday by projecting from the buttresses large baulks of timber, from which were sprung others which stretched across the entire span of canal. The canal men 'mudlarks' of which the company have a supply on hand, and others on that side, mustered in force and in unmistakable language threatened what they would do if any attempt was made to cross their incline or put a foot on their ground. The railway men and navvies equally strong drew themselves up in battle array. Watch fires were lighted and sentinels placed however to guard the works, and we trust soon to be able to report the opening of this much needed communication.

Although the obstacles placed in the way of the building of the line by the Shropshire Union were eventually overcome, the problems of the S&B were not yet at an end. The girder erected across the Windmill incline, weighing 95 tons, and 32 feet in length, crashed causing considerable damage. Various efforts were made to lift the girder, which all proved to be futile. In the end they had to cut this large structure in two, and only then could they lift it back in place by a suitable chain obtained from Edge's chain works at Coalport.

One station was built on the line - Madeley Court - named after the nearby Court House, once the home of the Lords of the Manor of Madeley. Sidings were laid from the Court station into the Court Ironworks formerly operated by the late James Foster, the Stourbridge ironmaster. The ironworks, erected in 1843, were surrounded by mines which linked into the works, and later into the S&B sidings by horse-drawn tramways.

The S&B's original plan was to form a junction with its main line at Shifnal, with a branch extending into Coalbrookdale via Madeley Court, and continuing on to Ironbridge. The

S&B's finances were always in a precarious state, consequently it had to be content with the shorter route from Madeley Junction to Lightmoor. The eventual plan for this branch, as submitted to the Clerk of the Peace at the Shirehall, Shrewsbury on 30th November, 1848, did not deviate from the line that was built. The only slight alteration was that the plan called for a double junction with the main line at Madeley Junction; however, only the east-facing part of this junction was built. Having reached Lightmoor the S&B then had a direct link with the Coalbrookdale Company's tramway system, and, as was seen earlier, with the Wgton&SJR. The access into the mines and furnaces met its needs, and the plan for extending into Coalbrookdale and beyond was abandoned.

According to the GWR minute book for 1855 the line was opened on 1st October of that year, but it would appear that the section of the line to Madeley Court had already opened by November 1854 as it was reported that arrangements had been made for coal and iron to be taken by rail to the Court Works at Madeley, for onward conveyance by canal to Coalport due to the fact that there was a water shortage in the canal between Donnington and Stirchley. The GWR, ever mindful of the presence of the LNWR in the area, made a survey in February 1855 for a railway to Coalport, leaving the Madeley branch at the Court Works. This move by the GWR was prompted by the fact that, by 1855, the Shropshire Canal was being operated under great difficulty, caused by subsidences and water shortages. The canal manager recommended the conversion of the canal to a railway, thereby giving the LNWR direct access to the River Severn at Coalport. The GWR plans never came to fruition, but the conversion of the canal to a railway by the LNWR was carried out in an Act of Parliament obtained in 1857.

A boost was given to the Madeley branch by the Madeley Wood Company opening up its Kemberton pit in 1864, a siding being laid from the branch into the colliery in the same year.

The Wgton&SJR joined the Madeley branch with an end-on junction at Lightmoor, allowing passenger trains to continue to Shifnal, following the opening of the Wgton&SJR to passenger traffic on 1st May, 1859. The GWR built a platform at Lightmoor for passenger accommodation which continued to be known as Lightmoor Platform, and was never referred to as a station in official documents.

For reasons unknown, on the opening of the line from Lightmoor to Buildwas on 1st November, 1864 the GWR immediately closed the platform at Lightmoor. It is difficult to understand why the GWR took this step for at this time Lightmoor was well populated, with two extensive rows of cottages 'Coker's Row' and 'Stable Row,' and the nearby community of The Finney. There were also four dwellings virtually adjoining the Platform with the grandiose name of 'The City'. No doubt for the GWR, like the other companies involved in the building of the line from Wellington to Craven Arms, the emphasis was on the conveyance of mineral traffic and the products of the local ironworks, with very little consideration being given to the travelling needs of the local inhabitants.

Chapter Four

Much Wenlock & Severn Jn (Lightmoor Extensions) Act

The relationships between the Wenlock companies and the GWR were sinking further into acrimonious depths. Dispute after dispute was arising: firstly, who was responsible for the cost of laying the siding into the Cannock Chase Shadwell quarries? Secondly, the Wenlock companies found that between Coalbrookdale and Ketley Jn they only had facilities for running over this section, not full running powers. Also, the age old question of the terms for the renewal of the lease with the GWR could not be resolved.

To add to their problems, a dispute had arisen between George Benson of the Lutwyche Estate and the Lilleshall Company. Benson was requesting a royalty of 6d. per ton of stone, but the Lilleshall Company was only prepared to pay 4d. per ton, in addition the company also requested a reduction in the rent. In consequence of this dispute, no limestone was being conveyed from Presthope over the line, which was having an adverse effect on the companies' finances.

In an endeavour to find their way out of this impasse, on 21st October, 1872 the Wenlock companies instructed their Engineer, John Fowler, to submit plans for a junction commencing at Lightmoor and continuing to a spoil bank near the Madeley Court Works, where a junction would be formed to link in with the LNWR Coalport branch. It is evident from these plans that the Wenlock companies were seeking the help of the LNWR in an attempt to make the GWR more amenable to their wishes. This link with the Coalport branch would give the Wenlock line access to the furnaces at Stirchley, Hinkshay and Blists Hill. The Directors of the Wenlock companies considered,'. . . that it was a great disadvantage to be at the mercy of the GWR, and it would be a great help if connection could be made with the LNWR'.

The Wenlock scheme went forward with the support of the Coalbrookdale Company, the Madeley Wood Company, and the ironworks on the eastern side of the coalfield. The GWR was strongly opposed to this scheme, as well may be imagined; it had no desire to see the LNWR encroaching on what it saw as its territory, and furthermore did not wish to have a company over which, at present, it had full operating control having direct links with the LNWR.

However, despite the GWR's protests, the Wenlock companies went ahead with their scheme in the full knowledge that they had the backing of the leading local industrialists. On 1st April, 1873 minutes of evidence were taken before the House of Commons Select Committee on Railway Bills, Mr Littler QC appearing for the promoters of the Bill, and Mr Rodwell QC appearing as Counsel for the GWR, which was petitioning against it.

The Coalbrookdale Company was prepared to subscribe £5,000 to this proposed scheme, as a siding from its Dawley Castle furnaces into the proposed line would give it access to the LNWR at Stirchley, thereby enabling the company to send and receive goods from other districts. W.G. Norris in his evidence stated that at present limestone from the Bradley Quarry, Much Wenlock, had to be sent to Horsehay station, and then transhipped into tramway wagons and conveyed a distance of two miles by horse-drawn tramway to their Castle furnaces. He stated that it would be impossible to transfer the limestone onto their tramway at Lightmoor as the gradient to the Castle furnaces was far too steep for conveying limestone on a horse-drawn tramway.

Evidence in support of the Bill was also given by John Arthur Anstice, a partner in the Madeley Wood Company, whose furnaces were situated at Blists Hill near Madeley, and from his evidence we get an insight into the problems facing the ironmasters in the Severn Gorge with regards to the transportation of essential supplies to their furnaces. Anstice stated that: 'We get our limestone from Westwood quarry on Wenlock Edge, it is conveyed over the Wenlock Company's line to a wharf on the river at Buildwas Junction, it is then transhipped on to barges on the river to Coalport, it is then transhipped again into tramway wagons and taken up a very steep incline to our furnaces at Bliss's Hill'.

The inclined plane referred to is the Hay Inclined Plane, which is now part of the Ironbridge Gorge open air Museum at Blists Hill. Anstice also mentions the fact that the river was 'stopped' for two or three months of the year due to flood or drought. This problem necessitated large stocks of limestone being stored at their furnaces. Much of the limestone was being brought into the coalfield from North Wales at a cost of 5s. 3d. per ton, Richard Groom, the Managing Director of the Stirchley furnaces, maintained that if he had direct access to the Wenlock quarries by this proposed line he could obtain the stone at a 1s. per ton cheaper. This sentiment was voiced by many other ironmasters who gave evidence.

Joseph Fogerty, who was Assistant Engineer in the construction of the Wenlock companies' lines, spoke vehemently in support of the proposed link with the LNWR. He highlighted the problems of transporting the limestone to Horsehay. On many occasions the train would have to set back into Lightmoor to make a fresh start due to the severity of the gradient. He also stated that on numerous occasions the local ironmasters had approached him concerning a link between Wenlock and the LNWR, but when he had raised the matter with the GWR they did not appear to be interested. He was also convinced that unless running powers were granted to the Wenlock companies, between Coalbrookdale and Lightmoor, the proposed extension to the LNWR would be useless.

Joseph Robinson, the London agent to the Coalbrookdale Company, stated that his company's minerals 'were very much worked out' and that ironstone for the Dawley Castle furnaces was being brought in from North Staffordshire, via the North Stafford line, the LNWR and the GWR to Horsehay, then transhipped on to the tramway wagons for the two mile journey to the Castle furnaces.

The GWR was accused of treating the Wenlock companies in a cavalier fashion and of making every endeavour to 'eat them up'. General George Forester was even stronger in his condemnations. He stated that 'the GWR were attempting to annihilate them, so that they could buy them up cheap'. James Grierson, General Manager of the GWR, spoke in opposition to the Bill. He said that the problem of the Wenlock limestone industry was not one of transportation, but one of quality of the stone, that was why many of the ironmasters were looking to North Wales for their supply.

Edward Wilson, the Engineer of the former West Midland Railway, also spoke in evidence against the Bill. He stated that, 'it would be inappropriate to build junctions both at Lightmoor and Madeley Court to link with the LNWR at Stirchley, due to the problems of mining subsidence in these particular areas'.

Despite the GWR's strong opposition, Royal Assent was given to the Bill on 21st July, 1873. Known as the Much Wenlock & Severn Junction (Lightmoor Extensions) Act, 1873, it gave the Wenlock companies powers to make a junction with the GWR's Lightmoor to Coalbrookdale branch, 74 yards west of the bridge carrying the railway at Lightmoor over the Lightmoor to Madeley road. The Extension consisted of Railways Nos. 1, 2, 3 and 4 (*see map p. 67*). They were now at liberty to link into the LNWR. In addition, the Act also gave them running powers over the branch from Coalbrookdale to Ketley Jn.

Following their success in obtaining this Bill the Wenlock companies were faced with protracted negotiations for the purchase of the land between Lightmoor and Stirchley. However, at the Directors' meeting held on 16th August, 1875 it was agreed to issue 2,400 shares at £10 each, and that 500 of these shares should be allotted to the Coalbrookdale Company. At this same meeting it was agreed to pay Joseph Fogerty the sum of £200 in respect of his charges and expenses in connection with the extension.

A blow was to befall this scheme, however. It was reported to the Directors at their meeting held on 24th July, 1876 that the Coalbrookdale Company had refused to accept the allotment of shares under the present circumstances. Those circumstances were the result of the rapid decline in the Shropshire iron trade of the 1870s. The fortunes of the Coalbrookdale Company's Dawley Castle and Lightmoor furnaces at this time were in the balance (*see Appendix Seven*); other ironmasters who had been supporters of this extension were also suffering from a decline in trade. Despite this set back, the Wenlock companies were determined to press ahead with their scheme, the Directors agreeing to take legal opinion regarding the Coalbrookdale Company's liability to take up the calls for shares made upon them. It would appear that no legal action was taken, for on 20th October, 1877 the Directors requested their Secretary to write to the Coalbrookdale Company and ascertain the likelihood of a revival in trade sufficient to fulfil their wish for the construction of this extension.

No favourable reply seems to have been received, for at their meeting held on 15th April, 1878 the Directors agreed that notices to treat given to owners of land required for the construction of the extension be withdrawn, and to cancel provisional agreements entered into with various landowners. The Directors considered that 'the failure of the Coalbrookdale Company to fulfil their assurance given to this Company, and the general depression in the Shropshire iron trade, [means that] the construction of the extension cannot be carried out'. The only gain to the Wenlock companies from the long and costly saga of the Lightmoor extension had been the granting of running powers from Coalbrookdale to Ketley Jn.

Railway No. 1
It was proposed that this line should leave Lightmoor 174 yards west of the bridge carrying the Lightmoor and Coalbrookdale branch over the road from Lightmoor to Madeley called Park Lane. Terminating in a field called the Near Moors, the property of ironmaster William Orme Foster.

Railway No. 2
Commencing with a junction with Railway No. 1 in the field called the Near Moors terminating by a junction with the Coalport branch of the LNWR 69 yards south of the bridge carrying that branch over an occupation road leading from Madeley (Court) station on the Madeley branch of the GWR to Madeley Court.

Railway No. 3
Commencing with a junction with Railway No. 1 in the field called Near Moors. Terminating in the Parish of Stirchley by a junction with the Coalport branch of the LNWR about 2 chains south of Stirchley station.

Railway No. 4
Commencing with a junction of the Madeley branch of the GWR at a point 284 yards west of a bridge carrying the Coalport branch of the LNWR over the GWR Madeley branch. Terminating with a junction with the Coalport branch 69 yards south of a bridge carrying this branch over an occupation road leading from Madeley (Court) station on the Madeley branch of the GWR to Madeley Court.

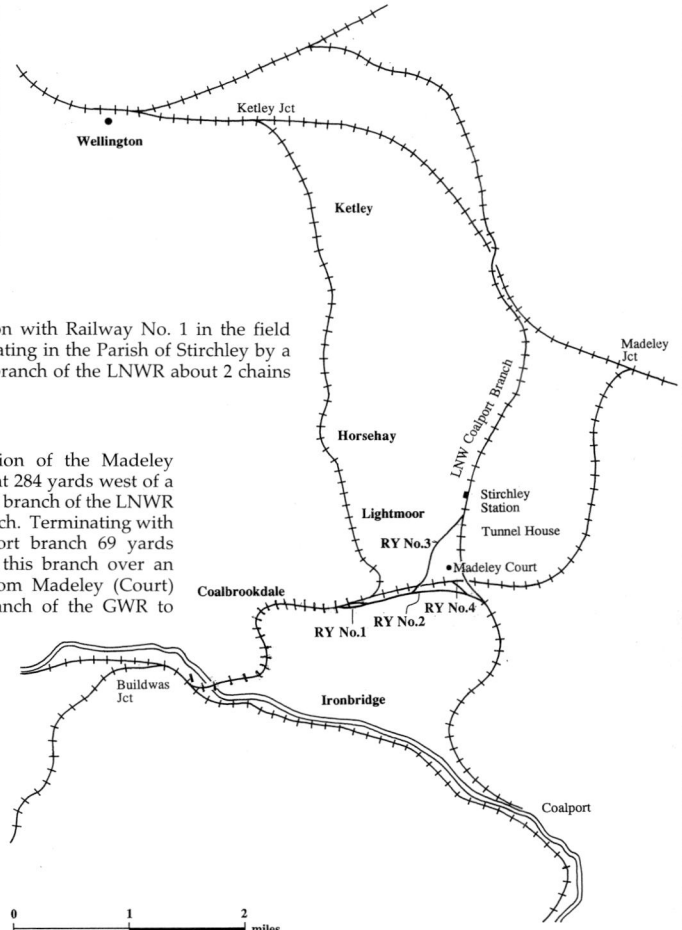

An LNWR Stafford to Shrewsbury train standing in the down platform at Wellington *c.* 1906. Note Wyman's newspaper and bookstall.   *Lens of Sutton*

A view of the up platform at Wellington in July 1909 with Wellington dignitaries awaiting the arrival of Princess Marie Louise of Schleswig Holstein. The reason for the visit being that the Princess had been invited to open the annual Orleton Hall fete.   *Author's Collection*

Chapter Five

Along the Line
The Route Described

This chapter describes the line during the period of the 1920s / early 1930s.

The market town of Wellington, until the coming of the new town of Telford, was second only to the county town of Shrewsbury, dominated by the famous Shropshire landmark, the Wrekin. A town where industry and agriculture met, in the streets could be seen the agricultural labourer with his 'york' straps fastened below his knees, mingling with the miner and furnace worker with his red neckerchief and whippet.

The prosperity of Wellington was no doubt due to its nearness to the mines and ironworks of the East Shropshire coalfield. Many industries became established both in and around the town in the 19th century, these comprised of brewing and malting, an extensive timber yard (owned by the Groom family), and the agricultural engineering firm of S. Corbett and Son. In the early part of the 19th century the town consisted of street traders, but in 1866 a market hall was constructed on the site of a former town hall. The cattle market was established in 1867, before this cattle were sold in the streets.

Wellington, as a railway junction was born out of an enforced agreement between the Shrewsbury & Birmingham, the London & North Western, and the Shropshire Union Railway & Canal companies. The agreement ensured that all traffic between Shrewsbury and Wellington should be pooled and divided equally between the three companies. The joint line between Wellington and Shrewsbury was opened on 1st June, 1849, the Shropshire Union line from Wellington to Stafford being opened on the same day. The Shrewsbury & Birmingham was only able to open its line as far as Oakengates station, some 2½ miles beyond Wellington, due to the fact that Oakengates tunnel was not completed. The rest of the line was opened throughout to Wolverhampton (High Level) on Monday 12th November, 1849. On 16th October, 1867 the Wellington and Market Drayton Railway was opened linking up with the isolated Nantwich & Market Drayton line, thereby affording Wellington a direct link with Crewe and Manchester.

Returning to the Wellington and Craven Arms branch, journeys commenced from Nos. 3 and 4 bay platforms crossing over the down main line on to the up main line just beyond the Wellington No. 2 signal box. Moving through a deep cutting Stafford Junction is passed and the train enters into solely Great Western territory. Squeezed in the 'V' between the Stafford line and the GWR line is passed on the left the Haybridge Iron Works (opened in 1864), making wire rods, and later iron and steel bars and sections. There were three sidings into the works off the main line controlled by a ground frame (there was a signal box here until 7th December, 1932).

Leaving the main line at Ketley Junction on the left, as the train climbs the 1 in 50 gradient to Ketley, passengers could see what was once the site of the old Waterloo Sidings. Passing under the narrow cast-iron bridge carrying a foot path from Ketley to Hadley, the Wrekin Foundry comes into view, better known locally as James Clay Ltd. The works moved from Wellington in 1924; they were renowned for their agricultural machinery, and implements. The line then crossed the A5 road at Ketley, here the closure of the crossing gates during shunting operations into Clay's sidings was the cause of much annoyance to many motorists making their way home in the evening. The range of buildings at Ketley consisted of a signal box next to the level crossing, with booking office and waiting room attached, also adjoining was the station master's house.

One lasting memory that many of the passengers would have had of the Ketley waiting room was of two very large framed advertisements, one extolling the Fishguard to Rosslare Steamship service of the GWR the other advising the travelling public of the advantages of joining the 'Railway Passengers Insurance Association', details of which might be obtained

Note: The Madeley branch is described in Chapter Six.

The 3.16 pm Wellington to Crewe, this train consisted of the last four coaches which were detached at Wellington from the 9.40 am Bournemouth to Birkenhead express. This train ran non-stop to Crewe and then on to Manchester (London Road). The stock alternated between Southern and Great Western stock, on this particular day it consists of Southern stock. The train is headed by Wellington locomotive 'Bulldog' class 4-4-0 No. 3417 *Lord Mildmay of Flete* passing under Springfield Bridge, Wellington and entering on to the Crewe branch on 7th June, 1938.

Brunel University Collection

An LMS 'Super D' 0-8-0 standing on the down main at Wellington on 21st June, 1947.

H.C. Casserley

BR Standard class '3' 2-6-2T No. 82006 curves away from Ketley Junction on 30th March, 1959 with the 5.50 pm Wellington to Much Wenlock service. *M. Mensing*

The 5.50 pm Wellington to Much Wenlock service is seen between Ketley Junction and Ketley hauled by a '57XX' class 0-6-0PT No. 3626 on 12th September, 1959. To the right can be seen the cutting where John Dickson constructed his private railway linking the Waterloo Sidings with the Ketley furnaces in February 1851. *M. Mensing*

The 7.05 pm Much Wenlock to Wellington train on 5th August, 1961 headed by '57XX' class 0-6-0PT No. 3744 as it passes the Wrekin Foundry shortly after leaving Ketley station. It is noticeable that at this time the last train of the day had been reduced to a single coach.

M. Mensing

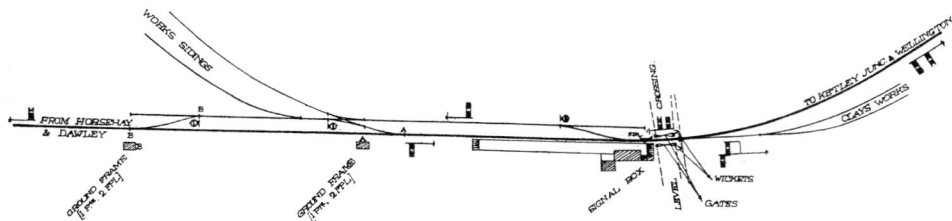

G.W.R. KETLEY STATION.

from the local station master. It was the practice of the GWR that all local station masters automatically became agents of this Insurance Association. Another feature of the waiting room was a large round oak table on which was a family bible of considerable size, placed there by James Keay a Wellington printer who resided at nearby Ketley Hall in the latter part of the 19th century. It was no doubt Keay's intention that waiting passengers should not pass the time in discussing idle pursuits, but turn their minds to the spiritual aspects of life.

Leaving Ketley station on a high embankment the passenger had the first view of the former industrial activity of the area, for stretching out from the line as far as the Ketley to Ketley Town road was a 'moonscape' of small slag mounds, created by the former Ketley Ironworks, and on the rise behind Ketley Hall can be seen the site of the former Ketley inclined plane. Ketley incline was at the end of the Oakengates to Ketley canal, built in 1787 to link the mines in the Oakengates area with the Ketley Ironworks. This inclined plane was the first to be successfully used on a canal in Great Britain.

Another sight from the carriage window below the slag tips, and a towering pennystone clay mound, was a half-timbered cottage where a local miner and his son could be seen extracting coal from a shallow shaft in the garden at the rear of the cottage by a rope and bucket. On leaving Ketley on the right was a long loop line off which went extensive sidings into the Sinclair Iron Company's works, these works having been set up in 1903 for the making of light castings.

Within two minutes of leaving Ketley the train would be pulling into Ketley Town Halt, which opened on 6th March, 1936 to serve the inhabitants of the newly-built estate of Sinclair Gardens. Leaving Ketley Town Halt, on the left the line follows the track bed of the tramway which ran from the Ketley Ironworks to Horsehay, also from the same side of the line a 'gin' pit could be seen with a horse wearily walking round winding the coal out of the mine shaft.

In contrast to the mine shafts and pit mounds, as the train progresses towards New Dale Halt the line passes the local beauty spot of Ketley Dingle, through which ran a stream, on either side of which had been planted trees and shrubs, an area much used as the annual venue for the local Sunday School 'treats' before seaside resorts became more popular. Also another feature of the Dingle was that on Bank Holidays during the early part of this century the trees would be adorned with candle-lit lanterns.

Still climbing, now at 1 in 45, the train reaches New Dale Halt, opened on 29th January, 1934 to serve the local mining community. The Coalbrookdale Company erected a settlement at New Dale following the installation by them (in 1759) of a short-lived furnace and foundry. The community consisted of a Quaker Meeting House, later to become a Wesleyan Chapel, and 28 back-to-back houses. Also on the right of the Halt could be seen the three-arched tramway bridge over the Ketley Dingle stream.

Just before arriving at the level crossing at Lawley Bank station, on the left was a small brickworks with three kilns, and at the side of the brickworks a drift or adit could be seen going into the hillside. This drift was driven in by the Wrekin Coal Company in the late 1920s to link into the workings of its colliery at Prince's End, Lawley Bank.

After passing over the level crossing the train arrives at Lawley Bank station, with its small wooden signal box and adjoining wooden waiting room. To the traveller on the branch Lawley Bank station always looked drab and uninviting, giving the appearance that a coat of paint on its wooden structure would never have been wasted. During the 1920s and throughout the 1930s, as each passenger train arrived at the station they would be greeted by a local character, all 3 ft 4 in. of him, little Billy Lloyd. Billy would be waiting on the platform with his small truck made out of an orange box with its two small wheels and wooden handles waiting to collect any parcel for delivery to the inhabitants of either Lawley or Lawley Bank.

On leaving Lawley Bank the line now rises sharply to 1 in 45 as it approaches Horsehay tunnel (59 yards). On a Saturday afternoon, or on a summer evening, in a field on the left of the line before reaching the tunnel, it would be possible to witness the miners indulging in their favourite sport of 'rabbit coursing'.

Ketley station in August 1932 showing the crossing gates over the A5 London to Holyhead road, and the substantial station master's house. The signals are the Ketley starter and the distant signal for Ketley Junction. *Real Photographs*

Ketley Town Halt looking towards New Dale, showing the Ketley distant signal. Note the shunting spur and stop block from the Sinclair Ironworks' sidings on the extreme right. *Lens of Sutton*

Ketley Town Halt had been built in 1936 and is seen here after the removal, in 1962, of its wooden shelter. On the left is the much overgrown shunting spur from Sinclair's sidings. Sinclair's Ironworks can be seen in the distance. *Lens of Sutton*

New Dale Halt had been built to serve the mining community of that name. Note the sleeper supports under the platform. The tramway constructed by Abraham Darby (II) in 1756 between Ketley and Horsehay ran at the rear of the Halt. *Ironbridge Gorge Museum*

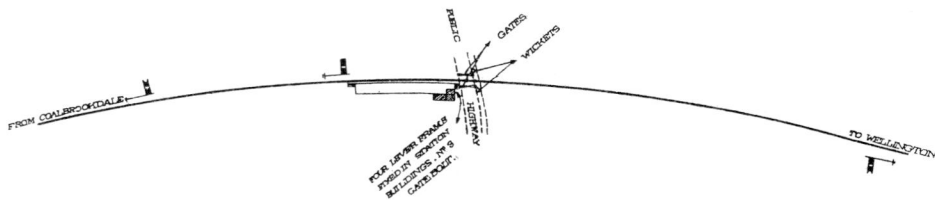

G.W.R. LAWLEY BANK.

FROM COALBROOKDALE

TO WELLINGTON

PUBLIC

GATES

WICKETS

FOUR LEVER FRAME
FIXED IN STATION
BUILDINGS . Nº 8
GATE BOLT.

HEADWAY

Lawley Bank station showing (*from left to right*) part of the signal box, booking office, waiting room, and parcels' storage shed. Just beyond the dilapidated fencing is the corrugated shed used as a signal lamp room.

Lens of Sutton

After leaving Horsehay tunnel the summit of that steep climb from Lawley Bank is reached, and immediately the train takes a sharp plunge down a steep drop of 1 in 40 leading into Horsehay & Dawley station. Before reaching the station the goods yard can be seen on the right with its 10 sidings and a spur. Horsehay yard was always a scene of great activity, shunting operations were continually being carried out by the Horsehay Company's own works engine. The train enters a shallow cutting below the goods yard to arrive at Horsehay & Dawley station. The signal box is separate from the rest of the station buildings which are of brick construction and consist of a booking office and general waiting room.

Dawley's claim to fame is that it was the birthplace of Capt. Matthew Webb, the first man to swim the English Channel in 1875. If Horsehay station never appeared to be crowded with passengers, one item which always adorned the station was pigeon baskets: during the pigeon racing season Horsehay was on the racing circuit.

A unique feature of the station was its 'milk ramp'. The approach to the station from the Horsehay to Dawley road was by a very steep slope not sufficiently wide to take a wheeled vehicle, in consequence of which the local farmers had difficulty in moving their milk churns from the road on to the platform. Following the increased competition from road transport for the haulage of milk, in 1925 the railway company installed a ramp from the road on to the station platform. This consisted of a brick ramp, on which were placed two rails, 18 inches apart. The milk churns were placed on to the rails and slowly lowered down the ramp to the platform. Sadly this facility had been introduced too late, as by the latter part of the 1920s much of the milk traffic conveyed on the branch had been taken over by road haulage.

On leaving Horsehay platform, under the wide-arched bridge carrying the Horsehay to Dawley road (and at one time the horse-drawn tramway carrying coal and iron stone into the old Horsehay furnaces), on the right was the extensive works of the Horsehay Company famous for its manufacture of bridges, girders and cranes. Emerging from Horsehay station in a deep cutting the line to Lightmoor Jn continues on a steep downward gradient. The passengers would suddenly be confronted by a scene of both former and present industrial activity; a landscape created by man. To the left of the waste tips and disused mineshafts on the Brandlee was a tall chimney stack towering above the derelict kilns and buildings of a pipe works, which operated until 1915, known by the sophisticated name of 'Days Automatic Waste Water Closet & Sanitary Pipe Syndicate Co. Ltd'. Just below was a group of industrial houses known as 'The Potteries', the central feature of which was an old pot kiln known as 'The Roundhouse' which was being used as a domestic dwelling. At this point rising sharply above the line to the right was a slag mass created from the Coalbrookdale Company's furnaces at Horsehay, which closed in 1886. This slag mound was a dominant feature of the area and ballast from here had been used on many parts of the GWR system.

Descending into the Lightmoor valley, high on the hillside is the turreted building of the Pool Hill School, built in 1845 by the Coalbrookdale Company for the children of its employees. Just beyond there may be seen the huge waste mounds of the Deepfield, Top Yard, and Springwell collieries dominating the whole of the valley. Reaching the small settlement of Doseley, on the right below the railway embankment may be seen the red and pale brick church of St Luke's built in 1845, the church being wedged in between Doseley Brick Works and Johnston's road stone quarry. From this point on the line the remains of the bed of the Coalbrookdale arm of the Shropshire Canal can be seen. Also below this vantage point on the high embankment can be seen a long row of industrial dwellings, Sandy Bank Row, better known locally as 'Dill Doll Row', built by the Coalbrookdale Company in the early 1830s to house its workers employed at the Horsehay and Dawley Castle furnaces.

The next stopping point is Doseley Halt with its crossing gates, small signal cabin, and crossing keeper's house. The Halt was opened on 1st December, 1932 when the railways generally were becoming concerned at the steadily increasing opposition from road transport. The GWR found that the inhabitants of Doseley no longer wanted to walk to Lightmoor or Horsehay to catch the train, all that was now necessary was to walk the few hundred yards to Little Dawley from where the Midland Red Bus Company had commenced to run a service

The Horsehay Company's 0-4-0 locomotive is seen in Horsehay goods yard *c.* 1924. *Left to right,* are Jack Wedge (GWR platelayer), George Woolford (Horsehay Co. shunter), Lloyd Jones (Horsehay Co. shunter), Howard North (Horsehay Co. maintenance engineer), Ben Evans (truck loader for the Coalmoor Sanitary Pipe Co.) and Jack Smith (GWR platelayer). The wagon next to the engine bears the name Maw & Co., Benthall. *Ironbridge Gorge Museum*

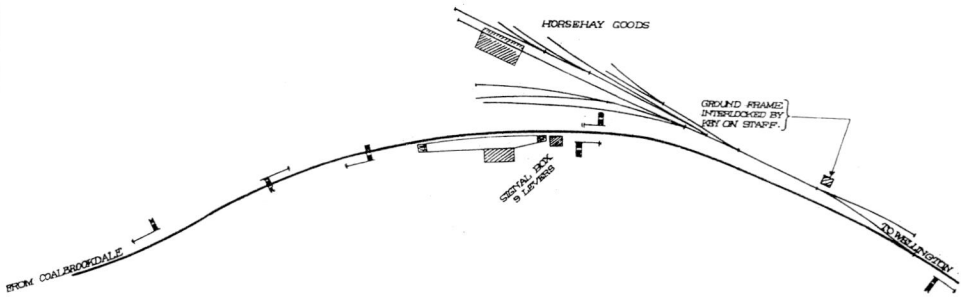

A railway turntable being constructed in the Horsehay Company's yard *c.* 1922. In the background can be seen the company's engine shed, and to the left Horsehay pool. *R. Stanley*

A scene which dominated the Horsehay area up to World War I was the sanitary pipe works on the Brandlee, its full title being Day's Automatic Waste Water Closet & Sanitary Pipe Syndicate Co. Ltd. A tramway connected this works with the GWR sidings at Horsehay.

Ironbridge Gorge Museum

Doseley Crossing cabin and Halt. Note the two oil lamps on the halt, these were attended to by the crossing keeper, in consequence there was no need for the guard to put down and take up the tilley lamp as was the case at other halts along the branch. The sharp gradient at the Horsehay end of the platform necessitated most passenger trains, especially when the rails were wet, having to back down over the crossing to get away on the level.   *Lens of Sutton*

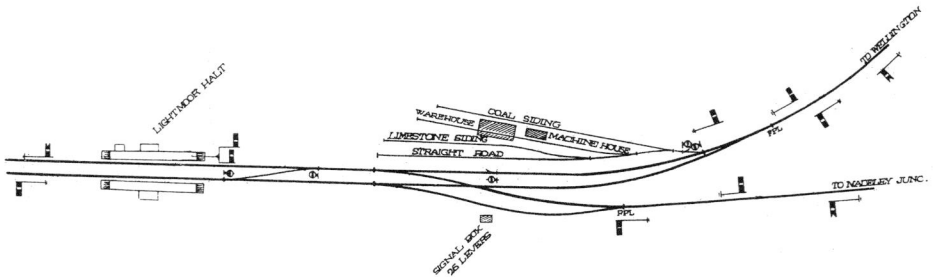

G.W.R. LIGHTMOOR JUNCTION.

to Wellington in the summer of 1932. To add further to the company's problems, within a few months of building the Halt a William Jackson started to run a private bus service from outside the Halt to Wellington on market days.

On leaving the Halt on the left rising sharply above is the huge mass of the spoil heap of the former Springwell Colliery which operated from the early 1790s to the mid-1880s. From this shaft both coal and ironstone had been mined. It was at the Springwell Colliery on the afternoon of 6th December, 1872 that eight miners lost their lives, due to the breaking of the pit chain as they were ascending the shaft. Looking out from the right of the train as it approaches the small hamlet of Gravel Leasows, the unique squatter settlement of Holywell Lane comes into view. The miners, furnace and brickyard workers, built their cottages on waste land to form this settlement within the Manor of Dawley Parva.

Also in Gravel Leasows the line passes the former Jubilee Primitive Methodist Chapel, known locally as 'The Pop Bottle Chapel', built in 1863 to serve the local mining community. Just below Gravel Leasows the line was cut through a pennystone pit mound, and on emerging from this grey surround there comes into view on the left a field by the name of the 'Bandridge Leasow', the 'Bandridge' being the boundary field of the once open-field system that operated in this part of the Manor of Dawley Parva. Passing over Dawley Parva level crossing with its small signal cabin and crossing keeper's house, the train passes over a cast-iron bridge, under which once ran the horse-drawn tramway linking the Lightmoor furnaces with the Dawley Castle furnaces. On rounding a sharp right-hand curve Lightmoor Junction is approached, where, to the left, trails in the Madeley branch adjacent to which was situated Lightmoor Junction signal box.

Lightmoor is a scene of contrasts. On the left can be seen the stacks of the Lightmoor Brick and Tile Works, belching its black smoke with a backdrop of pennystone pit mounds, and the slag tips of the former Lightmoor furnaces, and on the right, until the late 1920s, could be seen the wide open spaces of the Rough Park golf course and the adjoining fields, undisturbed by any former industrial activity. On arrival at Lightmoor the line becomes double track; the station at Lightmoor was opened on the 12th August, 1907, and was known as Lightmoor Platform. The platforms were wooden and the waiting rooms were of corrugated iron with a pagoda roof. The booking office was below the platforms at road level. The gents' urinal at the south end of the up platform was unique, it consisted of cast-iron plates with a cast-iron filigree top, and provided accommodation for one person only.

Leaving Lightmoor on the down line, on a gradient of 1 in 50, the train passes over another horse-drawn tramway linking the Lightmoor Brick and Tile Works with the Coalbrookdale Ironworks. The line now passes through the Lightmoor Dingle with its tree-lined pit pounds on either side. As the train emerges from the trees, above and to the left are the large stone blocks holding back the waters of the Coalbrookdale Company's New pool. This pool was used as a reservoir for the rest of the operating pools in the Coalbrookdale valley. Emerging from the cutting created by the stone block retaining wall, the old mill appears; this was erected by the Darby family in the middle of the 18th century to grind the corn for the inhabitants of Coalbrookdale. Until the late 1920s the remains of an old water wheel could be seen on the side of the mill. After crossing the Cherry Tree Hill road bridge, rising sharply above the line to the right is the densely wooded Vane Coppice, down which an inclined plane was laid in 1793-4 linking the Coalbrookdale arm of the Shropshire Canal at Brierly Hill with the Coalbrookdale Ironworks.

Taking a sharp left-hand curve into the head of the Coalbrookdale valley the train arrives at Green Bank Halt, taking its name from the estate which surrounds it. The Halt was opened on the 12th March, 1934. After crossing the Coalbrookdale-Wellington road the train enters the tree lined valley of Coalbrookdale over a 26-arch viaduct, to the right of which is the Sunnyside Estate, the home of the Darby's, the Quaker ironmasters. To the left, on the floor of the valley, is the famous ironworks. Entering upon the viaduct the train crosses over the Upper Furnace pool; the traveller on the line in the early 1930s would have gazed down from the viaducts to the left on to what was known as the Upper Works, consisting of pattern shops, belt repair

The 26-arch viaduct viewed from the site of the former Brierly Hill inclined plane c. 1925. The viaduct carried the Lightmoor extension between Lightmoor and Coalbrookdale built by the GWR and opened for traffic on 1st November, 1864. At the north end of the viaduct can be seen the Green Bank Farm, to the left of the viaduct can be seen the old mill and the coke hearth. The small building in the centre with the tall chimney is the former toll house at the bottom of Jiggers Bank on the Wellington-Coalbrookdale toll road.

Ironbridge Gorge Museum

shops and moulding rooms. Little did the traveller know that under this mass of buildings lay the furnace where, in 1709, Abraham Darby (I) revolutionised the iron industry by smelting iron with coke as a fuel. In his wildest dreams that same traveller could never have envisaged that 60 years hence this valley would be designated a World Heritage Site.

As the train passes down the valley under Captain's Coppice, looking across to the east side of the valley can be seen the imposing Holy Trinity Church built in 1854, and the blue brick building of the Literary and Scientific Institution built by the Coalbrookdale Company in 1859. Immediately below in the works might be seen locomotive No. 5 carrying out shunting operations, this being one of the six locomotives built by the Coalbrookdale Company. Rounding a sharp right-hand curve Coalbrookdale station is reached, with its sidings going off on a steep downward gradient into the works.

On arrival at Coalbrookdale station the passenger is struck by the design and layout of the station buildings, with its yellow brick and tiled roof, a stark contrast to the drab, uninteresting designs of the station buildings encountered between Ketley and Lightmoor Junction. From here on the journey enters the domain of that interesting character Joseph Fogerty, the Assistant Engineer who was responsible for the building of the remainder of the line, and whose influence is to be seen in all the station buildings between Coalbrookdale and Harton Road.

Leaving Coalbrookdale, to the left can be seen the stone block viaduct built into the rock of the Ironbridge Gorge below Benthall Edge, carrying the Severn Valley line. The train now enters a deep cutting in which it passes over Chune's Crossing, so named after the family who once farmed the adjacent land. This is merely an occupation crossing going to a smallholding and a sand hole beyond. In the crossing keeper's house there was a repeating block bell and indicator, and near the front door of the house were two levers which operated signals protecting the crossing gates. From time to time reviews were made of the crossing with view to dispensing with the services of the crossing keeper, but each time the same conclusion was reached that: 'Due to bad sighting of the crossing by approaching trains, it is not considered desirable to make any change'. As the train emerges from the cutting the passenger is afforded a wonderful view eastwards of the Ironbridge Gorge through which the River Severn flows, and although scarred by industry in former years, it has done little to detract from the rural charm of this beautiful valley, with its houses clinging to the side of the Gorge, dominated by the Old Lodge, once the hunting lodge of the Priors of Wenlock Priory, and St Luke's Church.

Passing over that great work of engineering, the Albert Edward Bridge built by the Coalbrookdale Company, on looking down from the bridge to the left the passenger could gaze down on to the Meadow Ferry, one of the last surviving ferries in the Gorge, with the ferryman conveying his passengers across the river in a punt boat, hauling on a wire strung from the river bank on either side. Also from the bridge could be seen a siding, making its way to the river side, where once the limestone was conveyed from Wenlock quarries. At the end of the siding are the remains of the quay where limestone was unloaded on to Severn barges for transportation down river for use in the Madeley Wood Company's Blists Hill furnaces. At the end of its life, this siding, thought to have been removed about 1931, was only used for the occasional wagon of coal destined for the steam engine which pumped water from the river to the water columns at Buildwas station.

After crossing the Albert Edward Bridge, the train briefly joins the Severn Valley line (opened on 1st February, 1862 by the West Midland Railway Company and linking the towns of Shrewsbury and Hartlebury). Approaching Buildwas station, towering above the river, are the steel stacks of the Ironbridge 'A' Power Station acting as a landmark at the end of the Severn plain before entering the Ironbridge Gorge. The opening of the power station on 13th October, 1932 brought new life to the Much Wenlock branch, with the daily scenes of coal trains coming in from the Staffordshire coalfields via the Madeley branch. There also followed a considerable increase in passenger traffic bringing in workmen to the power station.

An aerial view of Coalbrookdale c. 1925 showing the Upper and Lower Works of the Coalbrookdale Company with the Wenlock branch snaking its way through the valley, also visible are the sidings extending from Coalbrookdale station into the works. Under the Wellington road on the right can be seen the narrow gauge tramway which ran from the works to the Severn Foundry on the side of the River Severn at Ironbridge.
Ironbridge Gorge Museum

Ivatt class '2' 2-6-2T No. 41201 crossing the viaduct at Coalbrookdale with the 5.45 pm Much Wenlock to Wellington train on 9th June, 1962. Note the strengthening roundels which are marked 'GWR 1902'. Traffic at this spot is much busier today than that depicted in the photograph. The fifth arch from the left is now the main entrance to the Ironbridge Gorge Museum's Coalbrookdale site. *M. Mensing*

Diesel railcar No. W55012 is seen operating the 5.50 pm Wellington to Much Wenlock service on 9th June, 1962 just south of Coalbrookdale viaduct. To the right can be seen the Coalbrookdale Company's Long Warehouse built in 1839 with its clock tower of 1843. To the right of the clock tower in the trees is the site of Brierly Hill inclined plane. *M. Mensing*

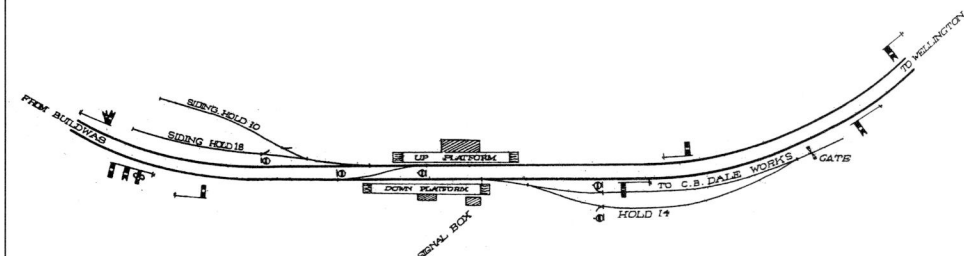

G.W.R. COALBROOKDALE.

'850' class 0-6-0 saddle tank No. 1947 at Coalbrookdale in the early 1890s on a passenger train bound for Wellington. No. 1947 was built at Wolverhampton in March 1887 and pannier tanks were fitted in 1922. The engine was eventually withdrawn in November 1938. Note the rape oil lamp containers on top of the four-wheel coaches.   *Ironbridge Gorge Museum*

A posed photograph of the Meadow Ferry on the River Severn below the Albert Edward Bridge at Buildwas *c.* 1898. To the left of the boat is the bearded ferryman holding on to the pulley wire, to the right can be seen the lad porter from Buildwas smoking a pipe. The local constabulary is also much in evidence. It would appear that in addition to operating the ferry, the ferryman also hired out pleasure boats on the river. *Ironbridge Gorge Museum*

The Albert Edward Bridge and River Severn at Buildwas *c.* 1908. To the left of the bridge can be seen the steam rising from the pumping engine house. The pumping engine was used for pumping water from the river to the water columns at Buildwas station. Note the boats in the foreground moored at Meadow Ferry. *Ironbridge Gorge Museum*

A Stephenson Locomotive Society Special approaching Buildwas Junction on 23rd April, 1955 headed by 'Dean Goods' 0-6-0 No. 2516. To the right is the Buildwas North end slack sidings with wagons from the power station, and to the left of the engine is the Severn Valley line.

H.F. Wheeler

Peckett 0-4-0ST shunting in the Ironbridge Power Station sidings at Buildwas in April 1959.

H.C. Casserley

Ironbridge 'A' Power Station, Buildwas. Opened on 13th October, 1932 by the Minister of Transport P.J. Pybus. *Ironbridge Gorge Museum*

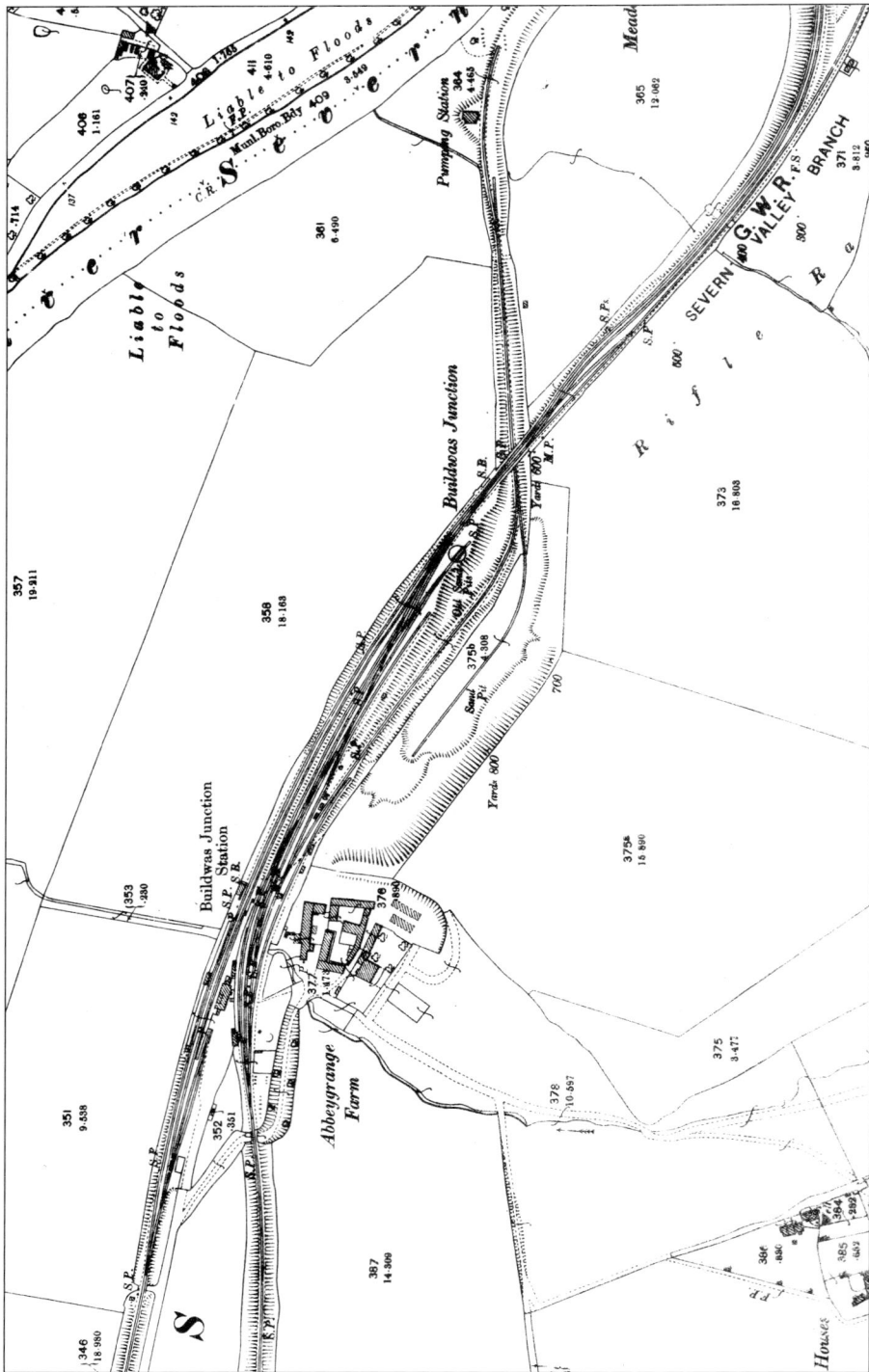

Buildwas Junction. Note the site of the Junction and Station signal boxes, also the sand pit sidings, and the pumping station sidings used by the Madeley Wood Company for the purpose of transferring limestone on to its barges on the River Severn for transhipment to its furnaces at Blists Hill.

Reproduced from the 25", 1882 Ordnance Survey Map

As the Wenlock branch train approaches Buildwas station the lines diverge; the Severn Valley continuing straight on towards the low level up and down platforms, the Wenlock branch diverging to the left and heading towards the (single) high level platform for the Wenlock-bound trains. Sandwiched in between the high and low level platforms were the station buildings, consisting of, booking office, waiting rooms, and station master's house (further details are in Chapter Six). The usual practice was for a Wenlock-bound branch train to proceed along the Wenlock loop (which paralleled the platform line), run on to the Wenlock branch and then reverse into the platform, backing on to a Wellington-bound train already standing in the single platform.

Buildwas station was two miles from the village, and the only sign of life outside the station was the day-to-day activity at the adjoining Grange Farm. Nevertheless, despite its isolation, Buildwas was never devoid of passengers: people changing trains, fishermen, families from Ketley, Horsehay and Dawley whose finances never allowed for the occasional train journey to the seaside, and who had to be content with a visit to nearby Sandy Beach for a paddle and a picnic by the side of the river. In addition there would be visitors to nearby Buildwas Abbey.

Leaving Buildwas the train starts its long arduous climb of 1 in 40 up Farley Dingle, to the right can be seen the river, meandering slowly before plunging into the Ironbridge Gorge, also the picturesque ruin of the 12th century Cistercian Abbey, with the remains of its fish ponds clearly indentifiable in the adjoining fields. Stretching out below is the road leading up the Dingle to Farley and Much Wenlock, and on the roadside can be seen the Buildwas Mill, one of three corn mills driven by the waters of the Farley Brook. Buildwas Mill was still being used to grind corn until 1928, but in the early 1930s the mill area was turned into the Buildwas estate timber yard, and the mill machinery used to drive the saw mill. Another familiar site at the commencement of the Dingle was the old timber-framed tithe barn which was part of the Mill Farm.

By now the passenger is fully aware from the sharp staccato blasts of the '44XX' class engine that the two-coach load is stretching the locomotive to its limits on this winding gradient through the limestone rocks. On the right, and well below the line, can be seen the small hamlet of Lawless Cross, with the Farley Brook charging over a waterfall in its haste to reach the Severn. Shortly after leaving Lawless Cross, on the right, was a yard which was a sight to behold for the steam enthusiast; there could be seen steam traction engines, steam rollers and threshing boxes, this being the home of the Shaw family, who were the local road and farm threshing contractors. An interesting feature of the Shaw's house which was attached to the yard, was that the front room of the house was used by the Primitive Methodists as a cottage meeting room. On the opposite side of the line is a deep chasm formed by quarrying for limestone, known as Norrey's Rock, once operated by Lord Forester. During heavy rains the Farley Brook would charge through this chasm in a raging torrent. Just beyond Norrey's Rock and on the same side the train is dwarfed by the high limestone block retaining wall, built to hold back the loose limestone rock which abounds in this area.

The echo of the exhaust from the engine now reverberates around the Dingle as the train continues its long, arduous climb towards Farley Halt. However, before reaching the Halt on the left is the old Farley Mill, the second of the Farley Brook mills. In addition to being water-powered it was also operated by steam. It closed as a flour mill in 1917 but continued as a corn mill until the mid-1920s. The mill was operated for many years by the Harper family, Caleb Harper was a substantial shareholder in the Wenlock and Severn Junction Railway.

On leaving the mill behind and taking a slight left-hand curve, Farley Halt is reached. Opened on the 27th October, 1934, the Halt was situated below the Rock House public house, and on the Buildwas to Much Wenlock road. The Halt is adjacent to a bridge carrying a road over the line into what was once the Bradley quarries; after passing under the bridge, a siding, controlled by a ground frame, goes off into the former quarry. As early as 1777 the Madeley Wood Company was extracting limestone from Bradley for use in its Bedlam furnaces; however, by 1832 the Coalbrookdale Company owned the quarry. In 1889 the company sold the quarry to Caleb Harper of the Farley Mill; by 1900 Harper had leased the quarry to Adam Boulton, who continued to operate it until its closure in 1931. Following its closure as a quarry

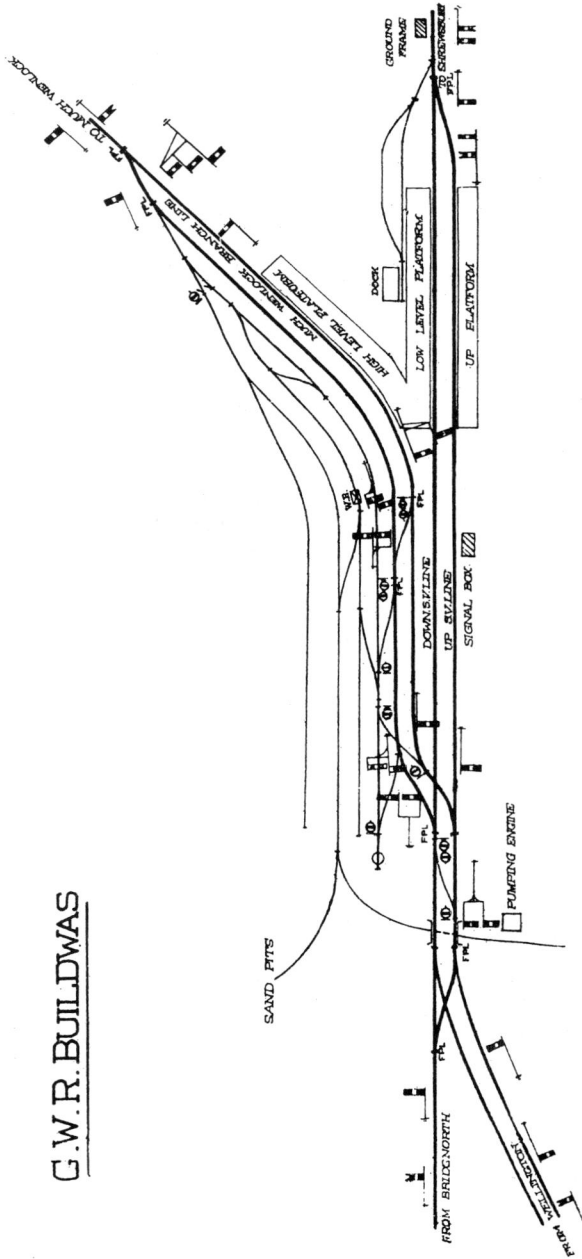

G.W.R. BULLDWAS

Buildwas station in August 1932 looking towards Ironbridge on the Severn Valley line. The cabin on the down platform to the left of the station buildings housed the electric staff instruments for the Buildwas to Wenlock section of the Wenlock branch.   *Real Photographs*

Buildwas Junction in August 1950 with '44XX' class 2-6-2T No. 4401 on the high level platform with a train for Wellington, and on the low level platform is '51XX' class 2-6-2T No. 4139 waiting to leave with a passenger train for Hartlebury. Wellington fireman, John Evison, looks down towards the Hartlebury train from the high level platform.   *Real Photographs*

The 11.17 am Wellington to Much Wenlock train hauled by '51XX' class 2-6-2T No. 4120 climbs through Farley Dingle between Buildwas and Much Wenlock on 30th March, 1959. To the left can be seen Lawless Cross and the old road where at this point a steep climb commenced through the Dingle. In the background can be seen the outline of Shropshire's famous landmark, The Wrekin. The train is traversing the route of the present road through the Dingle.
M. Mensing

Farley Halt looking towards Much Wenlock. Under the bridge can be seen the points leading into the Bradley quarry sidings. Through the trees on the right can be seen the outline of the former 'Rock House' public house.
H.C. Casserley

TO CRAVEN ARMS

GROUND FRAME
3 LEVERS

TO BUILDWAS

MESSRS BOULTON & Cº LOADING PLATFORM & KILNS.

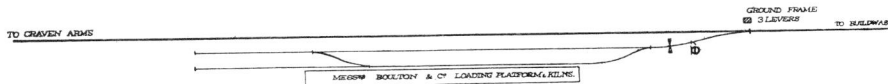

Farley siding in 1932. The buildings once formed part of the Coalbrookdale Company's Bradley quarry. At the time of the photograph it was being operated by Waths Dairy of Birmingham manufacturing cheeses. In 1938 this was turned into a petrol storage terminal.

Author's Collection

Farley Crossing with '14XX' class 0-4-2T No. 1414, a Stourbridge engine, specially commissioned for the the filming of Mary Webb's novel *Gone to Earth* on 20th June, 1949.   *Alderson Collection*

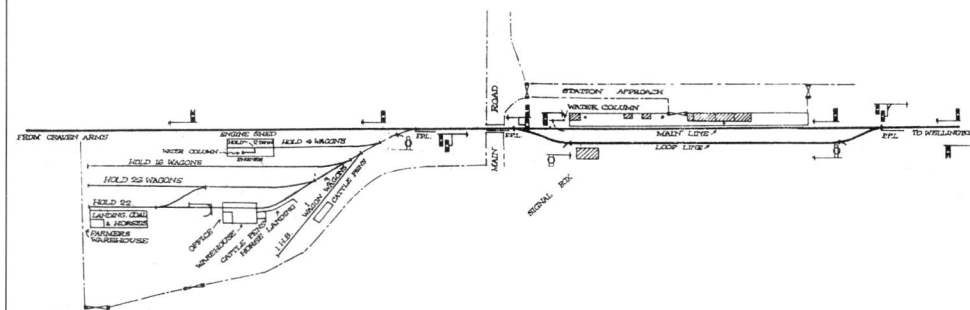

G.W.R. MUCH WENLOCK.

The view of Much Wenlock goods yard from the station on 10th September, 1949. The trees and shrubs were planted shortly after the opening of the line by Dr Willliam Penny Brookes, Wenlock's great benefactor.

H.C. Casserley

the buildings adjacent to the sidings were taken over by the Waths, Dingle Dairies of Birmingham and used as a creamery, producing cheeses until it closed in 1938. By this time the war clouds were beginning to gather, and the buildings and quarry were taken over by the Ministry of Defence, who turned the area into a petrol storage installation.

Shortly after leaving the quarry sidings, the train comes to Farley Crossing over which went a track to the Bradley and Newhouse farms, and on to the small hamlet of the Wyke. Still climbing, and about half a mile from Farley Crossing, on either side of the line are limestone quarries; to the left is the former Standhill quarry, and to the right the Shadwell quarry. Limestone was being extracted from the Standhill quarry in the 1830s, by 1848 a William Roper was renting the quarry from Sir Watkin Williams Wynn. When the line was opened the quarry was being operated by the South Wales & Cannock Chase Coal and Coke Co. On the opening of the line sidings were put in to serve the quarry, but by 1903 these had been lifted. The Shadwell quarry (on the right) was also operated by the Cannock Chase Company, and when the line was built sidings were laid into the quarry, but these were also removed some time between 1904 and 1912. The company continued to operate the quarry until 1910; by 1912 it was owned by M.A. Boswell; in 1925 it was being operated by Tarslag Ltd.

On leaving the quarries the gradient eases momentarily as the train enters a conifer tree-lined embankment, and on emerging from the trees it enters the single platform at Much Wenlock, with its imposing Gothic stone building. On the opposite side to the platform, and adjacent to the parallel loop line, which had no platform, there could be seen a beautiful rockery, with large limestone boulders interspersed with shrubs and alpine plants, flanked by a row of rhododendron bushes. In the centre of the rockery was a fountain, which alas had long ceased to operate. The cost of landscaping the station area had been borne by the Vice Chairman of the Wen&SJR, Dr William Penny Brookes. (For further detail of the station, see Chapter Six.) The ancient Borough of Wenlock is a town of great historical interest with its black and white timber-framed houses, the ruins of its ancient Cluniac Priory, and its 16th century Guildhall, which rests on the oaken arches of the buttermarket and which houses a whipping post and portable stocks. On starting away from the station the train crosses Sheinton Road bridge, and on the left can be seen the goods yard (the site of the original passenger station) with its shed and loading deck, and engine shed (closed 31st December, 1951).

Now starts the long climb on to Wenlock Edge, passing on the left a reservoir which provided the water for the column at Wenlock station. The next stop is Westwood Halt opened on 7th December, 1935. The Halt served the small hamlet of Westwood, with its few cottages and a farm, the unmanned level crossing being a road which led into the farm yard. On leaving Westwood the end of the long climb is reached, and starts to level out to Westwood Sidings. These sidings served the Westwood quarry and were controlled by east and west end ground frames. When the line opened limestone was being extracted for use in the Madeley Wood Company's furnaces. Horse-drawn tramways ran from the quarry on to a loading ramp above the sidings. The quarry was bought by C.R. Kane in 1933.

On arrival at Presthope station, a mile further on, its complete isolation is striking, the only sign of habitation being the station master's house standing on a ridge above the station. Although isolated, its importance is magnified by the number of sidings (a mini-marshalling yard on a branch line), because of the extensive quarrying formerly carried out by the Lilleshall Company in this area. A siding 1½ miles long ran from the station sidings into the Lilleshall quarries. Prior to World War I a special train left Presthope each day for the Lilleshall Company's furnaces at Priors Lee. However, by the early 1920s the company had ceased quarrying operations in the Presthope area.

Leaving Presthope station, to the left of the train was a large outcrop of limestone rock on which were three limekilns, this outcrop with its kilns forming a most dramatic entrance to the 207 yds-long Presthope tunnel driven through the limestone rock. On emergence from the tunnel the passenger is rewarded with a panoramic view of the beautiful Ape Dale with its irregular field patterns and isolated farms with the gently rising backcloth of the Stretton Hills in the distance. A sight never to be forgotten on a winter's morning with the snow-capped hills dominating the Vale.

Much Wenlock station.

Reproduced from the 25″, 1926 Ordnance Survey Map

Much Wenlock station in 1908 with its ivy covered station master's house and station buildings, to the left of the platform is the loop line, in the distance can be seen the GWR signal box opened in 1893, and to the right the original West Midland signal box, the cover of which was placed over the ground frame in 1867. *Shropshire Museum Service*

Much Wenlock station looking towards Buildwas on 18th June, 1949 with the Linden Fields bridge in the distance. Note the local limestone forming the base of the platform.

Real Photographs

An 1870s photograph of Much Wenlock football team, with the station in the background, completely devoid of its later ivy covering, and before the gardens opposite the platform were laid out.   *Shropshire Museum Service*

The forecourt of Much Wenlock station *c.* 1960. The building was designed by Joseph Fogerty.
Note the 'Wen and the Lock' below the finial on the station master's house.   *R.S. Carpenter*

Much Wenlock goods yard. To the left are the cattle pens and the grain store attached to the goods shed. To the right is the engine shed and water tank. The water tank was fed by a pipe connected to a reservoir situated roughly half-way between Wenlock and Westwood Halt.
Shropshire Museum Service

Another view of the goods yard at Much Wenlock; it was here that the temporary station was built following the opening of the Wen &SJR on 1st February, 1862. *Pat Garland*

Westwood Halt in 1954. The crossing gates can still be seen, the nameboard still stands but the halt shelter has been removed.   *Shropshire Museum Service*

G.W.R. WESTWOOD SIDING. [PRESTHOPE.]

G.W.R. PRESTHOPE

Presthope station on 4th August, 1932. On the extreme right can be seen the Lilleshall Company's former mineral line into their limestone quarry.   *Mowat Collection*

The Lilleshall Company's standard gauge mineral railway linking its limestone quarries on Wenlock Edge with Presthope station.

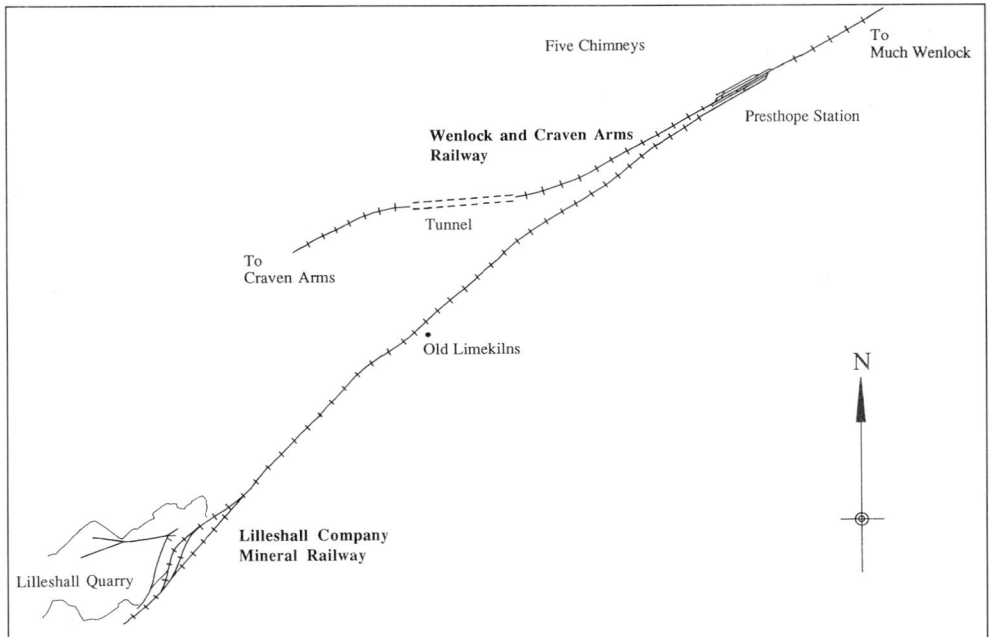

G.W.R. LONGVILLE

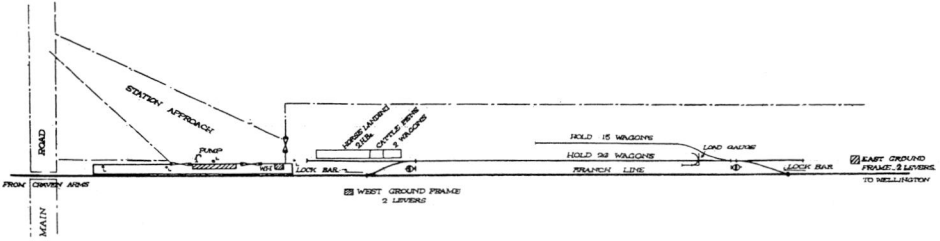

Longville station *c.* 1930. It is apparent from the number of milk churns on the platform that road haulage had not fully captured the milk traffic from this section of the branch.

Mowat Collection

The course of the line now drops dramatically as the train approaches the isolated Easthope Halt, opened on 4th April, 1936. The Halt is built clinging to the side of the Edge Wood and served the isolated farms and village of Easthope which was some 2½ miles away on the other side of Wenlock Edge. The train continues through the Edge Wood where a variety of bird and wild life could be seen. Foxes and rabbits abounded, and on occasions the journey could be further enlivened by the sight of a deer dashing into the wood, or a buzzard soaring above having strayed from the Stretton Hills. The line continues to fall at 1 in 100 towards Longville station; before reaching Longville with Edge Wood to the left still above, the remains of a timber siding can be seen, with the rails lifted, but still with great stacks of timber stacked neatly nearby. The siding was opened in 1919 and timber was brought down from the wood by horses and chains to the sidings.

Longville station, a single platform with its red and yellow brick booking office and waiting room, served a few cottages, a farm, an Inn, and the nearby Lutwyche Hall, the home of the Benson family, who did so much to promote the building of the line between Much Wenlock and Craven Arms. The station also served the villages of Cardington, Holdgate, Shipton and Stanton Long. The platform was on the up side, and the station buildings consisted of a general waiting room, ladies' waiting room of brick and goods warehouse lock-up. There were two sidings, and a horse landing for two horse boxes, and a cattle landing for two wagons. There was no signal box, Longville being an intermediate station on the Presthope to Rushbury staff section. There were east and west ground frames, access to both being obtained by a key on the Presthope-Rushbury staff.

After leaving Longville the line passes under the densely wooded Longville Coppice, and over Coates Crossing with its crossing keeper's house. Since the line was built the house had always been occupied by the Rushbury station master, and it was the duty of the station master's wife to operate the crossing gates as and when a farm cart from the nearby Coates Farm required to go into the fields under Coates Wood. Later, after the abolition of the Rushbury SM's post, it became the duty of the Longville station master's wife.

The line has now levelled out into Ape Dale, and soon enters Rushbury station with its avenue of fir trees on either side, the station in every respect being similar to that of Longville. To the right of the station, about a ¼ mile distant, is the village dominated by the tower of St Peter's Church and the nearby castle mound, all remains of the castle having long since gone. Rushbury still retains its packhorse bridge over the Eaton Brook and the station served the villages of Rushbury and Munslow. The signal box was at the north end of the platform, the box containing the locking frame only, the electric train staff instruments being situated in the booking office. The station was not a crossing place. The station buildings consisted of a booking office, general and ladies' waiting room, and a lamp room. The staff were just the station master and a signalman, the latter being required to assist with station duties. A ground frame was situated at the east end of the station, and gave access to two sidings, a horse landing and cattle pens. In the station yard there was a cart weighbridge. At the Craven Arms end of the platform there was a water column.

On leaving the station the train passes under the roadway which formed part of the Roman road, with a steep rise from the station leading on to Roman Bank and over Wenlock Edge into the Corve Dale. Still passing under the densely wooded Edge Wood, to the left, and nestling under the wood, can be seen the small hamlet of Eaton-under-Heywood, and the embattled tower of the 12th century church of St Edith; the hamlet consists of one farm, the rectory and one cottage. Soon the train enters Harton Road station, the last on the branch. The station is as isolated as the hamlet of Eaton, all that can be seen from the train is a farm, and the station master's house. Harton Road served the hamlets of Ticklerton, Halton, Soudley, Eaton, Westhope and Burwood, most of these (in 1922) each having a population of 50 people, Eaton and Burwood having only 40. The station consisted of the usual buildings: booking office, general and ladies' waiting room and a lamp room. The staff consisted of the station master and one gate woman, she being employed at Wolverton Crossing, which was situated between Harton Road and Marsh Farm Jn. There was one double-ended siding which held 10 wagons,

Coates Crossing between Longville and Rushbury. This was the home of the Longville and Rushbury station master. Note the well kept garden and the telephone box attached to the telegraph pole. *Author's Collection*

Rushbury *c.* 1930 looking towards Much Wenlock. *Mowat Collection*

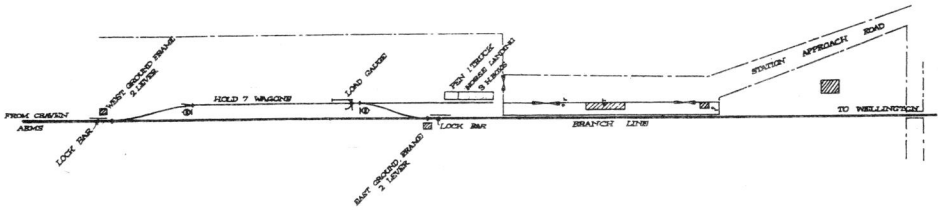

G.W.R. HARTON ROAD.

Harton Road station *c.* 1930 looking towards Craven Arms. The ground frame cabin can be seen to the left of the platform, and the sidings to the right.

Mowat Collection

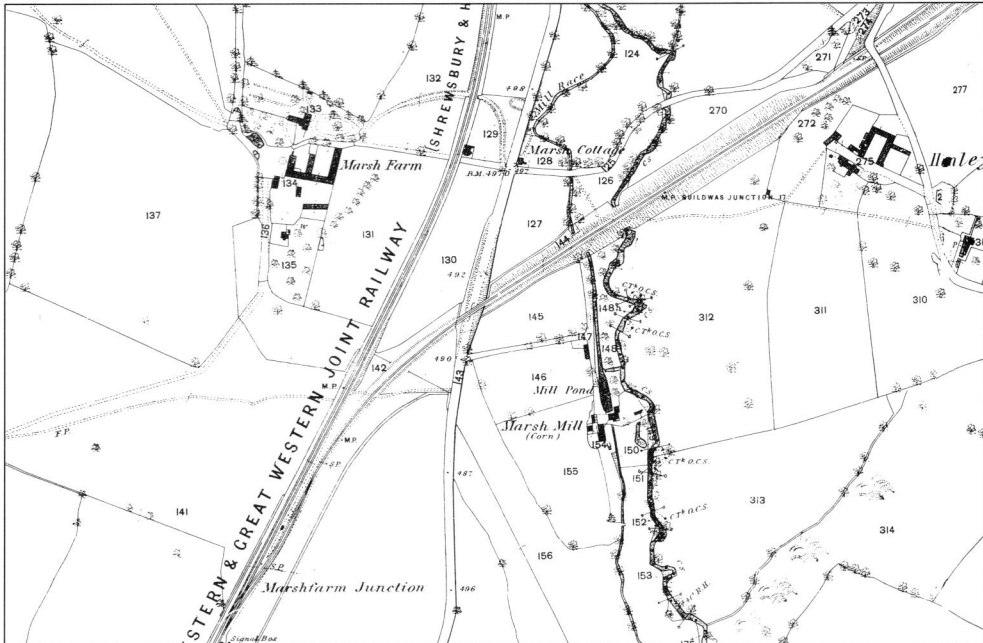

Marsh Farm Junction. *Reproduced from the 1882, 25" Ordnance Survey Map*

Stretford Bridge Junction, Craven Arms in July 1935. Note the signal box carries the name Bishops Castle Junction. To the left was the line to Bishop's Castle and to the right the main line to Shrewsbury. *Author's Collection*

access to which was from either the east or west ground frames. The ground frames were controlled by the key on the Rushbury to Marsh Farm Jn staff. Also in the sidings was a cattle pen, which held one wagon and a horse landing for three horse boxes. One scene of activity that could be witnessed at the station was when the local estate farmers conveyed coal from the yard to the home of the local Lord of the Manor, as part of their statutory estate duty.

A well known person who could be seen alighting at Harton Road station during the early 1920s was Eric Blair, better known as George Orwell, the novelist and essayist, made famous by his two best known novels *Animal Farm* and *Nineteen Eighty Four*. His visits were to enable him to spend his holidays with his friends the Buddicombe's, who resided at nearby Ticklerton Court.

Shortly after leaving Harton Road there is a long straight stretch across Henley Common, this was once part of the common field system attached to the small hamlet of Henley. Across the common and into a tree-lined deep cutting; as the train weaves in and out of the trees and cuttings between Harton Road and Marsh Farm Junction brief glimpses can be seen of a tower rising well above the trees to the left of the line; this is the well known Shropshire landmark 'Flounders Folly', a mid-19th century folly. After negotiating its stone staircase tourists would be rewarded with commanding views of the surrounding Shropshire and Border countryside.

The line now crosses the main Church Stretton to Ludlow Road and soon approaches Marsh Farm Jn signal box and turns on to the main Shrewsbury to Hereford line. On the main line there was an up goods loop, brought into use in July 1910, on the site of a former up refuge siding. On entering the junction, and looking across the fields, a familiar sight would be a farmer on horseback, rounding up his flock of Clun Forest sheep, a reminder to the passenger that this is Welsh Border country. Not long after joining the main line the train stops at Wistanstow Halt, the village being 1¾ miles from the Halt.

Before entering Craven Arms station, on the right was Stretford Bridge Jn, for the Bishop's Castle Railway. In the early 1930s the Wenlock branch train could be brought to a stand here, whilst a Bishop's Castle Railway mixed train was allowed to pass, with its former GWR '517' class engine and its chain-braked ex-LNWR four-wheeled coaching stock, an open-planked wagon, a cattle truck and a Bishop's Castle brake van. Many interesting stories surround this ill-fated little line, which was commenced in 1863, but due to financial difficulties was not completed to Craven Arms until 1866. Shortly after opening, surplus lands and some movable effects were sold by the creditors, and the company was placed in the hands of a Receiver in Chancery, where it remained ever after. The line was closed to traffic in May 1935.

After passing Stretford Jn and Long Lane Crossing, to the right is the carriage and engine shed, and to the left the goods shed and yard. The train pulls in on the down platform at Craven Arms, and after taking water the engine runs round the two coaches, and backs into the bay at the north end of the platform, this also being used by the Bishop's Castle trains.

Craven Arms owes its existence to the coming of the Shrewsbury and Hereford Railway in 1852. It is truly a railway town created out of the hamlet of Newton. The S&H line passed through the Onny Valley, its route taking it past Shropshire's famous beauty spot Stokesay Castle, and past a coaching inn named after the Lord of Manor the Earl of Craven, prompting the S&H to give the station the name of Craven Arms. The station was opened for traffic on 20th April, 1852. The parish name of Stokesay was added to the station's name a little later.

The importance of Craven Arms as a railway centre was given added impetus by the opening of the Knighton Railway in 1861. Although only a branch it was in reality to be the embryo of the LNWR's march upon Swansea. Various small companies were involved in the construction of the line between Craven Arms and Swansea, these later being absorbed into the LNWR or operated jointly by the LNWR and GWR.

On 1st July, 1862 Craven Arms station came under the joint ownership of the LNWR, GWR and West Midland Railway. The station consisted of up and down main line platforms, with booking office, general and ladies' waiting room, together with refreshment rooms on the down side. Also on the downside was the station master's house. The up side consisted of general and ladies' waiting rooms only. The north and south end bays were on the down side. The north

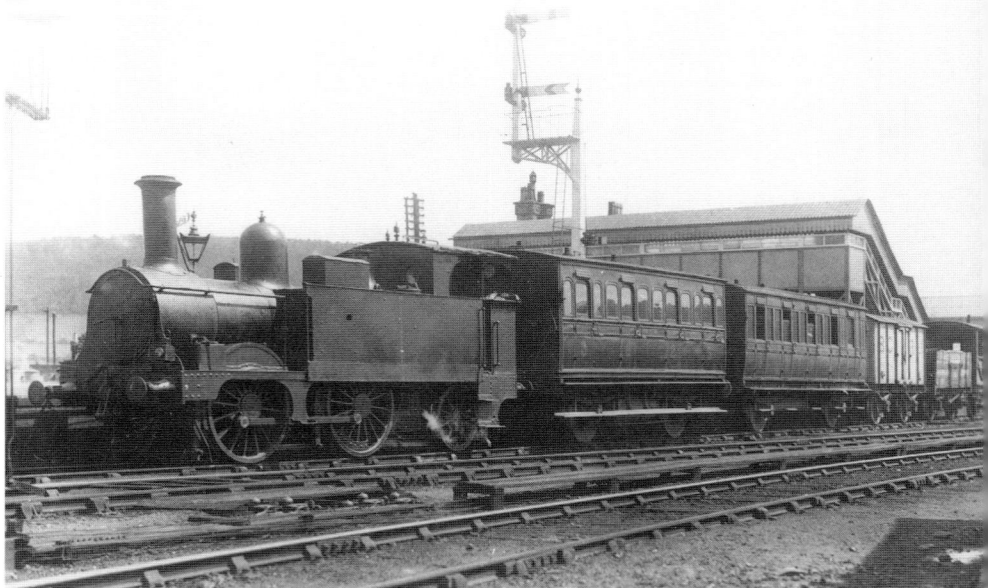

A Bishop's Castle mixed train standing in the Wenlock bay at Craven Arms *c.* 1931 headed by Bishop's Castle Railway 0-4-2T No. 1. Note the first coach consists of a third class compartment at either end and two second class in the middle.   *R. Carpenter*

A Bishop's Castle mixed train headed by No. 1 standing in the down platform at Craven Arms on 8th October, 1931.   *R. Carpenter*

Craven Arms station from the air, showing the engine shed and carriage sidings.

Aero Pictorial Ltd

Craven Arms station up and down platforms looking towards Ludlow. At the end of the down platform is the water tank and column, and to the right in the distance is the Central Wales Junction signal box. *David Lawrence*

A North to West of England express passing through Craven Arms in 1906 hauled by 'Bulldog' class 4-4-0 No. 3403 *Trinidad*. *Lens of Sutton*

The 10.10 am Shrewsbury to Hereford train at Craven Arms on 10th September, 1949 hauled by 'Castle' class 4-6-0 No. 5097 *Sarum Castle*. *H.C. Casserley*

A southbound goods passing through Craven Arms on 10th September, 1949 hauled by '28XX' class 2-8-0 No. 2878. *H.C. Casserley*

A southbound goods making its way through Craven Arms hauled by an ex-LMS '8F' class 2-8-0 No. 48665 on 10th September, 1949. *H.C. Casserley*

end bay was utilised by the Bishop's Castle and Wenlock branch trains. The south end bay was used by the Central Wales local trains operating between Craven Arms and Llandovery.

The Station signal box was at the north end of the down platform, and controlled the north end bay, the engine shed roads and carriage shed sidings. The Central Wales Junction signal box was situated just off the south end of the up platform, and controlled the south end bay and the Central Wales junction.

In 1861 an engine shed was built to house one locomotive operated by the Knighton Railway Company. By the late 1860s four locomotives were stationed here and a new stone shed was built to accommodate them. Carriage cleaning and maintenance for carriages working over the Central Wales line was carried out at Craven Arms. The facilities for this service were greatly improved by the building of a new carriage shed in 1907. The goods shed and offices together with extensive sidings were situated on the down side, just a little way north of the down platform.

From the mid-1870s a considerable amount of coal traffic passed through Craven Arms to the North-West following the opening of several small lines in South Wales. Traffic was boosted yet again in 1888 with the introduction of a through express between Bristol and the North-West.

With the coming of the railway, Craven Arms soon became the centre for sheep, cattle and horse sales. Between August and October each year large store sales were held of Clun and Kerry breeds of sheep. There was also an annual sale of Ayrshire cattle. However, the sale that brought real life to the town was the annual horse fair when the horse dealers would descend from the Welsh hills and surrounding towns and villages. The bargaining was done in both Welsh and English, and the scene was greatly enhanced by the colourful bargaining techniques of the dealers. The sales consisted mainly of Welsh ponies, many of them in the latter part of the 19th century and the early part of the 20th century destined to be conveyed by rail to the mines of the East Shropshire coalfield.

Whilst sitting in the auto-trailer awaiting the return journey at 5.10 pm, this being the last train of the day from Craven Arms to Wellington, the passenger is able to reflect on the diversity of this branch: from the family digging for coal in their back garden at Ketley; to the farmer rounding up his sheep in the rural surrounds of Marsh Farm Jn. In between are the towering pit mounds, slag heaps, decaying pit-winding engine houses of the East Shropshire coalfield, followed by the rural charm of Farley Dingle, Wenlock Edge and the distant Stretton Hills.

An ex-LNWR 2-4-2T No. 46727 backs on to a Central Wales train standing in the Central Wales bay at Craven Arms on 10th September, 1949.   *H.C. Casserley*

Chapter Six

Operating the Line

(In this chapter it is proposed to deal first with the line between Wellington and Craven Arms and treat the Madeley branch as a separate entity afterwards.)

Wellington

The joint station at Wellington provided a microcosm of railway operations at a small market town. Most of the Paddington to Birkenhead expresses stopped there, as did the Birkenhead-Dover, and the Birkenhead-Bournemouth expresses - the latter alternating each day with Great Western and Southern stock. There would also be a through LMS train from Shrewsbury to Stafford, and each weekday one through train from Swansea to Stafford. In the summer months the Aberystwyth to Birmingham excursions, mainly hauled by the 'Dukedogs', could also be seen. Apart from these through services, there was also the hustle and bustle associated with branch line terminus stations, for not only was it the terminus for the Wenlock branch, but it also served the Market Drayton and Crewe branch, and the LMS Coalport branch.

There were also two extensive goods yards, although these were not jointly operated. The Town goods yard, on the east of the Shrewsbury side of the station was operated by the GWR, and the Queen Street yard, on the west of the station, operated by the LMS. The station is dominated by All Saints' parish church, on the eastern side, and by its high retaining wall, towering above the engine shed roads and carriage sidings. To the west, there are high retaining walls again, above number three and four bays, surmounting which was a walled pathway on to steps leading down to the station approach.

The station and yards were controlled by four signal boxes, which were open continuously. Approaching Wellington from Wolverhampton was No. 1 box, better known as 'Stafford Junction', which controlled the line to Stafford, and the Coalport branch. This was the eastern boundary of the joint line. On entering the station from Wolverhampton and emerging from under the King Street bridge, to the right was No. 2 signal box, which controlled No. 3 and 4 bays, and the eastern end of the Crewe platform loop. The old LNWR-type signal box was demolished in March 1953 and replaced by a modern brick-built box erected with the sole intention of replacing the other three signal boxes. However, this was not accomplished until the early 1970s. At the west end of the down platform was No. 3 box, which controlled the roads into the engine shed and carriage sidings, and the west end of the Crewe loop platform, and the eastern access to both the Queen Street and Town goods yards. At the extreme west end of the layout was No. 4 box, or 'Market Drayton Junction' which controlled the Market Drayton and Crewe branch, and the western ends of both goods yards.

Returning to the station, this consisted of down and up main line platforms, and down and up through roads. On the north side of the up platform (an island) was the platform for the Crewe and Market Drayton trains. On the south side of the down platform, and connected to it, were Nos. 3 and 4 bays, from which the Coalport and Wenlock and Craven Arms branch trains started.

When waiting on Wellington station, whether as a rail enthusiast or a disinterested passenger, there was always plenty to occupy the mind. There were the Paddington expresses, hauled by a 'Castle', 'Saint', or 'Hall', with their gleaming chocolate and cream coaches adorned with destination boards, occupying a good length of each coach, proclaiming to the travelling public whence they had come and to where they were bound. Each headboard announced the same - 'Paddington-Leamington-Birmingham-Wolverhampton-Shrewsbury-Wrexham-Chester and Birkenhead [for Liverpool]'. As a small

Wellington station on 3rd August, 1935. Passing under the Victoria Road bridge is 0-6-0PT No. 2713 hauling the 6.25 pm Ketley to Wellington goods. The driver is Bill Bevan and the fireman is Ivor Machin. Bill Bevan was easily distinguishable by the fact that he always wore a trilby hat at work, never the railway issue or cap. The train standing in the up platform is the 4.25 pm Birkenhead to Paddington express. The signal box in the distance is Wellington No. 2 box opened in 1881 and closed in March 1953 when it was replaced by a modern brick-built box.

R. Carpenter

The 3.10 pm to Craven Arms about to leave No. 3 bay at Wellington on 7th September, 1951 hauled by '44XX' class 2-6-2T No. 4401. This train was worked by Wenlock men who would return with the 5.10 pm ex-Craven Arms arriving in Wellington at 6.37 pm.   *H.C. Casserley*

The 3.10 pm to Much Wenlock standing in No. 4 bay at Wellington on 13th December, 1958, headed by '57XX' class 0-6-0PT No. 9774. It would appear that the steam heating is having very little effect, as most of the steam is escaping from under the coaches.   *M. Mensing*

The 4.30 pm to Much Wenlock standing in No. 4 bay at Wellington on 4th July, 1959, with pannier tank No. 9630.   *M. Mensing*

Wellington, No.4 bay, on 21st April, 1962 with pannier tank No. 9639 waiting to leave with the 5.50 pm to Much Wenlock.   *M. Mensing*

boy, the author, having just accomplished the long journey on the Wenlock branch from Horsehay to Wellington, gazed in wonder at these destination boards, boasting of the towns and cities which the express served, not understanding why they never included the name of Wellington, for it seemed every bit as important a railway junction as the others.

Up until 1931 the 2.10 pm Paddington to Birkenhead included three slip coaches, one was detached at Banbury, a second at Leamington Spa and the last at Wellington. This coach was slipped by the slip guard at Ketley Jn, eventually being brought to a stand at Wellington No. 2 box home signal on the main line. The station pilot standing in the down platform would then be allowed to proceed on to the down main and couple up to the slip coach and bring it into the down platform. The rules would not allow a slip coach to negotiate points from the main line into the down platform under its own momentum. On a number of occasions, when an over-zealous guard had applied the vacuum brake too fiercely, bringing the coach to a stand in the section, the driver on the station pilot would be issued with a 'wrong line order' to enable him to proceed into the section on the wrong road in order to retrieve the stranded slip coach. The slip coach would stay in the Town goods yard overnight, returning to Paddington the next morning attached to the rear of the 11.02 am express from Wellington. After 1931 the 2.10 pm stopped at Wellington.

Mention has been made of the Bournemouth and Dover trains and their stock. The 9.40 am Bournemouth to Birkenhead arrived in Wellington at 2.50 pm. The last four coaches of the train were detached, and these then formed the 3.16 pm to Crewe and Manchester (London Road). This was a fast train to Crewe, stopping only at Market Drayton. The train was worked by Wellington men in the 1920s usually with a 'Barnum' class locomotive, and in the 1930s by a 'Bulldog' class.

A unique operation, which was to be seen daily at Wellington, was the method by which they dealt with the Wenlock and Coalport branch trains. The train would run into No. 3 bay. After the passengers had alighted, the engine would then propel the coaches out of the bay up the inclined spur on to the stop block. The shunter would then put the hand brake on in the guard's van, release the vacuum in the coaches, and uncouple the engine, which would then drop back into No. 3 bay. The points would then be reset for No. 4 bay, the shunter would release the hand brake in the van and allow the coaches to glide slowly into the bay. The engine would then run back up the spur, the points again being set for No. 4 bay, allowing the engine to drop back on to the coaches.

The engine shed operations were also clearly visible from the Crewe loop platform: engine cleaning, preparation, fire dropping, and tube cleaning. Up until 1949 the archaic method of coaling the engines by a bucket and winch could still be seen. This system required two men on the winch, which was then slung manually over the bunker or tender of the engine. In 1949 this method was replaced by an electric winch system.

Wellington did not have the luxury of a train enquiry office until the 1920s. If passengers were in doubt about a particular train, they would approach an old gentleman sitting in his wicker invalid chair at the approach to the booking office. Undoubtedly he had been a former railwayman for he was always dressed in his railway uniform, and peaked cap.

A custom which was carried out on one day each year was the placing of a chain across the entrance to the station approach from Church Street, indicating to the public at large that it was a sufferance road, and not a public right of way. Wellington was blessed with two refreshment rooms, one a rather commodious one, on the down platform, and a much smaller one on the up platform. These were franchised out to Messrs Hughes of Welshpool, as were many of the refreshment rooms in the Northern division of the GWR.

Haybridge Sidings

These sidings were on the north side of Wellington No. 1 signal box and they served the Haybridge Steel Works. Up until 1932 the sidings were controlled by a normally switched-

Ketley station *c.* 1908. It would appear that the photograph was taken during the summer as the gentleman with the umbrella appears to be shading himself from the sun's rays. To the left is Ketley Wesleyan Chapel. The building adjoining the tree was a shop displaying various types of ropes made by Burroughs Brothers, at the rear of the shop was their rope walk. Note that at this time the signal box was not connected to the booking office, but just prior to World War I a small brick building was erected linking the two together.   *Ironbridge Gorge Museum*

'51XX' class 2-6-2T No. 4158 is seen at Ketley with a passenger train bound for Wellington in May 1957. The photograph shows the signal box, booking office and station master's house.
Real Photographs

out signal box situated on the down side adjoining the Hadley Road bridge. The only goods train that called there was the 3.05 pm from Wellington to Horsehay, which called on Mondays, Wednesdays and Fridays. On one of these days the Ketley signalman was required to walk from Ketley to Haybridge to operate the signal box. Following the completion of the shunting operations he would ride back in the guard's van to Ketley. During the Ketley signalman's absence from the station box, the Ketley station master would take over.

In 1932 the Haybridge box was closed and a ground frame was put in at the entrance to the sidings. This frame was operated by the guard of the goods train. The ground frame was actually controlled by the signalman from Wellington No. 1 box, who upon the release of a lever in the box allowed the guard to operate the ground frame.

Ketley Junction

The Junction signal box was situated on the up side of the main line, just a little south of what were formerly the Waterloo Sidings. Crossing on to the single line of the Wenlock branch, trains commenced a sharp climb of 1 in 50 towards Ketley. Ketley Jn to Ketley was operated under the electric train staff regulations.

Ketley

There was one platform on the down side of the line, the signal box being situated at the north end of the platform. The branch here crossed the busy A5 London to Holyhead road. The level crossing gates were interlocked with the signals, but were operated by hand. Passenger and parcels traffic only was dealt with at the station, three days a week the GWR parcels delivery van would come out from Oakengates to deliver the parcels in the Ketley area.

There were two private sidings, one of which was on the down side of the line on the Wellington side of the station serving Clay's Works. This was established at Ketley in 1924 and made agricultural implements and cast-iron rainwater goods. The works later became the Wrekin Foundry Ltd. The up side goods running loop held 42 wagons, off which there was a private siding into Sinclair's Ironworks. Up until 1924 there were two ground frames, one at the south end of the station platform gave access to the loop sidings, and also direct access into the private sidings of the Sinclair Iron Company. This ground frame was removed in 1926, access to the loop and sidings then being controlled from the signal box. The other ground frame was situated at the south end of the running loop and also gave access into Sinclair's private sidings. Goods trains coming into Ketley from Horsehay and stopping for the purpose of shunting at Sinclair's were met by the signalman, who would obtain the staff (later token) from the fireman; he would then detach the token from the leather pouch, in later years it was the metal holder, place it in the ground frame lock to release the levers to turn the points for the up loop.

The two goods trains which carried out shunting operations at Ketley were the 11.25 am from Wellington to Much Wenlock, and the 3.05 pm from Wellington to Horsehay. Invariably these two goods trains would require a bank engine for the steep gradient between Ketley Jn and Ketley. This was usually provided by the Wellington Yard shunter; if this engine was not available the station pilot engine would be utilised. On arrival at Ketley the goods would be turned into the loop opposite the platform, the engine would be uncoupled and turned out on to the branch single line at the ground frame at the entrance to Sinclair's private sidings. The engine would then run round the train and enter the loop at the north end at the rear of the guard's van. The train would then be propelled to the top of the loop, the wagons for Ketley at the front of the train would be detached and secured. The rest of the train with wagons for Horsehay would then be allowed to drop back controlled by the guard, by this time the engine would be standing in the works' sidings. Immediately the train, under the

Horsehay goods yard *c.* 1928. The roofs of the buildings in the foreground are part of the Horsehay Company's works. To the right of the photograph the Horsehay Company's engine is propelling two wagons along the Horsehay to Dawley road, in the background can be seen the houses in Spring Village. *Ironbridge Gorge Museum*

An early photograph of Horsehay & Dawley station. Note the porter standing by the ground frame levers on the platform, indicating that the photograph was taken before the signal box was built in 1883. *Ironbridge Gorge Museum*

control of the guard, was clear of the works' points, the engine would reverse out and hook on to the front of the train. It would then propel the train out of the loop at the north end past the signal box, and over the level crossing on to the running line, ready to proceed to Horsehay.

A complete survey of the stations on the Wenlock branch was done in the early part of 1925, no doubt brought about by the increasing concern of the railway companies at the road competition which was beginning to rear its head, particularly that of the operations of the Birmingham and Midland Motor Omnibus Company (Midland Red). The operation of this company began seriously to affect the passenger traffic at Ketley, Lawley Bank, Horsehay, Coalbrookdale, and Much Wenlock. However, during the latter part of the 1920s, the GWR and the LMS met this increasing competition not by open hostility, but by closer co-operation with the Midland Red, culminating in an agreement dated 15th April, 1930, which gave the LMS a 30 per cent controlling share, and the GWR a 20 per cent controlling share in the bus company.

In 1921 considerable pressure was being placed on the Sinclair Iron Company by the GWR to increase the size of its sidings. It was claimed by the railway company that the limited space available was not sufficient to meet the requirements of the increased amount of traffic from the works, which necessitated in the railway company's engines being used for dealing with the traffic for an excessive amount of time. Despite this request it does not appear that the Sinclair Iron Company made any attempt to meet the wishes of the GWR.

In 1924 the passenger receipts for Ketley were £734, parcels £336, goods traffic £21,158. The goods traffic came under the direct control of the goods manager at Horsehay.

The line from Ketley Jn to Lightmoor Jn was operated under the single line block working system, the sections being Ketley Jn to Ketley, Ketley to Horsehay, and Horsehay to Lightmoor Jn. Up until 1921 these sections used the Webb-Thompson Electric Train Staff instruments, however a fault occurred in this system between Ketley and Horsehay (*see page 137*). The train staff system was removed and replaced by the electric key token; this necessitated the tokens being placed in a leather pouch or metal holder.

Lawley Bank

At Lawley Bank there were level crossing gates which crossed the road leading from the village of Lawley to Lawley Bank. There was a bell and keyless disc provided in the crossing box. This station served the hamlets of Lawley, Lawley Bank, Malins Lee, New Dale, and New Works. Only passenger and parcels traffic was dealt with here, goods traffic for this area being dealt with at Horsehay.

The Wrekin Coal Company had a drift mine near to the station, this drift linking into their colliery, which was about 1¾ miles distant. In 1923 the Wrekin company made application to the GWR for a siding into the area surrounding the drift mine, which was just a little way south of the station, to enable it to build a brick and sanitary ware works. The works was eventually erected but the request for a siding never materialised. From Lawley Bank the line continues on a ruling gradient of 1 in 45 up to Horsehay Tunnel; the ground above the tunnel carries the road from Dawley to Wellington.

Horsehay & Dawley

On approaching the points for the goods yard at Horsehay there was one of the many stop boards to be seen on the branch. The standard gradient instructions, as laid down in 1879 by G.N. Tyrell the then GWR superintendent of the line, were observed, with the following addition on the Wenlock branch: '. . . that when a goods train consists of more than eight wagons and two vans it must be brought to a stand at the head of the incline'. These

Horsehay station *c*. 1912 showing the signal box, waiting room and booking office. Note the enamel sign advertising Nectar Tea and the post and lamp focused on to the staff setting down post. The children must have felt privileged to pose for Mr Alcock the Ironbridge photographer.
Ironbridge Gorge Museum

Dawley Parva Crossing ground frame. This ground frame until the mid-1880s controlled the sidings into the former Lightmoor furnaces. Once known as Lightmoor Road, the gates at this point guarded the road between Little Dawley and Lightmoor. *Ironbridge Gorge Museum*

instructions must have been amended later because on the boards it stated quite specifically: 'That All Goods and Minerals Must Stop Dead Here'. This stop board was placed at the summit of a gradient of 1 in 40 on the way down from Horsehay to Lightmoor Jn.

Horsehay & Dawley station served the area of Horsehay, Dawley, Coalmoor, Doseley, and Little Wenlock. The platform was on the down side, with the 9-lever signal box situated at the Ketley end of the platform.

In the goods yard there were 10 sidings and a spur, and a loading bank was provided between two sidings in the yard. Two sidings led from the yard one into the Horsehay Ironworks, and the other into the slag tip sidings. Following the end of World War I the GWR ceased to use its own truck weighbridge, and instead used the Horsehay Company's weighbridge for which they paid a shilling per wagon. Likewise they also made use of the Horsehay Company's locomotive for the yard shunting, for which they paid £7 per week.

The General Strike of 1926 prompted the Horsehay Company to offer the use of its shunting engine to operate services between Horsehay and Wellington. Despite the fact that the GWR was desperately in need of volunteers and help in any way, they obviously did not consider it wise for the Horsehay Company to operate trains over this route. The superintendent of the line's log for 6th May, 1926 has the following terse comment: 'that this offer was not taken up'.

There was a two-storey goods shed here, 70 ft long, with accommodation for the Goods Department clerks and checker. The deck in the warehouse could accommodate three wagons, and there were two cranes of 30 cwt. capacity. The principal traffics dealt with, both at the station and the goods yard, before the onslaught of road competition, were castings, road stone, sanitary pipes, milk, pigeons and general goods. The parcels traffic was delivered and collected by a private agent.

Horsehay was famous for its bridge building works, and many thousands of passengers carried by the GWR have passed either under or over one of the many bridges constructed at Horsehay, each bridge carrying the iron roundel worded 'Built at Horsehay, Shropshire, England' and the date. In addition to traversing the bridges the Great Western passengers would also be travelling on another commodity provided at Horsehay: 'ballast'. This was extracted from the huge slag heap which dominated the landscape around Horsehay, the slag having been deposited by the Coalbrookdale Company's Horsehay furnaces during its industrial activity between 1755 and 1886. Up until World War II it was common to see a ballast train leaving the yard at Horsehay each week destined for some distant part of the GW system. In addition to the ballast trains another familiar sight was to see a special train leaving with its two, or sometimes three, special low loader 'Macaw' wagons loaded with bridge girders, or a crane with a guard's van at each end. A Swindon inspector would be required to travel with each of these trains to its destination, wherever that may be.

Dawley Parva Crossing Ground Frame

The reason for the word 'ground frame' on the crossing cabin is to be found in the undergrowth a little way to the south of the crossing (the Lightmoor side), on the right of the line. Here can be found the shallow cutting which carried the sidings into the former Lightmoor furnaces, the sidings being laid into the furnace site in 1858. In 1880 one train only was booked to stop there and that was the 5.45 am goods ex-Wellington, and then only if the train was not conveying a full load. The reason for this ruling can be well understood when looking at the 1 in 45 gradient on which the train would stand whilst the engine was carrying out the shunting operations in the sidings. In the event of the goods not being permitted to stop, the wagons for the furnace site would have had to be left in the yard at Lightmoor, and picked up by the 11.52 am goods ex-Much Wenlock which would then proceed to Dawley Parva Crossing and carry out the necessary shunting operations.

In 1921 Tarslag Ltd approached the GWR with a view to opening up the sidings again for the purpose of extracting the slag from the former Lightmoor furnace site for road mending

An unidentified '72XX' class 2-8-2T banks an oil train over the viaducts at Coalbrookdale *c.* 1955.
Don Houlston

Coalbrookdale station in 1899. On the right are the sidings into the Coalbrookdale works. Note the tall home signal post, this was to enable the train crew to have a sighting of the signal when approaching the sharp curve into the station. Standing on the down road is an early non-vacuum goods brake van. It is interesting to note the uniform of station master William Marshall standing on the left of the photograph. He is wearing the flat uniform hat and not the round hat which we associate with GWR station masters, the reason for this being that well into the early part of this century at many of the smaller stations they were referred to as 'station inspectors'.   *Ironbridge Gorge Museum*

purposes. However, nothing came of this approach and the sidings were just left to fade into obscurity under the undergrowth. In 1882, the year before the furnaces closed, no goods trains were booked to stop, neither were there any shunting operations carried out there.

Lightmoor Jn

Lightmoor Jn was the termination of the single lines from Ketley Jn and from Madeley Jn, and was the commencement of the double line to Buildwas. The branch from Madeley Jn came in on the down side of the line at which was situated the wooden signal box with its 25 levers. This box however was demolished in 1951 and was replaced by a brick-built box which was built a little way to the north end of the up platform.

Lightmoor served the scattered cottages tucked in behind the pit mounds, and the small hamlets with strange sounding names like The Finney, The Dell Hole, The City, The Stocking, Stable Row, and Coker's Row.

The goods yard was at the north end of the platform, and the sidings came in off the line from Horsehay. There were four roads in the yard, which were the coal road, warehouse road, limestone sidings, and straight road. On the warehouse road there was the weighing machine house, and the warehouse which was of wooden construction; the narrow gauge tramroads operated by the Coalbrookdale Company linked its Shutfield and Lightmoor Tile Works directly with the loading bay at the warehouse. In the early 1920s it would appear that the warehouse was leased to the Coalbrookdale Company for the purpose of storing its tiles prior to dispatch by rail.

Before the opening of the line from Buildwas to Lightmoor in November 1864 limestone from the Coalbrookdale Company's quarries was brought down the River Severn from Buildwas to the Loadcroft Wharf at Ironbridge, where it was loaded into the small trucks, and brought by horse-drawn tramway up through Coalbrookdale and the Lightmoor Dingle to the limestone wharf at the Lightmoor goods yard. Here it was transferred into standard gauge wagons for dispatch to the Horsehay furnaces.

Leaving Lightmoor the line enters on to a double track on a falling gradient of 1 in 50 towards Coalbrookdale.

Coalbrookdale

At Coalbrookdale there were up and down platforms, with the signal box situated at the Lightmoor end of the down platform. The signal box was only opened during shunting operations into the Coalbrookdale works, or into the coal sidings on the up side of the line. Number 1 siding leading into the works held 20 wagons, and No. 2 held twelve. Great Western engines were not allowed beyond the gate into the works, all shunting operations in and around the works and to the gate into the sidings were carried out by the Coalbrookdale Company's own locomotive, which up until the early 1930s would have been 0-4-0 No. 5 built by the company. This locomotive has now been restored and is to be seen in the Ironbridge Gorge Museum of Iron at Coalbrookdale. The goods agent's office was situated some considerable distance from the station and yard, it was on the Wellington Road adjacent to the main entrance to the Coalbrookdale works.

Catch points existed 344 yards on the Buildwas side of the station on the up line. On leaving Coalbrookdale the line continues to fall at 1 in 50 towards Buildwas.

Buildwas Junction

Buildwas was a double junction station with a through line from Shrewsbury to Worcester (the Severn Valley line), and the branch line from Wellington to Marsh Farm Jn. There were four block telegraph sections as follows:

Double line from Buildwas to Coalbrookdale
Single line from Buildwas to Ironbridge (Severn Valley)
Single line from Buildwas to Much Wenlock
Single line from Buildwas to Cressage (Severn Valley)

The station consisted of high and low level platforms, the former (a single platform) was used for the Wellington to Much Wenlock trains in each direction, and the trains from Ironbridge and Shrewsbury on the Severn Valley line used the low level platforms.

The first signal box at Buildwas was probably a hut covering a ground frame. On 4th February, 1886 the GWR authorised the installation of the block telegraph between Buildwas and Wenlock, at a cost of £67 6s. 2d. On 16th November, 1887 more signalling work was authorised, which involved the renewal of locking apparatus and signals, also the erection of two signal boxes, the total cost of this major work being £2,080. The Station signal box was situated a little way south of the up platform on the Severn Valley line, this box controlled the station and the Wenlock branch. The Junction signal box was situated adjacent to the up road of the Severn Valley line near the sidings for the Meadow Wharf and pumping station. This box controlled the junction with the Severn Valley line and the branch to Coalbrookdale and Wellington. In 1922/23 the two boxes were demolished and replaced by a central box which had 66 levers, this box being extended in 1931 to accommodate 113 levers, the additional levers being required for the newly-built power station sidings.

The station buildings on the low level (Severn Valley line) consisted of a small passenger shelter on the up side, on the down side there was the booking office, general waiting room, ladies' waiting room, store room and lamp hut. On the high level platform there was just a passenger shelter. The station master's house was also situated on the low level platform on the down side; in 1924 he was paying a weekly rent of 5s. 11d. The station staff consisted of the station master, one junior clerk, two signalmen, two shunters, two porters, one lad porter and one male crossing keeper. The crossing keeper was employed on the Severn Valley line at a crossing on the Buildwas to Wenlock road.

Three water columns were provided, one at the Worcester end of the Severn Valley up platform, one at the Shrewsbury end of the Severn Valley down platform, and one at the Wenlock end of the high level platform. There was also an engine turntable in the yard, and a pump house on the up side of the line near to the junction of the Severn Valley and Wenlock branch lines. The siding leading to the pump house was once used by the Madeley Wood Company, and the Cannock Chase Coal and Iron Company for transporting their limestone to their Severn Wharf near the Albert Edward Bridge.

Prior to the opening of Ironbridge Power Station at Buildwas in 1932 the siding accommodation at Buildwas consisted of three sidings on the down side of the Severn Valley line, these were as follows:

No. 1 Siding	17 wagons
No. 2 Siding	43 wagons
No. 3 Siding	45 wagons

These sidings were accessible to up and down trains, a load gauge was provided over No. 1 siding, and there was also a truck weighbridge on this same siding.

In 1932 with the opening of the power station, Buildwas was to be transformed from a rural junction nestling in the Severn valley into a great concourse of coal sidings with shunting activities being carried on throughout the day. The daily scene of activity was enhanced by the power station's two industrial locomotives, a Peckett 0-4-0 and a Bagnall 0-4-0.

When the two signal boxes were in operation the electric train staff instruments were situated in each box. Following the erection of the new central box the electric staff instruments were then sited in a cabin situated on the down low level platform, these instruments controlled the Wenlock branch. The Severn Valley line staff instruments were sited in the central signal box.

Bradley Sidings

The sidings were situated on the down side of the line, entrance to which was controlled by a three-lever ground frame unlocked by the key on the Buildwas to Wenlock train staff. There were two lines into the sidings, at the north end was a crossover and also a loading bay. When the sidings were used for the purposes of the limestone quarry, the crossing keeper from Farley Crossing would have to be in attendance to assist the guard during shunting operations, leaving his wife to look after the crossing.

When the former quarry became a petrol depot large storage tanks were built into the quarry, the area around the tanks being landscaped and allowed to blend into the surrounding countryside. From these tanks feed pipes led into a central pipe extended between the sidings, from this central pipe arms were attached which could be placed over each tanker for the purpose of filling them.

With the opening of the petrol depot in 1938 considerable relaxation took place in the type of motive power which could be used between Buildwas and Farley. All engines in the 'blue' group such as the '78XX', '28XX', '53XX', '63XX', '73XX', and the 2-6-2 tanks '41XX', '51XX', '61XX' and '81XX' could be seen negotiating the precipitous climb of 1 in 40 through the Farley Dingle; considerable difficulties were experienced by the enginemen as they endeavoured to coax these large engines around the sharp curves especially in wet weather. In fact, later on all engines in the 'red' group, with the exception of the '47XX' class, were allowed to work to the depot. These engines were also allowed to work to Wenlock for the purpose of taking water.

All the petrol trains came in via Shrewsbury, and then ran via the Severn Valley line to Buildwas, and upon arrival at Buildwas the train had to be accompanied by the shunter on duty at Buildwas up to Farley to assist the guard with the shunting operations.

Much Wenlock

There was one platform at Wenlock on the up side of the line, with an adjacent running loop, able to be used by freight trains for crossing purposes. The station buildings were of brick and Wenlock limestone, and comprised of a booking office, general waiting room, ladies' waiting room, corrugated parcels hut, corrugated lamp hut, and a guards' room. The guards' room situated at the Presthope end of the platform was in fact the first signal box at Wenlock, this box being completed in 1867 shortly after the opening of the line. In February 1886 the Great Western authorised the block telegraph system between Wenlock and Buildwas, prior to this the train staff and ticket system had been in operation. During the later period of 1888 the whole of the signal work was renewed, including renewal of locking appliances and signals. A new signal box was constructed opposite the old one and adjacent to the loop line and opened in January 1893.

The station master's house was also on the platform, for which, in the early 1920s, a rental of 7s. 8d. per week was paid. The station staff in the mid-1930s consisted of: station master; one clerk; three passenger guards; one porter-guard; two signalmen; one checker; one porter; one male crossing keeper (Farley Crossing); one gatewoman (Farley Crossing).

Access to the goods yard (the site of the first terminus station) was by way of the facing points just south of the Sheinton Road bridge on the down side of the line. There were three

Much Wenlock station with its original signal box, and an early GWR semaphore signal. These early semaphore signals were constructed with a slot in the post for the arm, 'danger' being shown by the arm in the horizontal position the 'all right' by it being out of sight within the post, and 'caution' by the half-way position.   *Ironbridge Gorge Museum*

Much Wenlock station showing the station master's house in August 1932. At the end of the platform on the right is the early West Midland Railway signal box of 1867 and opposite it the replacement box of 1893.   *Real Photographs*

Wenlock station on 10th September, 1949 with '57XX' class 0-6-0PT No. 9639 waiting to leave with the 9.22 am to Craven Arms. This train would be worked by Wenlock men to Presthope where they would change over with Wellington men working the 8.20 am goods ex-Wenlock. The Wellington men would then continue with the passenger train returning with the 11.10 am ex-Craven Arms. Note on the left the old signal box where a ground frame was fixed in 1864, eventually covered in 1867. Looking out from the signal box on the right is Fred Groves the signalmen. *H.C. Casserley*

Much Wenlock goods shed *c.* 1960. This building had been constructed using the local limestone. *R. Carpenter*

main sidings with the capacity to hold 58 wagons. Over No. 3 siding was a loading gauge, also provided in the yard was a cart weighbridge. The importance of agriculture to this market town is evidenced by the fact that the yard contained two large cattle pens, and accommodation for 13 horse boxes.

The goods warehouse consisted of an office and deck accommodation, for dealing with two wagons, together with a crane of 30 cwt capacity. The principal traffic dealt with was livestock, general merchandise, and timber. Goods and parcels for the town and surrounding rural area were collected and delivered by an Agent.

The engine shed sidings could hold four wagons, while the engine shed had a capacity for two engines, with a corrugated iron engineman's cabin and coal stage. At the side of the shed was situated a water column.

Westwood Sidings

After reaching the summit of the steep climb from Wenlock there is a steady descent to Presthope. At the beginning of this descent, on the up side, were Westwood Sidings. Up to the early 1920s access could be gained from both north and south ground frames, into the long sidings which ran adjacent to an equally lengthy loading bay. (Originally there had been a signal box here, but the date of its removal is uncertain.) The north end bay was later taken out, when the length of the sidings, and loading bay were considerably reduced. The North GF closed on 17th June, 1928 but the South GF remained until the line closed in 1963. Like many other sidings on the branch goods trains could only call here when they were not fully loaded. In the later days of the branch the 8.20 am goods ex-Wenlock only called on Mondays, Wednesdays, and Fridays putting in one empty wagon and taking out one loaded wagon of limestone.

Presthope

At Presthope there was one platform on the up side of the line, and the station buildings consisted of a booking office, general waiting room, ladies' waiting room, and goods lock-up. The station master's house was on the up side of the line on the embankment just north of the platform; in 1921 his rent was 3s. 11d. per week. The signal box, also on the up side, only contained the locking frame, the electric train staff instruments being situated in the booking office. Prior to 1881 a ground frame was attached to a stage in the goods yard from which the points and signals were operated. A long loop line opposite the platform line enabled two freight trains, or a passenger and a freight train, to cross here.

The station staff consisted of the station master and one signalman, the signalman was required to assist with the station duties.

On entering Presthope station and gazing out on to the down side of the line there was evidence of its former glory, brought about by that one product, 'limestone': the length of its sidings, its crossovers, shunt signals, and the line vanishing into the trees as it made its way to the Lilleshall Company's quarries. The sidings provided accommodation for 135 wagons, not taking into account the accommodation provided by the Lilleshall Company's line.

There was an extensive landing for horses; which also included cattle pens. In the yard behind the station buildings was a cart weighbridge, and in the sidings a truck weighbridge.

Easthope (or Longville) Siding

Situated between Easthope Halt and Longville was the Easthope Siding, laid by 1919. The siding was for the convenience of the timber fellers on the Lutwyche Estate, to save them having to haul their timbers to either Presthope or Longville stations.

The siding was only accessible to goods trains running in the direction of Craven Arms. When it was necessary for a train to call, the station master at Longville had to notify the station master at Presthope. The former would then arrange for a porter to meet the train and unlock the gate into the sidings; the key on the Presthope-Rushbury staff would then unlock the ground frame controlling the siding. All empty wagons for the siding had to be forwarded to Presthope. It would appear that the siding only had a very short life for by 1927 it had ceased to be used.

Gradients

In view of the severity of its gradients, rigid instructions were issued concerning train operation on the branch. In the early days before the introduction of the continuous brake, each goods train had to have two brake vans, one attached to the engine, and the other at the rear of the train, and each van had to be accompanied by a guard. A similar arrangement applied to passenger trains. In the event of a passenger train having more than eight coaches, additional brake carriages had to be attached. Many of the trains were mixed (passenger and goods' stock), with the exception of mineral and timber wagons which were not allowed to be attached to passenger trains.

No goods train was allowed to exceed nine loaded wagons between Buildwas and Wenlock, and between Wenlock and Buildwas 16 loaded wagons and two brake vans was the maximum load. This restriction operated from the opening of the line until the opening of the oil terminal at Farley at the beginning of World War II.

Various experiments with the continuous brake system were carried out by the GWR between 1876 and 1880, eventually it came out in favour of the Sanders Automatic Vacuum system which was reported on favourably by Colonel Rich of the Board of Trade following experiments carried out between Swindon and Didcot in 1878. This system, with various modifications, eventually appeared as the Great Western Automatic Vacuum brake.

It was not, however, until 1883 that the automatic brake appeared on the Wenlock branch, and even after this date the GWR continued to use the non-vacuum brake coaches, and where three or more of these coaches were used on a train it was still necessary to have an additional brake. As late as 1889 passenger trains were still running over the branch with non-vacuum brake coaches. It was 1895 before all branch passenger coaches were operated by the continuous vacuum brake.

Signalling

With the opening of the Wgton&SJR from Ketley Jn to Horsehay in 1857 this section was operated on the 'one engine in steam' principle. Following the opening of the continuation of the branch to Lightmoor and on to Madeley Jn, Spagnoletti's single needle system was used.

From its opening in 1862 the Wen&SJR worked on the 'one engine in steam' principle between Wenlock and Buildwas, this also applied when the line was extended to Presthope in 1864 by the WenRC.

When the line was opened throughout from Ketley Jn to Marsh Farm Jn the single line sections of the branch were operated on Spagnoletti's single needle system, with the exception of that between Buildwas and Wenlock, which still continued to operate on the 'one engine in steam' principle due, no doubt, to the severity of the incline on this part of the branch. The double line between Lightmoor and Buildwas, following its opening on 1st November, 1864, was operated on the time interval system, however, by 1884, the Block Telegraph system was in operation on this section.

In 1869 the train staff and ticket system was operating on the single line sections of the branch, the train staff working being as follows:

The electric token for the Ketley to Horsehay section of the Wenlock branch. In 1920 these tokens replaced the Webb-Thompson electric train staff between Ketley Junction and Lightmoor.
Author's Collection

The electric key token for the Horsehay to Lightmoor Junction section of the Wenlock branch.
Author's Collection

Ketley Junction signal box, to the rear of the box is the Haybridge housing estate, Hadley. In the distance to the right of the box is the Haybridge steelworks. *Ironbridge Gorge Museum*

The new signal box at Lightmoor Junction completed in 1951. The original signal box was situated on the Madeley branch. To the left is the line to Horsehay and to the right is the Madeley branch. Note the picking up and setting down staff posts. *Ironbridge Gorge Museum*

Buildwas Junction bracket signal on the Wenlock branch facing Buildwas station. Reading from left to right are signals for the platform, through road and sidings. In the distance can be seen the Severn Valley line, coal sidings and Ironbridge 'A' Power Station. The wooded slope is Marn Wood.   *R. Carpenter*

Between	*Form of Staff & Ticket*	*Colour of Staff & Ticket*
Ketley Jn & Lightmoor Jn	Round	Green
Lightmoor Jn & Madeley Jn	Square	Red
Buildwas & Wenlock	Six-Sided	Yellow
Wenlock & Presthope	Round	White
Presthope & Marsh Farm	Six-Sided	Blue

The staff would have been wooden, about a foot long, and each staff was fitted with a brass plate inscribed with the name of the section to which it applied. There was only one staff to each section, but there could be any number of tickets, these tickets were locked in a box which could only be opened by a key extending from the end of the staff. The driver could not enter a staff section unless he was in possession of the staff, or had a properly made out ticket and had been shown the staff. In the event of the driver going into the section with a staff on his train then no train could follow him, but when he arrived at the end of the section a train waiting could take the staff back. If the driver went into the section on the authority of a ticket then any number of trains could follow him, each with a ticket. The final train in that direction would take the staff; having arrived at the end of the section the driver would hand over the staff which would then allow trains to run in the other direction. Until 1865 the train staff or ticket was always carried by the guard.

The train staff and ticket system continued to operate on the branch until 1896, when the Webb-Thompson electric train staff machine was introduced. The staff was a large iron tube about 23 in. long by 1¼ in. diameter; on the end of the staff were two brass plates on which were inscribed the name of the station at either end of the staff section.

When the electric train staff was introduced on to the branch the staff sections were altered as follows:

> Ketley Jn to Ketley
> Ketley to Horsehay
> Horsehay to Lightmoor Jn
> Lightmoor Jn to Madeley Jn
> Buildwas to Wenlock
> Wenlock to Presthope
> Presthope to Rushbury
> Rushbury to Marsh Farm Jn

As previously mentioned, in 1921 a fault was found in the electric train staff system operating between Ketley and Horsehay. It was found that after a staff had been removed from the instrument to allow the train to proceed into the section, if the signalman at each end of the section held down their plungers simultaneously a further staff could be withdrawn at the Ketley end. Following this discovery the electric train staff system was withdrawn between Ketley Junction and Horsehay and replaced by the electric token system. The metal tokens were placed into a leather pouch with a hoop attached to enable the fireman to pick them up or put them down on the lineside staff posts. The leather pouches were eventually replaced by the less cumbersome metal token holders.

By 1928 the whole of the sections between Ketley Jn-Lightmoor Jn-Madeley Jn were operating on the electric token system. However the single line between Buildwas and Marsh Farm Jn continued to use the electric train staff system until the closure of the line.

Over the years requests had been made by landowners whose estates joined the line between Longville and Harton Road for facilities to be provided for the loading of timber at any point on the line, to save having to haul either to Longville, Rushbury or Harton Road stations. The railway company could never see its way clear to accede to these requests. However, after World War I with the clouds of universal road haulage looming on the horizon, the company at last agreed to make these facilities available. The railway company

MUCH WENLOCK BRANCH.

UP TRAINS.

		WEEK DAYS.										
		1	2	3	4	5	6	7	8	9	10	11
		Pass.	Pass.	Gds.	Pass.	Gds.	Gds.	Pass.	Gds.	Pass.	Gds.	Pass.
Miles	STATIONS.	a.m.	a.m.	a.m.	a.m.	noon.	p.m.	p.m.	p.m.	p.m.	p.m.	p.m.
	Presthope … … … dep.	…	…	…	…	…	…	…	…	…	…	…
	Much Wenlock … … dep.	7 35	9 20	10 10	10 55	12 0	2 0	3 25	5 30	7 0	6 20	7 40
3¾	Buildwas … … … arr.	7 50	9 35	10 30	11 10	12 25	2 35	3 40	5 50	7 15	6 40	8 0

DOWN TRAINS.

		WEEK DAYS.										
		1	2	3	4	5	6	7	8	9	10	11
		Pass.	Pass.	Gds.	Pass.	Gds.	Gds.		Pass.	Gds.	Gds.	Pass.
Miles	STATIONS.	a.m.	a.m.	a.m.	a.m.	p.m.	p.m.	p.m.	p.m.		p.m.	p.m.
	Buildwas … … … dep.	8 5	9 45	10 35	11 20	12 55	2 30	3 25	4 0	…	6 20	7 40
	Much Wenlock … … arr.	8 20	10 5	10 50	11 40	1 10	3 15	3 40	4 20	…	6 40	8 0
	″ … … dep.	…	…	…	…	…	1 30	…	…	4 45	…	…
3¾	Presthope … … … arr.	…	…	…	…	…	…	…	…	5 5	…	…

The Driver in charge of the Wenlock Branch Engine will carry a Train Staff, and no Engine or Train must proceed upon this Branch without such Staff. See page 55.

No Train to exceed 8 Loaded Wagons Up or 16 Wagons Down this Branch.

The Wenlock Engine to make a Special Trip to Presthope and back, or Buildwas and back, at 8.30 a.m., when required.

Extracts from the Working Timetable for 1864 on the Wenlock branch between Buildwas and Much Wenlock, and Buildwas and Presthope.

MUCH WENLOCK BRANCH.

	WEEK DAYS.							
	1	2	3	4	5	6	7	8
	Pass.	Pass.	Pass.	Pass.	Pass.			
STATIONS.	a.m.	a.m.	a.m.	p.m.	p.m.			
Much Wenlock … … dep.	7 40	9 20	11 5	3 25	6 25	…	…	…
Buildwas … … … arr.	7 55	9 35	11 20	3 40	6 40	…	…	…

	WEEK DAYS.							
	1	2	3	4	5	6	7	8
	Pass.	Pass.	Pass.	Pass.	Pass.			
STATIONS.	a.m.	a.m.	a.m.	p.m.	p.m.			
Buildwas … … … dep.	8 5	9 40	11 30	3 56	7 40	…	…	…
Much Wenlock … … arr.	8 25	10 0	11 50	4 15	8 0	…	…	…

The Driver in charge of the Wenlock Branch Engine will carry a Train Staff, and no Engine or Train must proceed upon this Branch without such Staff. See page 55.

The Wenlock Branch Engine will work Goods and Mineral Traffic between Wenlock and Buildwas Junction according to instructions.

No Train to exceed 8 Loaded Wagons Up or Down this Branch.

had already provided a timber siding at Easthope, in addition it installed occupation key boxes at Longville and Harton Road stations. These key boxes allowed the respective station masters to withdraw a key from the box, as long as any P.W. Dept gangers working in the section had replaced their keys into the boxes in the section in which they were working (the key being required as their authority to operate a trolley in the section). After having withdrawn the key the station master would show this to the driver of the timber train and this would authorise him to proceed into the section. The regulations laid down that the Longville station master must have his key replaced in the box by 4.10 pm, likewise the Harton Road station master must have his replaced by 4.20 pm, in order to allow the gangers to withdraw their keys, thus enabling the gang to return home on their trolleys.

With the severe gradients it was a common site to see bank engines working over the branch, these being allowed to work between Wellington and Horsehay, Buildwas and Much Wenlock, and Buildwas, Lightmoor Jn and Horsehay.

Passenger Train Operation

Although no operating agreement had been reached between the Wgton&SJR and the GWR at the date of opening, the GWR commenced to operate the line with its own staff and rolling stock. The first passenger train to operate on the branch left Madeley Court at 7.05 am on the 2nd May, 1859 for Wellington via Lightmoor. The first train in the down direction was the 10.10 am Wellington to Shifnal over the Madeley branch arriving in Shifnal at 11.00 am. A train left Madeley at 12.20 pm for Shifnal, after which there was a gap until a train which left Wellington at 4.30 pm arriving in Shifnal at 5.20 pm. In the other direction were the 12.50 pm and the 6.50 pm services from Shifnal to Wellington (via Lightmoor) making a total of three trains each way.

From the commencement of the line there was also a Sunday service advertised, this in fact only amounted to one train each way, one leaving Wellington at 3.05 pm arriving at Shifnal at 4.00 pm, and returning from Shifnal at 6.30 pm and arriving in Wellington at 7.10 pm.

By 1863 two additional trains had been added to the timetable, albeit on Mondays and Thursdays only. On Mondays a train left Madeley at 6.55 am via Lightmoor for Wellington, this was undoubtedly for the cattle market which was held at Wellington on this day. The additional Thursday train was for Wellington's general market. Also in 1863 the Sunday service had been increased to two trains each way between Wellington and Shifnal.

From its official opening day on 1st February, 1862 the Wen&SJR branch from Wenlock to Buildwas ran six passenger trains each way, the first leaving Wenlock at 7.40 am and the last leaving Buildwas at 7.40 pm at night. Each of the six trains was booked to connect with the Severn Valley trains to Shrewsbury. With the opening of the Lightmoor extension to Buildwas on 1st November, 1864 the first up train was the 7.08 am from Buildwas to Wellington via Horsehay arriving in Wellington at 7.41 am. The opening of this extension meant that the trains over the Madeley branch no longer ran via Horsehay to Wellington. Also the Sunday service was increased to four trains each way. There were two trains each way between Wellington and Coalbrookdale via Shifnal, and two more each way between Shifnal and Coalbrookdale only.

In 1865 the first train was 8.20 am from Wellington arriving at Buildwas at 9.03 am followed by trains at 12.30 and 5.20 pm, the last train being 8.20 pm arriving in Buildwas at 8.53 pm. The engine then went 'light' to Wellington via the Severn Valley line and Shrewsbury to enable the branch between Ketley and Coalbrookdale to close immediately after this last train. The first up train from Buildwas to Wellington was at 7.08 am arriving in Wellington at 7.41 am, others being at 11.45 am and 3.15 pm, the last train leaving at 7.40 pm and arriving in Wellington at 8.10 pm. By 1867 a further train had been added on Saturdays only this being the 10.15 pm ex-Wellington arriving in Buildwas at 11.10 pm, the lengthy schedule explained by the fact that the train was run 'mixed' (passenger and goods). This train returned as the

Wellington and Severn Junction.

MADELEY AND COALBROOKDALE AND MUCH WENLOCK AND CRAVEN ARMS BRANCHES. (SINGLE LINES.)

UP TRAINS.

The Single Line between Ketley Junction and Madeley Junction, and Buildwas Station and Marshbrook Junction is worked by Train Staff.

THE TRAIN STAFFS WORK AS UNDER:—

	Form of Staff and Ticket.	Color of Staff and Ticket.
between Ketley Junc. and Lightmoor Junc.	Round	Green
" Lightmoor Junc. and Madeley Junc.	Square	Red
" Buildwas and Madeley Junc.	Six-sided	Yellow
" Buildwas and Wenlock	Round	White
" Wenlock and Presthope	Six-sided	Blue
" Presthope and Marshbrook Junc.		

WEEK DAYS.

Miles from Craven Arms	STATIONS.	1 Pass. a.m.	2 Gds. a.m.	3 Gds. a.m.	4 Pass. a.m.	5 Gds. a.m.	6 Gds. a.m.	7 Pass. p.m.	8 Gds.&Pas. p.m.	9 Gds. p.m.	10	11 Pass. p.m.	12 Gds. p.m.	13 Gds. p.m.	14 Pass. p.m.	15 Pass. p.m.	16 Gds. p.m.
	Craven Arms ... dep.	8 15	…	…	…	…	…	…	…	2 20	…	3 40	…	…	5 50	6 45	…
3¼	Marsh Farm Junction	…	…	…	…	…	…	…	…	2 25	…	…	…	…	…	6 53	…
5½	Harton Road	…	…	…	…	…	11 15	…	…	CR	…	…	…	…	…	6 57	…
8¼	Rushbury	…	…	…	…	…	11 25	…	…		…	…	…	…	…	7 6	…
10¼	Longville	…	…	…	…	…	11 32	…	…		…	…	…	…	…	7 12	…
	Lilleshall Siding	…	…	…	…	…	11 43	…	…	2 40	…	…	…	…	…		…
14	Presthope	9 42	…	…	…	…	11 52	1 5	…		…	…	…	…	7 21	7 21	…
	Westwood	…	12 10	…	…	…	12 10		…		…	…	…	…			…
17	Much Wenlock ... { arr. / dep.	8 53	…	…	…	12 20	12 35		…	2 45	…	3 40	4 15	…	7 29	7 30	8 40
	S. W. & C. Co.'s Siding	…	…	…	…		CR		…		…		CR	RR			CR
	Bradley	8 28	7 40	…	10	10 11 15	12 55	1 14	CR	3 0	…	3 50	4 23		5 59	7 39	8 55
20¼	Buildwas ... { arr. / dep.	8 30	7 50	…	10	10 15 11 40	1 20	1 15 / 1 20	CR	3 20	…	4 10 4 16	4 30		6 0 / 6 5	7 40	9 10
21¼	Coalbrookdale	8 35	…	9 45	10 20	10 15 11 55	CR		3 45		…	4 30				7 44	CR
21¾	Coalbrookdale Works	…	…	9 55		10 24	1 39	1 24	3 49	3 35	…	4 21	4 45	RR	6 7 / 6 10	7 46	9 25
23	Lightmoor ... { dep.	8 39	8 5		10 24 11 55	10 25 12	1 40	1 25	CR	CR	…	4 26	4 50	5 25	6 9	7 49	9 25
	Madeley ...	8 40	8 10	CR	10 25 12					4 5	Main Line.	4 35					CR
24	Madeley Junction	…	8 35	10						CR		4 40					
27	Shifnal ... { arr. / dep.	…	8 47	10 25			2 1b		3 58	4 20	4 50			CR	6 10		9 40
29	Hollinswood ...	…	9 0	10 50			2 20		4 3					5 05 40			
	Dawley Parva	8 45		11 5	10 30 12 15		CR	1 30	CR						6 15	7 54	CR
23¾	Horsehay	8 49	…		10 34		1 55	1 34	3 45					CR	6 18		9 40
24¼	Lawley Bank	8 54	…		10 39		CR	1 39						6 0	6 24	8 0	9 55
25¼	Ketley Works	8 57	…		10 42		2 1b	1 42	3 58					6 5	6 27	8 5	10 0
26¼	Ketley Junction	…	…				2 20								6 30		
27	Wellington ... arr.	9 0	…		10 45			1 45	4 3	4 50		4 40					6 10

SUNDAYS.

STATIONS.	Pass. a.m.	Pass. p.m.
Craven Arms ... dep.	7 30	6 40
Presthope	7 45	6 55
Much Wenlock	7 50	7 5
Buildwas	7 55	7 5
Dawley Parva	8 10	7 20
Horsehay	8 15	7 25
Lawley Bank	8 20	7 29
Ketley Works	8 24	7 32
Wellington	8 28	7 35

R.R. Between Lightmoor and Horsehay.   When this conditional trip is not run, the 4.15 p.m. Train from Bradley Siding will arrive at Wellington at 6.40 p.m.

Wellington & Severn Junction Working Timetable for 1869.

DOWN TRAINS.

WEEK DAYS.

Distance from Hollinswood.	Distance from Wellington.	STATIONS.		1	2	3	4	5	6	7	8	9	10	11	12	13	14	15	16	17		
				Gds.	Gds. &Pas	Pass.	Pass.	Gds.	Pass.	Gds.	Gds	Pass.	Gds.	Gds	Pass.	Gds.	Pass.	Pass.	Gds	Pass.		
				a.m.	a.m.	a.m	a.m.	a.m.	a.m.	a.m.	p.m.	p.m.	p.m.	p.m.	p.m.	p.m.	p.m.	p.m.	p.m.	p.m.		
...	...	Wellington	dep.	5 15	...		9 20	9 30	11 0	...	...	2 25	2 45	...	4 30		...	6 50	7 0	8 35	...	...
...	1	Ketley Junction	"	5 25	...	...	9 23	9 40	11 3	...	...	2 29	2 55	...	4 33	...	...	6 53	7 10	8 38	...	...
...	1½	Ketley	"	—	...	...	9 25	—	—	...	...	2 33	—	...	4 35	...	...	6 56	—	8 41	...	...
...	2½	Ketley Works	"	—	...	...	—	9 50	—	...	...	—	CR	...	—	...	...	—	CR	—	...	...
...	3	Lawley Bank	"	—	...	...	9 29	—	—	...	...	2 38	—	...	4 39	...	...	7 0	—	8 47	...	...
...	4	Horsehay	"	5 55	...	...	9 34	10 5	11 11	...	12 25	2 43	3 10	...	4 43	5 10	...	7 5	7 20	8 52	...	...
...	5	Dawley Parva	"	6 10	...	...	—	CR	—	...	CR	--	—	...	—	—	...	—	CR	--	...	...
...	...	Hollinswood	"	—	...		—	—	—	11 40	—	—	—	...	—	—	...	—	—	—	...	...
...	...	Shiffnal	arr.	—	...	...	—	—	—	—	—	—	—	...	—	—	...	—	—	—	...	...
			dep.	—	...	9 20	—	—	—	—	—	—	—	...	—	RR	5 0	—	—	—	...	...
1	...	Madeley Junction	"	—	...	9 24	—	—	—	11 46	—	—	—	...	—	—	5 6	—	—	—	...	...
3¼	6¼	Madeley	"	—	...	9 29	—	—	—	11 56	—	—	—	...	—	—	5 15	—	—	—	...	...
5	5½	Lightmoor	arr.	6 15	...	9 33	9 39	10 15	11 15	12 10	12 40	2 48	3 20	3 45	4 47	5 20	5 20	7 10	7 35	8 58	...	...
...	...	Lightmoor	dep.	6 25	...	9 34	9 40	10 20	11 16	12 20	—	2 49	...	—	4 48	...	5 21	7 11	7 50	8 59	...	...
6½	7	Coalbrookdale	"	—	...	9 40	9 44	--	11 20	—	—	2 54	...	—	4 53	...	5 25	7 15	CR	9 5	...	...
6¾	7¼	Coalbrookdale Works	"	CR	...	...	—	CR	—	12 30	—	—	...	—	—	...	—	—	CR	—	...	...
7½	8	Buildwas	arr.	6 35	...	...	9 49	10 35	11 25	12 35	1 0	3 0	...	3 55	4 58	...	5 30	7 20	8 5	9 10	...	...
			dep.	6 50	...	...	9 50	10 45	11 45	1 15	...	3 5	...	4 0	5 0	...	5 31	7 40	8 15	9 11	...	...
...	...	Bradley	"	CR	...	...	—	CR	—	CR	...	—	...	4 8	—	...	—	—	—	—	...	...
...	...	S. W. & C. C. Co.'s Siding	"	CR	...	...	—	CR	—	CR		—	...	...	—	...	—	—	CR	—	...	...
11	11½	Much Wenlock	r.	7 10	...	...	9 59	11 0	12 0	1 30	...	3 15	...	...	5 9	...	5 40	7 50	8 30	9 20	...	...
			dep.	...	7 15	...	10 0	...	...	1 35	...	...	...	...	5 10	...	...	...	...	...	...	...
...	...	Westwood	"	...	CR	...	—	...	...	CR	...	...	...	...	—	...	...	...	...	...	...	...
14	14½	Presthope	"	...	7 35	...	10 7	...	...	2 10	...	...	...	...	5 19	...	...	...	...	...	...	...
...	...	Lilleshall Siding	"	...	—	...	—	...	...	2 15	...	...	...	...	—	...	...	...	...	...	...	...
17	17½	Longville	"	...	7 45	...	10 15	...	...	...	...	...	...	...	5 28	...	...	...	...	...	...	...
19¾	20¼	Rushbury	"	...	8 5	...	10 23	...	...	...	...	...	...	...	5 37	...	...	...	...	...	...	...
22¼	22¾	Harton Road	"	...	8 15	...	10 33	...	...	...	...	...	...	...	5 46	...	...	...	...	...	...	...
24¾	25¼	Marsh Farm Junction	"	...	8 25	...	10 37	...	...	...	...	...	...	...	5 51	...	...	...	...	...	...	...
28	28½	Craven Arms	arr.	...	8 35	...	10 45	...	...	...	...	...	...	...	6 0	...	...	...	...	...	...	...

LILLESHALL COMPANY'S PRESTHOPE SIDING.
This Single Line is worked by one Engine.

SUNDAYS.

STATIONS.		1	2	3	4	5	6	7	
			Pass.		Pass.				
			a.m.		p.m.				
Wellington	dep.	...	9 0	...	7 50	...	...	...	...
Ketley Junction	"	...	9 7	...	7 53	...	...	...	...
Ketley	"	...	9 10	...	8 0	...	...	...	...
Ketley Works	"	...		...		...	...	...	...
Lawley Bank	"	...	9 15	...	8 5	...	...	...	...
Horsehay	"	...	9 20	...	8 10	...	...	...	...
Dawley Parva	"	...	...	...		...	...	...	...
Hollinswood	"	...	...	...	...	...	...	...	...
Shiffnal	arr.	...	...	...	...	...	...	...	...
	dep.	...	...	...	...	...	...	...	...
Madeley Junction	"	...	...	...	...	...	...	...	...
Madeley	"	...	...	...	...	...	...	...	...
Lightmoor	arr.	...	...	...	...	...	...	...	...
Lightmoor	dep.	...	...	...		...	...	...	...
Coalbrookdale	"	...	9 33	...	8 23	...	...	...	...
Coalbrookdale Works	"	...	...	...	...	...	...	...	...
Buildwas	arr.	...	9 40	...	8 30	...	...	...	...
	dep.	...	9 45	...	8 33	...	...	...	...
Bradley	"	...	...	...	...	...	...	...	...
S. W. & C. C. Co.'s Siding	"	...	...	...	...	...	...	...	...
Much Wenlock	r.	...	10 0	...	8 50	...	...	...	...
	dep.	...	...	...	...	...	...	...	...
Westwood	"	...	...	...	...	...	...	...	...
Presthope	"	...	...	...	...	...	...	...	...
Lilleshall Siding	"	...	...	...	...	...	...	...	...
Longville	"	...	...	...	...	...	...	...	...
Rushbury	"	...	...	...	...	...	...	...	...
Harton Road	"	...	...	...	...	...	...	...	...
Marsh Farm Junction	"	...	...	...	...	...	...	...	...
Craven Arms	arr.	...	...	...	...	...	...	...	...

R.R. Run when required between Lightmoor and Horsehay.

The Gradients on the Line being heavy, and there being several level crossings, great care will be required in working these Branches, and two Guards will accompany every Train, with two Break Vans or Break Carriages: one to be placed next the Engine, and the other last on the Train.

When a Goods Train consists of more than eight Wagons and two Vans, it must be brought to a stand at the summit of the Incline (both on the Up and Down Journeys), in order that the Guards may pin down the necessary number of Breaks before descending the Incline in either direction, which must be done with extreme caution.—If a Passenger Train consists of more than eight Carriages and two Break Vans, additional Break Vans must be placed on the Train, namely, one Break for every four Carriages. All Wagons and Goods for Stations on these Branches, except Madeley, to be put off at Wellington. Goods may be sent by any Passenger Train, but not Minerals, Mineral Wagons, or Timber Trucks. All Wagons and Goods for Madeley to be put off at Shiffnal. Lines across the Columns denote the Stations at which the Trains are appointed to meet and cross each other.

No Train to exceed 8 Loaded Wagons Up the Wenlock Branch, or 16 Wagons with 1 Break Van, or 20 Wagons with 2 Break Vans and Guards Down the Wenlock Branch.

Up Goods Trains must not leave Presthope or Wenlock until the Guard has fastened down such a number of Wagon Breaks as will ensure, in the opinion of the Engineman, the stoppage of the Trains at any point between Presthope, Wenlock, and Buildwas. C.R. To stop if the Train has not a full load on. D On Saturdays, the 8.30 p.m. Train from Wellington will leave at 9.0 p.m., and be 25 minutes later at all Stations than the times shewn. It will cross the 8.40 p.m. Goods Train from Wenlock at Lightmoor.

No two Engines to be allowed in the Lilleshall Company's Presthope Siding at the same time.

Wellington & Severn Junction Working Timetable for 1869.

NOTICE OF
SPECIAL ARRANGEMENTS
ON
WELLINGTON & SEVERN JUNCTION
BRANCH,
On WHIT-TUESDAY, MAY 18th, 1875.

ON WHIT-TUESDAY, MAY 18,

SPECIAL TRAINS will run between WELLINGTON and MUCH WENLOCK, as under:—

	a.m. A	a.m. B	RR noon. C	p.m.	RR p.m.			RR D	p.m. E	p.m. F	p.m. G	RR H
Wellington ....dep.	9 0	10 45	12 0	—	10 50	**Much Wenlock**...dep.		11 1 0	5 45	6 45	8 40	9 40
Ketley Junction	9 7	10 48	12 13		10 55	**Buildwas**		11 10	5 55	6 55	8 52	9 50
Ketley	9 7	10 52	12 1			**Coalbrookdale**......		11 15	6 0	7 5	9 3	10 0
Lawley Bank	9 14	10 57	12 12			**Lightmoor**		11 28		7 12	9 1	9 10 5
Horsehay	9 18	11 2	12 17			**Horsehay**				7 18	9 15	10 11
Lightmoor	9 23	11 8	12 21		11 25	**Lawley Bank**				7 25	9 20	10 18
Coalbrookdale	9 27	11 13	12 26	6 10	11 30	**Ketley**				7 30	9 25	10 25
Buildwas	9 32	11 20	12 32	6 15	11 36	**Ketley Junction**		11 45		7 35	9 30	10 30
Much Wenlock	9 40	11 30	12 40	6 25	11 45	**Wellington**		11 50		7 40	9 35	10 35

A—Cross 8.15 a.m. Passenger Train from Much Wenlock at Ketley Junction, and 9.0 a.m. Passenger Train from Craven Arms at Much Wenlock.

B—Cross 9.0 a.m. Passenger Train from Craven Arms at Ketley Junction, and 11.0 a.m. RR Special Passenger Train from Much Wenlock at Buildwas.

C—Cross 11.0 a.m. Special Train from Much Wenlock at Ketley Junction, and 12.40 p.m. Goods Train from Much Wenlock at Much Wenlock.

D—Cross 9.30 a.m. Ordinary Train from Wellington at Much Wenlock, 10.45 a.m. Special Passenger Train from Wellington at Buildwas, 11.12 a.m. Ordinary Train from Wellington at Lightmoor, and 12.0 noon RR Special Passenger Train from Wellington at Wellington.

E—Cross 4.25 p.m. Passenger Train from Wellington at Much Wenlock.

F—Cross 6.53 p.m. Passenger Train from Wellington at Lightmoor Junction.

G—Cross 8.10 p.m. Passenger Train from Wellington at Lightmoor Junction.

H—Cross 8.40 p.m. Passenger Train from Wellington at Much Wenlock.

RR—These Trains will run only if required.

The 11.12 a.m. Ordinary Train from Wellington to Much Wenlock will call at Ketley and Lawley Bank on Tuesday, May 18.

A Special Train will also run between MUCH WENLOCK & CRAVEN ARMS, as under:

	I p.m.			p.m.
Much Wenlock ... ...dep.	8 0	Craven Arms ... ...dep.		9 15
Presthope ... ... ,,	8 7	Marsh Farm Junction ... ... ,,		9 23
Longville ... ... ,,	8 13	Harton Road ... ... ,,		9 27
Rushbury ... ... ,,	8 20	Rushbury ... ... ,,		9 35
Harton Road ... ... ,,	8 28	Longville ... ... ,,		9 43
Marsh Farm Junction ... ... ,,	8 35	Presthope ... ... ,,		9 53
Craven Arms ... ...arr.	8 45	Much Wenlock ... ...arr.		10 0

I This Train will be in connection with the 6.53 p.m. from Wellington.

The 8.55 a.m. Goods Train from Wellington to Much Wenlock, 11.52 a.m. Much Wenlock to Dawley Parva, 1.0 p.m. Dawley Parva to Buildwas, the 4.45 p.m. Bradley to Wellington, the 7.0 p.m. Wellington to Much Wenlock, and the 8.10 p.m. from Much Wenlock to Wellington will not run on Tuesday, May 18, and Inspector SHIPWAY must arrange for the Engine and Guards to be utilised for the Special Passenger Trains.

The Special Trains will consist of about 9 coaches and 3 vans, and the Ordinary Trains throughout the day must be strengthened if necessary; but the Trains must not consist of more than 12 vehicles. The extra coaches in the Ordinary Trains must be formed in the centre of the Train, one pair of the carriages, which are fitted with continuous breaks, being formed in the front, and the other pair in the rear. The Special Trains must have a Break-van in front and another in the rear, and a Break-Coach in the centre of the Train. Every Train, whether Special or Ordinary, must have at least one Break and Guard to every four coaches, and no Train must consist of more than 12 vehicles.

☞ Station-Masters are to send to Superintendent's Office a Return of the Bookings by each Special and Excursion Train immediately after its departure, giving number of Passengers, and Receipts by each Class.

☞ The Station-Masters to see that the Mineral and Goods Trains are shunted, and kept clear of the above Trains.

JAMES KELLEY,
Superintendent of Northern Division.

H. Y. ADYE,
Superintendent of Worcester Division.

CHESTER, *May* 14, 1875.

Special working instructions between Wellington and Much Wenlock in respect of the Wenlock Olympian games on Whit Tuesday 18th May, 1875.

11.15 pm goods from Buildwas arriving in Wellington at 11.50 pm, the train to call only at stations ordered by Mr Rimmer the then station master at Buildwas.

Following the opening of the line between Wenlock and Craven Arms in December 1867, the first passenger train to leave Wellington was the 8.20 am arriving in Craven Arms at 10.05 am; this was the only down direction train to run direct between the two towns. The following trains from Wellington, the 11.15 am, 2.25, 5.30 and 8.30 pm only running to Wenlock. In the middle of the day a train left Wenlock at 1.00 pm arriving in Craven Arms at 1.55 pm. Finally a 6.45 pm departure from Shifnal running via the Madeley branch arrived in Craven Arms at 8.45 pm. In the up direction the first train left Wenlock at 6.35 am arriving in Wellington at 7.25 am. The first through train to leave Craven Arms for Wellington was the 11.45 am arriving in Wellington at 1.35 pm, the only other through train being the 6.45 pm from Craven Arms.

In 1869 there were two trains leaving Wellington for Craven Arms at 9.00 am and at 4.30 pm, trains in the opposite direction left Craven Arms at 9.00 am and 6.45 pm. There was also a mixed goods and passenger train which left Craven Arms at 11.05 am which took 3¼ hours to reach Wellington. The Sunday service by this time had been reduced to two trains each way, a 7.30 am from Wenlock to Wellington, returning from Wellington at 9.00 am and a 6.40 pm from Wellington which returned from Wenlock at 7.50 pm.

On examining the passenger timetables for the 1860s and 1870s, the drastic changes which took place from year to year indicate how the GWR was endeavouring to evolve a service to suit the economic needs of the industrial and rural community which it had to serve. For example, the timetable for 1868 shows that the first passenger train from Craven Arms was the 7.30 am which ran over the Madeley branch to Shifnal. By 1872 the first train to leave Craven Arms was the 9.00 am, which ran to Wellington. During this period major changes in passenger train times were also made to the trains between Wellington and Wenlock. It was not until the 1880s that a more stable timetable began to emerge.

By 1883 the Sunday service had been reduced to one train each way between Wellington and Wenlock. The morning train left Wellington at 9.00 am arriving at Wenlock at 9.45 am. Upon arrival at Wenlock the Wellington men who had worked this train would be required to book off, and book on again in the evening to work the 6.30 pm back to Wellington, arriving there at 7.25 pm. During the period that the enginemen and guard booked off away from their home station they would not have been paid.

Throughout the 1880s the 7.00 am service from Wenlock to Craven Arms was a mixed train, in consequence of which any passengers travelling by this train were subject to a 1½ hour journey time to Craven Arms. In 1892 this mixed train had been brought forward to leave Wenlock at 6.25 am.

In April 1906 the *Wellington Journal* carried the headline 'Travelling Transformation'; the article went on to describe at great length the new form of transport which was to be introduced on to the Wenlock and Madeley branches - this was the steam 'rail motor'. The GWR introduced these single saloon coaches in 1903 each coach powered by the small 0-4-0 engine built into one end of the vehicle. A driving cab was provided at both ends so that the unit could be operated easily in either direction. Most of these railmotors were fitted with retractable steps to enable passengers to be picked up and set down at raised platforms which the GWR built to serve small communities between stations. The article in the *Wellington Journal* went on to say that it was the intention of the railway company to build these raised platforms along the branch. However, no evidence remains to suggest that this intention was ever carried out. Trailers were also attached to the railmotors in their first few weeks of operation, but these soon proved to be too much for the motive power on the gradients between Buildwas and Wenlock, and between Buildwas and Lightmoor Jn.

The timetable for April 1906 shows that all passenger train services over the branch were now operated by the 'one class' railmotors. This also brought about another innovation in the time table; this was that some of the trains from Wellington to Wenlock and Craven Arms (and back) were routed via Shifnal. The Sunday service still continued to be operated by the engine and

A steam railmotor climbs through Farley Dingle on its way to Much Wenlock in May 1906. The span of operations of these steam railmotors on the branch proved to be very short due to the severe gradients they had to encounter. The other problem was on Wellington market days - when a trailer was added difficulty was experienced in getting away from stations situated on gradients. *Ironbridge Gorge Museum*

Craven Arms station in 1906 showing the steam railmotor and trailer which were being operated on the Wenlock branch during this year. In the bay can be seen the Bishop's Castle Railway goods train with its former GWR tank engine. *G.M. Perkins*

WELLINGTON, MUCH WENLOCK AND CRAVEN ARMS. (Week Days only.)

Miles		a.m.	a.m.	a.m.	p.m.	p.m.	p.m.	p.m.	p.m.	Saturdays only. p.m.
	Wellington .... dep.		8 17	11 20	1 35	3 0	4 30	5 25	7 40	10 25
1¼	Ketley .... ,,		8 22	11 25	1 40	3 5	4 35	5 30	7 45	10 30
3	Lawley Bank ...... ,,		8 26	11 30	1 45	3 10	4 40	5 35	7 50	10 35
4	Horsehay and Dawley ,,		8 31	11 35	1 50	3 15	4 44	5 40	7 54	10 40
5¼	Lightmoor Platform ,,		8 35	11 40	1 55	3 20	4 48	5 45	7 58	10 44
7	Coalbrookdale ...... ,,		8 39	11 44	1 59	3 24	4 51	5 48	8 0	10 47
8¾	Buildwas { arr.		8 43	11 48	2 3	3 28	4 56	5 51	8 4	10 50
	Buildwas { dep.		8 55	12 7	2 20	3 30		6 5	8 15	10 52
11¼	Much Wenlock ...... ,,	6 30	9F20	12 18	2 31	3 45		6 20	8 30	11 4
14½	Presthope .... ,,	6 38	9 30			3 55		6 30		
18	Longville .... ,,	6 45	9 40			4 5		6 40		
20½	Rushbury .... ,,	6 50	9 45			4 10		6 45		
22½	Harton Road ...... ,,	R	9 50			4 15				
28¼	Craven Arms and Stokesay arr.	7 5	10 5			4 30		6 55		

		a.m.	a.m.	a.m.	a.m.	p.m.	p.m.	p.m.	p.m.	p.m.	Saturdays only. p.m.
	Craven Arms and Stokesay ... dep.			7 50	11 5			4 50			8 0
	Harton Road .... ,,			8 1	11 17			5 6			8 7
	Rushbury .... ,,			8 6	11 22			5 10		7 6	8 18
	Longville .... ,,			8 15	11 27			5 18		7 13	8 26
	Presthope .... ,,			8 23	11 34			5 25		7 25	8 32
	Much Wenlock { arr.			8 34	11 43			5 35		7 35	8 36
	Much Wenlock { dep.		7 5	8 41	11 50	1 35	3 0	5 43		7 45	8 40
	Buildwas { arr.		7 12		12K 3	1 42	3 7	6 4		7G55	8 46
	Buildwas { dep.		7 15			1 45	3 15				
	Coalbrookdale ...... ,,	6 25	7 20	8 57	12K 7	1 50	3 19	6 9	5 8		
	Lightmoor Platform ,,	6 28	7 24	9 1	12K10	1 54	3 23	6 13	5 11		
	Horsehay and Dawley ,,	6 35	7 33	9 8	12K17	2 0	3 30	6 19	5 17		
	Lawley Bank ...... ,,	6 40	7 38	9 13	12K20	2 5	3 36	6 24	5 21		
	Ketley .... ,,	6 45	7 43	9 18	12K25	2 10	3 42	6 28	5 25		
	Wellington .... arr.	6 50	7 48	9 24	12K30	2 15		6 35	5 30		

F—Arrive 9.6 a.m.   G—Saturdays excepted.   K—Runs 6 minutes later on Saturdays.   R—Calls at Harton Road to set down Passengers on notice to the Guard at Rushbury.

Extract from the passenger timetable of 1922.

The 7.50 am ex-Craven Arms to Wellington approaching Much Wenlock on 10th September, 1949 hauled by '44XX' class 2-6-2T No. 4409. This train was worked by Wenlock men who would return with the 11.10 am ex-Wellington to Much Wenlock.   *H.C. Casserley*

The well wooded valley of Coalbrookdale showing the Coalbrookdale Company's lower works and the Literary & Scientific Institute. Making its way to Coalbrookdale station on a ledge hewn out of the Captain's Coppice is the 4.40 pm Wellington to Much Wenlock on 9th June, 1962, headed by Ivatt class '2' 2-6-2T No. 41201.   *M. Mensing*

coaches, this being the only time that any one could travel first class. The railmotors were shedded at Wenlock which meant that the three passenger guards stationed at Wenlock were replaced by four motor rail conductors as they were termed. The conductors were as follows:

Name	*Transferred from*
A.J. Greenway	Evesham
H. Carter	Kidderminster
W.J. Evans	Cressage
W.A. Osborne	Worcester

The 'transport revolution' on the branch was soon to prove a failure, due to the gradients and the fact that the single unit proved unable to cope with the number of passengers on market days. Later in 1906 this service was withdrawn.

Despite the fact that the line served an industrial community, no workmen's train was provided until 1919 when an empty stock train left Wellington at 6.00 am for Horsehay returning from there at 6.35 am. By 1922 the empty stock left Wellington at 5.50 am and was extended to Coalbrookdale, this train being further extended to Buildwas in 1933.

By 1928 the complexities of the earlier passenger timetables had given way to a more settled timetable. In the down direction there were two through trains from Wellington to Craven Arms, and five between Wellington and Wenlock and one early morning train leaving Wenlock at 6.30 am for Craven Arms. When extended in 1933 an empty stock train left Wellington at 5.20 am for Buildwas, this forming the 6.05 am workmen's train from Buildwas to Wellington. There were also two Saturdays-only trains, one was a mixed workmen's train from Ketley to Wenlock, and the other was the 10.00 pm from Wellington which arrived in Wenlock at 10.50 pm. In the up direction there were three through trains between Craven Arms and Wellington, and three from Wenlock to Wellington, the workmen's train from Buildwas to Wellington at 6.05 am, also another train from Buildwas to Wellington at 4.55 pm. The Saturdays-only train left Wenlock at 8.00 pm for Wellington.

In addition to its normal passenger services the branch also provided excursion trains for the local residents. There were the annual events like the Shrewsbury Flower Show, The Wenlock Olympian Games, and the Craven Arms May Fair. In 1933 a Saturdays-only service from Buildwas to Wolverhampton and Birmingham was introduced, leaving Buildwas at 4.50 pm, and arriving back in Buildwas at 1.16 am on Sunday morning.

In the first week in September a mass exodus took place from Ketley, Lawley Bank, and Horsehay when many of the locals made their way to the hop fields at Tenbury Wells in Worcestershire. This was in fact for many people their annual holiday. A festive air seemed to prevail in these three areas on the departure day.

Cis Jones, who was signalman at Ketley in the 1930s, recalls his memories of the hop pickers' departure day from Ketley station:

It was a red letter day at Ketley when the hop pickers left here for Tenbury Wells. I can see them now - men, women, and children wending their way up to the station from Ketley Brook, Ketley Offices, and Forge Row. They would have every conceivable piece of luggage from a brown paper parcel tied with string, to an old tin chest. Some would also have tea chests covered with brightly coloured wallpaper, these tea chests would be conveyed to the station on wheelbarrows, or on two-wheeled trolleys made out of orange boxes. This was in the days of mass unemployment and the luxuries of these people were few, in fact in that assortment of luggage, for many of them it would contain their worldly wealth. This event for them was their annual holiday.

The train would consist of five coaches, and was always double-headed; after Ketley it would pick up at Lawley Bank, Horsehay then on to Buildwas and down the Severn Valley line to Bewdley. It would then go on to the Tenbury branch for Tenbury Wells.

The hop pickers would be away for about three weeks, and while they were away their living conditions would be pretty rough. Their living accommodation would be in the sheds and barns around the hop fields.

When they returned not only did they have their various pieces of luggage, but they also had other things which they had collected. I well remember going into the guard's van to unload the luggage on one occasion when they returned, and one box which I started to unload seemed to move about, and in that box was a little pig which one family had brought back with them. Many of the men would come back well oiled after sampling the delights of the Tenbury beer.

Passenger train operation on the branch did not always run smoothly, as is evidenced by the following report in the *Wellington Journal* dated 14th May, 1932 under the heading 'Coalbrookdale':

An accident occurred on the railway on May 6th when the front wheel of the engine of the 12 o'clock train from Coalbrookdale to Wellington suddenly became detached shortly after passing over the viaducts. The engine left the metals and some 40 chairs were broken and many sleepers torn up before the train came to a standstill. Fortunately no one was injured, and the passengers were able to proceed to their destination by a passing lorry. The traffic was conducted on the down line, and the engine was hoisted into position by a large crane. The obstruction was cleared at 7.00 pm.

It would appear that the railway company was not too concerned about the passengers' welfare and comfort, by virtue of the fact that they did not organise a coach, but allowed them to continue their journey in the back of a passing lorry!

A further experiment was made in March 1936 with one of the company's AEC diesel railcar units between Wellington and Wenlock. This however did not get beyond the experimental stage, again the severity of the gradients, and the fact that a trailer could not be attached on market days, being the crucial factors.

Freight Train Operation

With the opening of the Wgton&SJR line from Ketley to Horsehay for goods traffic in March 1857, the Coalbrookdale Company's Horsehay furnaces were given access to the main rail network. This facility was already in existence for the Ketley Iron Company who had been connected by Dickson's private siding from the Waterloo Sidings on the Shrewsbury and Birmingham Railway into the Ketley works. Before the line was opened for passenger traffic in May 1859 there was no booked freight working between Wellington and Horsehay, the goods trains running as and when required.

Not until the opening of the line between Wellington and Lightmoor Jn and Shifnal, via the Madeley branch, do we see a working timetable for goods train operations.

In 1862 there was considerable freight activity, from Wellington there were eight goods trains, one Wellington-Madeley, one Lightmoor-Shifnal, and another Wellington-Lightmoor. Between Wellington and Horsehay there were five goods trains, of these three ran during the night, leaving Wellington at midnight, 1.20 am and another at 2.20 am.

There were also a number of goods trains in the opposite direction. One left Horsehay at 2.15 am arriving in Wellington at 2.35 am, the next was the 9.00 am from Horsehay to Wellington. From Lightmoor there was a goods at 3.30 pm calling at Lightmoor Road, Horsehay and Ketley arriving in Wellington at 4.30 pm. From Madeley a goods left at 9.15 pm and ran via Lightmoor arriving in Wellington at 10.00 pm.

In 1862 there were three goods trains, calling at what was then known as Lightmoor Road Sidings, these were the sidings serving the Lightmoor furnaces. By the late 1860s, these sidings were very little used. By the mid-1870s it was no longer called Lightmoor Road but Dawley Parva, the sidings being used for the purpose of bringing out furnace slag which was being used for road mending and railway ballast.

With the opening of the line from Lightmoor to Buildwas in 1864 the first goods train left Wellington at 5.50 am for Buildwas, another at 6.25 am and the last at 6.35 pm. From the opening of the line between Wenlock and Buildwas, in 1862 there had been no *booked* freight train working on this section, the engine working a freight train between passenger trains according to instructions. However, following the extension of the branch from Wellington to reach Buildwas in 1864 booked working for goods trains between Wenlock and Buildwas was introduced (and to Presthope when this section opened a month later).

In 1867 the Lilleshall Company's limestone sidings at Presthope were opened, following which there were three goods trains from there to Buildwas the first one leaving at 1.20 pm and the last at 5.20 pm. By this time there was more than 'one engine in steam' working between Presthope and Buildwas, for in addition to the Wenlock engine the Wgton&SJR engine was also working the 12.45 pm from Buildwas to Presthope and 2.05 pm from Presthope to Wenlock.

By 1869 there was mixed train working between Wenlock and Shifnal over the Madeley branch, services being the 9.15 am-ex Wenlock and from Shifnal the 11.15 am and 3.15 pm to Wenlock. Also during this year we see the introduction of the 11.30 am ex-Presthope conveying limestone to the Meadow Wharf at Buildwas for conveyance down river for the Madeley Wood Company's furnaces at Blists Hill. In 1869 the South Wales and Cannock Chase Company's sidings were opened at the Shadwell quarry at Wenlock. Also at this time there was a daily goods train from the Coalbrookdale Company's sidings at the Bradley quarry leaving there at 4.15 pm for Lightmoor, no doubt conveying limestone for use at the Lightmoor and Dawley Castle furnaces.

The closure of the Lightmoor and Dawley Castle furnaces in 1883 had an adverse effect on the goods train operations on the branch, and by 1885 the Dawley Parva sidings had closed.

From the opening of the line between Wenlock and Craven Arms in December 1867, cattle from the stations along the line for Wellington Market on a Monday were conveyed by a mixed train. However by 1886 an engine and two guard's vans left Wellington at 5.45 am for Craven Arms to work the 9.15 am thence, stopping at all stations to Buildwas to pick up cattle and arriving in Wellington at 11.00 am. This service was replaced in 1895 by an empty cattle wagon train which left Shrewsbury at 4.20 am via the Severn Valley line to Buildwas, and then on to the Wenlock branch for Craven Arms dropping off the empty cattle trucks at each station. The train would then return from Craven Arms at 8.30 am picking up the loaded cattle trucks at each station between Harton Road and Buildwas, and usually being banked from Buildwas to Horsehay. By 1932, due to increased road competition, this cattle train had been discontinued, and from then until the beginning of the World War II the odd cattle truck could be seen attached to the rear of the 8.50 am ex-Craven Arms 'mixed' which ran on Mondays only.

By the beginning of World War I in 1914 goods trains were only booked to call 'if required' at both the Lilleshall Company's sidings at Presthope, and the South Wales and Cannock Chase Shadwell sidings at Wenlock. By 1921 both these sidings had ceased to be used.

In 1922 a cattle train was introduced which ran on alternate Mondays leaving Wenlock at 10.45 am for Craven Arms; this train only had a short span of life for by 1927 it had been discontinued. From 1927 until the closure of the line to Craven Arms there was only one goods train in each direction between Wenlock and Craven Arms; this was the 8.20 am ex-Wenlock which arrived at Craven Arms at 10.50 am and returned from there at 11.30 am, arriving in Wenlock at 2.40 pm.

The 13th October, 1932 was a day of special significance for the branch, being the day on which Ironbridge Power Station was opened at Buildwas by the then Minister of Transport, Mr P.J. Pybus. The Minister and other dignitaries were conveyed from Wellington to Buildwas in three saloon coaches, and a dining car, hauled by a Dean standard goods engine. To the local population residing alongside the line their memories did not centre around the opening of the power station, but the opulence as portrayed by the saloon coaches, and the dining car with its red shaded lamps on each dining table, and its tasselled velvet curtains.

The opening of the power station breathed new life into the freight train working on the branch. The Ironbridge Power Station was designed to burn Midlands 'slack' and South Wales 'duff' and the network of railway lines converging on Buildwas helped to facilitate

Wellington and Severn Junction.

MADELEY AND COALBROOKDALE AND MUCH WENLOCK AND CRAVEN ARMS BRANCHES.

DOWN TRAINS.

Distance from Buildwas	STATIONS		1 Pass. a.m.	2 Pass. a.m.	3 Pas&Gds. a.m.	4 Gds. a.m.	5 Pass. a.m.	6 Gds. a.m.	7 Pass. a.m.	8 Gds. p.m.	9 Gds. p.m.	10 Pass. p.m.	11 Pass. p.m.	12 Pass. p.m.	13 Gds. p.m.	Sun. 1 Pass. a.m.	Sun. 2 Pass. p.m.
…	Craven Arms	dep.															
…	Marshbrook Junction	"	7 30						11 45		2 15			6 10			
…	Harton	"	7 40						11 55		2 30			6 20			
…	Rushbury	"	7 45						12 10		2 40			6 25			
…	Longville	"	7 55						12 20		2 55			6 35			
…	Lilleshall Siding	"	8 5								3 0			6 46			
…	Presthope	"	8 15					12 30		3 10			6 55				
…	Westwood	"							12 30		3 30						
…	Much Wenlock	{arr.	8 25				11 5	11 50	12 40							7 30	
…		dep.	6 35	8 30			11		12 45	2 20		3 25			7 55		
…	Bradley Siding	{arr.	6 48	8 45	9 15				1	2 50		3 40		7 5	8 15	7 45	6 55
…		dep.	6 50	8 50	9 20		11 20	12 10	1 5			4 5	5 50	7 20	8 30	7 50	7 5
…	Buildwas	{arr.	6 57	8 56	9 32				1 10	3 20		4 5		7 35	8 40	7 55	
…		dep.			9 55										8 50		
1	Coalbrookdale	"			9 58										9 0		
1¼	Coalbrookdale Works	"	7 2	8 59	10 10	10 15			1 14	3 35	4 9	4 9	5 54	7 39			
2¼	Lightmoor Junction	{arr.	7 3	9 0	10 11	10 25			1 15	3 52	4 10	4 10	5 55	7 40			
3	Madeley	"		9 14		10 30							6 0				
6	Madeley Junction	{arr.		9 18		10 50				4 7			6 6				
8¼	Shiffnal	{dep.				11 5							6 10				
…	Shiffnal	"	7 9		10 18				1 20	4 22		4 15		7 44	9 10	8 10	7 20
3	Hollinswood	"	7 14		10 28				1 24			4 19		7 48		8 15	7 25
4	Dawley Parva	"			10 33												
5	Horsehay, for Dawley	"			10 38				1 28			4 24		7 52	9 25	8 20	7 29
6	Lawley Bank	"	7 20		10 43							4 27		7 54	9 28	8 24	7 32
6½	Ketley Works	"	7 22		10 46				1 30			4 30		7 57	9 35	8 28	7 35
…	Ketley	"															
…	Ketley Junction	"															
8	Wellington	arr.	7 25		10 50				1 35								

Extract from the Working Timetable of 1892.

UP TRAINS.

Distance from Hollinswood.	Distance from Wellington.	STATIONS.		WEEK DAYS. 1	2	3	4	5	6	7	8	9	10	11	12	13	14	15	SUNDAYS. 1	2	3	4	5	6	7
				Gds.		Pass.	Gds.	Pass.	Pass.	Gds. & Pas	Pass.	Gds.	Gds. & Pas	Gds.	Gds.	Pass.	Pass.	Pass.				Pass.			Pass.
				a.m.		a.m.	a.m.	a.m.	a m	a.m.	p.m.	a.m.	p.m.	p.m.	p.m.	p.m.	p.m.	p.m.				a.m.			p.m.
...	...	Wellington	dep.	4 30		8 20	9 0			11 15			2 25			5 20		8 30				9 0			7 50
...	1	Ketley Junction	„	4 40		8 23	9 5			11 18			2 29			5 23		8 33				9 7			7 53
...	1¼	Ketley	„	—		8 26	—			11 21			2 33			5 25		8 36				9 10			8 0
...	2½	Ketley Works	„	CR		—	9 15			11 25			—			—		—				—			—
...	3	Lawley Bank	„	—		8 30	—			11 30			2 38			5 30		8 42				9 15			8 5
...	4	Horsehay, for Dawley	„	5 0		8 35	9 30			11 36			2 43			5 35		8 47				9 20			8 10
...	5	Dawley Parva	„	5 5		—	—			—			—			—		—				—			—
...	...	Hollinswood	„	—		—	—			—		11 40	—			—		—				—			—
...	...	Shiffnal	arr.	—		—	—	9 45		—		—	—			—		—				—			—
			dep.	—		—	—			—		—	—			—	6 45	—				—			—
1	...	Madeley Junction	„	—		—	—	9 51		—		11 46	—			—	6 51	—				—			—
3¾	6½	Madeley	„	—		—	—	10 0		—		11 56	—			—	7 0					—			—
5	5½	Lightmoor Junction	arr.	5 10		8 40	9 36	10 6		11 41		12 10	2 48			—	7 5	8 53				—			—
			dep.	5 20		8 41		10 7		11 55		12 20	2 49		3 50	5 40	7 6	8 54				—			—
6¼	7¼	Coalbrookdale Works	„	C R		—				—		12 30	—		—	5 41	—					—			—
6½	7	Coalbrookdale	„	—		8 46		10 11		12 5		—	2 54		—	5 45	7 13	9 0				9 33			8 23
7½	8	Buildwas	arr.	5 30		8 50		10 15		12 10		12 35	3 0		4 0		7 20	9 5				9 40			8 30
			dep.	5 45		8 55		10 20	11 30	12 15		1 5	3 5		4 5		7 30	9 10				9 45			8 33
...	...	Bradley Siding	arr.	5 55		—		—	—	—		—	—		—		—	—				—			—
...	...	Much Wenlock	arr.	6 5		—		10 30	11 45	12 35		1 25	3 15		4 25		—	9 20				10 0			8 50
			dep.			9 10					1 0	1 35					7 45								
...	...	Westwood	arr.			—					—	CR					—								
...	...	Presthope	„			9 20					1 10	1 50		4 15			8 0								
...	...	Lilleshall Siding	„			—					—	1 55		CR			—								
...	...	Longville	„			9 30					1 20			4 35			8 10								
...	...	Rushbury	„			9 40					1 30			4 50			8 20								
...	...	Harton	„			9 50					1 40			5 0			8 30								
...	...	Marshbrook Junction	„			9 55					1 45			5 15			8 35								
...	...	Craven Arms	arr.			10 5					1 55			5 30			8 45								

The Gradients on the Line being heavy, and there being several level crossings, great care will be required in working these Branches, and two Guards will accompany every Train, with two Break Vans or Break Carriages: one to be placed next the Engine, and the other last on the Train.

When a Goods Train consists of more than eight Wagons and two Vans, it must be brought to a stand at the summit of the Incline (both on the Up and Down Journeys), in order that the Guards may pin down the necessary number of Breaks before descending the Incline in either direction, which must be done with extreme caution.—If a Passenger Train consists of more than eight Carriages and two Break Vans, additional Break Vans must be placed on the Train, namely, one Break for every four Carriages. All Wagons and Goods for Stations on these Branches, except Madeley, to be put off at Wellington. Goods may be sent by any Passenger Train, but not Minerals, Mineral Wagons, or Timber Trucks. All Wagons and Goods for Madeley to be put off at Shiffnal. Lines across the Columns denote the Stations at which the Trains are appointed to meet and cross each other.

Buildwas and Much Wenlock.—The driver in charge of the Wenlock Branch Engine or Train will carry a Train Staff, and no Engine or Train must proceed upon this Branch without such Staff. See Instructions, page 57. No Train to exceed 8 Loaded Wagons Up the Branch, or 16 Wagons with 1 Break Van, or 20 Wagons with 2 Break Vans and Guards Down the Branch.

Up Goods Trains must not leave Presthope or Wenlock until the Guard has fastened down such a number of Wagon Breaks as will ensure, in the opinion of the Engineman, the stoppage of the Trains at any point between Presthope, Wenlock, and Buildwas. C.R. To stop if the Train has not a full load on. D On Saturdays, the 8.30 p.m. Train from Wellington will leave at 9.0 p.m., and be 30 minutes later at all Stations than the times shewn. E The 8.30 p.m. Goods on Saturdays will leave Buildwas at 9.0 p.m., and will be 30 minutes later at all Stations than the times shewn. It will cross No. 14 Passenger Train at Lightmoor as usual. *Meadow Wharf.*—A Train will leave Buildwas at 12.40 p.m. for Meadow Wharf, returning at 12.50 p.m. for Buildwas.

Extract from the Working Timetable of 1892.

WELLINGTON AND SEVERN JUNCTION.

MADELEY, COALBROOKDALE, MUCH WENLOCK, AND CRAVEN ARMS BRANCHES.

DOWN TRAINS—WEEK DAYS ONLY.

Commences June 11th, 1929.

Distance from Wellington. M.C.	Distance from Shifnal. M.C.	STATIONS.	Ruling Gradient 1 in	Station No.	Time allowances for Ordinary Freight Trains See page 2. Point to Point Times.	Allow for Stop.	Allow for Start.	Empty Coaches & Workmen. B	Light Engine. G	Goods. L See note	Goods. M	Passenger. B	Goods. M	Passenger. B	Goods. M See Note	Passenger.	Goods.	Passenger.	Goods.	Passenger. B	Goods. M	Passenger. B	Goods. M	Passenger. B	Pass. SO

Wellington dep. — Ketley Junction — Ketley — Lawley Bank — Stop Board — Horsehay (Dawley) — **Hollinswood,** arr. — **Shifnal** dep. — **Madeley Jc.** — Kemberton — Mad'ly(Sal'p) — Lightmoor Jo.arr. — Lightmoor Jc. dep. — Stop Board — Lightmoor P'form — **Coalbrookdale** arr. — **Buildwas** dep. — Bradley Siding — **Much Wenlock** arr. — **Much Wenlock** dep. — Westwood Siding — Presthope — Lilleshall Siding — Longville — Rushbury — Harton Rd. — Marsh Farm Junc. — **Craven Arms** arr.

Notes:
- **L** Leaves G. W. Yard 6.45 a.m. Arrives Horsehay 7.5 and Lightmoor Junction 7.20 a.m.
- **S** Starts from Goods Yard and arrives Ketley 11.34, Horsehay 12.2 p.m. and Coalbrookdale 12.50 p.m.
- **N** Traffic from the Market Drayton Branch and Wellington for the Severn Valley Line must be worked via Shrewsbury
- ‡ Calls at Harton Road when required to set down Passengers only. Guard to collect Tickets from Passengers alighting.

See page 70 for altered times when Special Trip run to Kemberton.

Arrive Westwood 8.55, Longville 9.55, Presthope 9.14, Longville 9.55, Rushbury 10.12, Harton Road 10.32.

Arrive Madeley Junction 1.55 p.m. Madeley 2.40 p.m.

See instruct. page 70 re working at Kemberton.

Urgent traffic only.

Single Line. Double Line. Single Line.

WELLINGTON AND SEVERN JUNCTION.—Madeley, Coalbrookdale, Much Wenlock, and Craven Arms Branches—continued.

UP TRAINS.—WEEK DAYS ONLY.

Distance from Craven Arms M.C.	STATIONS.	Rolling Gradient 1 in	Point to Point Times	Allow for Stop.	Allow for Start.	Passenger (Work'n) A.M.	Passenger A.M.	Passenger A.M.	Goods A.M.	Mixed MO A.M.	Goods A.M.	Passenger A.M.	Goods P.M.	Passenger A.M.	Goods A.M.	Passenger P.M.	Goods P.M.	Passenger P.M.	Goods P.M.	Goods P.M.	Passenger P.M.	Passenger P.M.	Light Engine P.M.	Passenger SO P.M.
3 16	Craven Arms ..... dep.				1			7 52		9 0										RR				8 0
5 69	Marsh Farm Junction "	200 R	7	1	1			7 57		9 3												6 52		
8 24	Harton Road "	100 R	6	1	1			8 3		9 20												7 0		
10 41	Rushbury "	100 R	6	1	1			8 9		9 45												7 10		
14 19	Longville "	100 R						8 14		9 58														
15 7	Lilleshall Siding "		11	1						10 16												7 20		
15 10	Presthope "	100 R						8 21		10 19								3 15		3 15				
	Westwood Siding "		2		1					10P20	10P20													
17 14	Stop Board top of Incline arr.	180 R			1			8 27		10 26					11 50				3 25		3 25		7 28		
17 14	Much Wenlock { dep.	43 F	7	2	1	7 5		8 32		10 36	10 30S	11 53		1 35		3 0				3 43		7t30	6t40	
17 21½	Stop Board top of Incline { arr. dep.		1 stop							10 37	10 31													
18 24	Bradley Sid'ng ..... { dep. arr.		3	2		7 13		8x39		10 46	10P33	12x1		1 43		3 8				5x51		7 58	6t47	8 8
20 35	Builwas " dep.	40 F	7	1	2	7 15		8 54		10 58	11 0	12 10				3 20								
21 48	Coalbrookdale ..... "	50 R	4	2	2	7 20		8 58		11 15	11 15	12 15				3 25								8 20
22 75	Lightmoor Platform "	82 R	9	1	2	7 24		9 2		11 25	11 19	12 19				3 29				4 0				8 25
23 0	Lightmoor Junc. arr.	60 R		1														4 28		5 10			7t10	8 29
1 5	Lightmoor Junc. dep.	100 R	4		1		6 25			11 30	11 30	12 20									4 0			
1 62	Madeley (Salop) "	640 R	2		1		6 28			11 55	11 35	12 25									4x45			
3 75	Kemberton "	82 R	7		1					12 33	11 50	12 35						4 20			4 48			
6 71	Madeley Junction arr.	150 F			1					1 0	12 50	12 45												
	Shifnal { dep. arr.	150 R	4x2 7	1	2	6 45						12 50						4 40		6 45	5 63			
24 51	Hollinswood { arr. dep.	40 R	12	1	1	6 50		9 0		11 11						3 34				5 18	5 23			8 34
25 5	Horsehay (Dawley) { dep.	45 R	4	1	2	6 33	7 30	9 7		11 50	11 40.					3 38				5 50			7 7	8 38
25 43	Stop Board "	45 F	6	1	1	6 40	7 38	9 14								3 43				6 P1	6 24			8 41
26 72	Lawley Bank "		1	1		6 45	7 43				11P22					3 48		5 10		6 29		7 56		8 46
27 77	Stop Board "	50 F	2			6 47	7 45	9 19			11x23					3 61				6 41	6 31			
28 44	Ketley "	132 F	1		1	6 49	7 48	9 21			11 44										6x14			
	Wellington arr.					6 50 7¾8	7¾8	9 23		12 42	11 50		2 18			3¾4				6 49	6¾4	8 10	7¾10	8 55

§ Depart Lightmoor Junction.

V Presthope arrive 1.10 p.m.   W RR Presthope to Westwood and back. Presthope depart 1.16 p.m. Westwood depart 1.20 p.m. Westwood arrive 1.20 depart 1.30,
Presthope arrive 1.35 p.m.   Y Convey Parcels traffic from Madeley.   ¶ Advertised 4.45 p.m.

RR For dates see local Notice.

Commencing June 11th, 1929, SX departs Buildwas 7.45 p.m., Wellington arr. 8.10 p.m.

B Commences June 11th, 1929.

Extract from the Working Timetable of 1928.

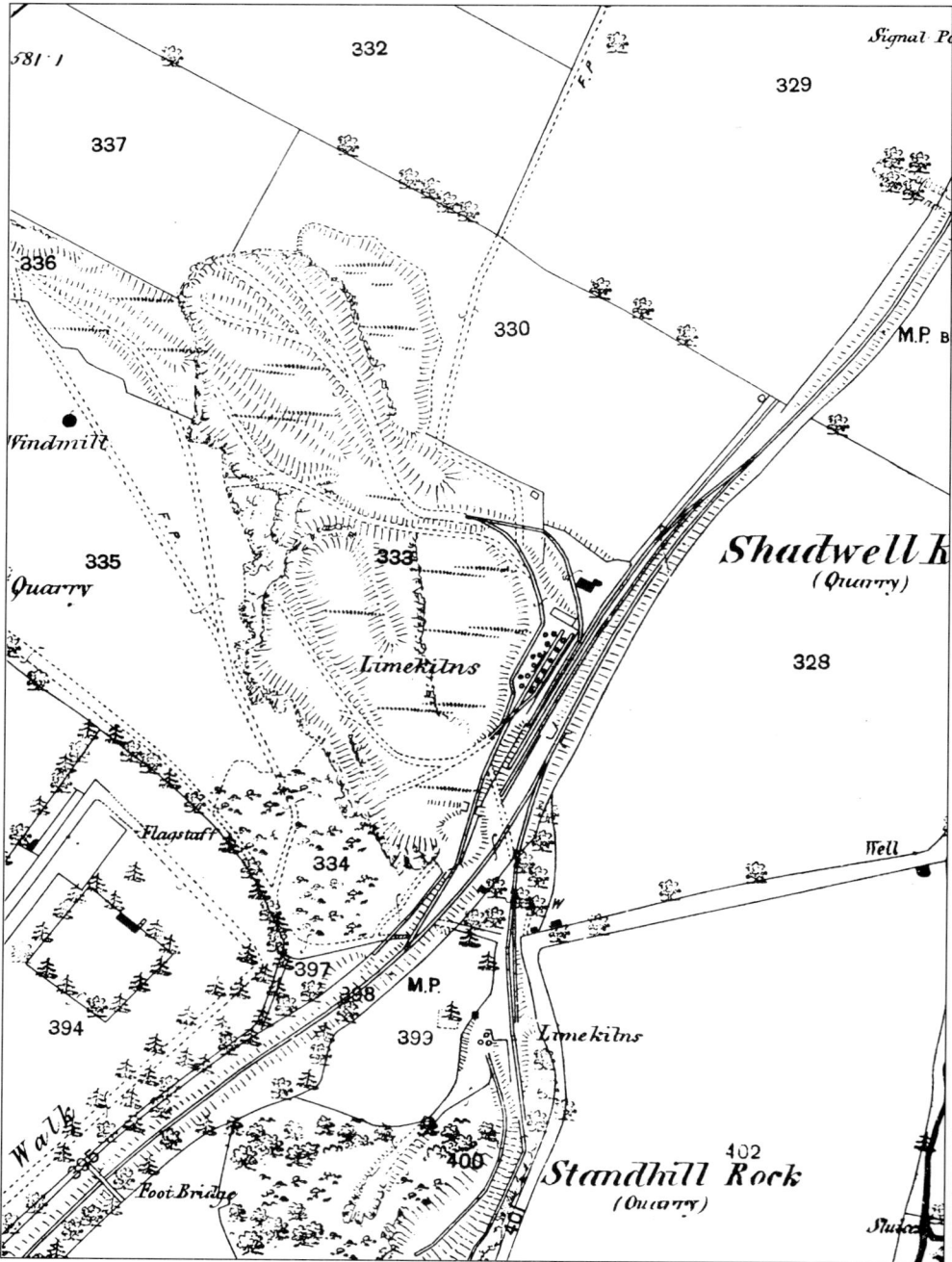

Shadwell and Standhill quarries, Much Wenlock.

Reproduced from the 25", 1882 Ordnance Survey Map

WELLINGTON AND SEVERN JUNCTION.

MADELEY, COALBROOKDALE, MUCH WENLOCK, AND CRAVEN ARMS BRANCHES.

Down Trains. — Week Days only.

Mile Post Mileage from Paddington R	Distance from Wellington	STATIONS	Ruling Gradient 1 in	B Empty C'ches and Workmen	B Pass.	B Pass.	B Pass.	B Mixed Train SO	B Pass.	B Pass.	B Pass.	B Pass.
M. C.	M. C.			a.m.	a.m.	a.m.	a.m.	p.m.	p.m.	p.m.	p.m.	p.m.
		WELLINGTON dep.	132 R.	5 30		7 0	8 17		3 0	4 30	5 45	7 40
166 63	1 5	Ketley Jct.	,,	5 32		7 2	8 19	12 4?	3 2	4 32	5 47	7 42
166 2?	1 47	Ketley	50 R.	5 35		7 5	8 22	12 45	3 5	4 35	5 50	7 45
165 71	1 77	Ketley T. Halt	45 R.	—		7 7	8 24	12 47	3 7	4 37	C5 52	C7 47
165 29	2 39	New Dale Halt	45 R.	—		7 9	8 27	12 50	3 10	4 40	5 55	7 50
164 67	3 1	Lawley Bank	45 R.	5 40		7 12	8 30	12 55	3 13	4 43	5 58	7 53
164 9?	3 58?	Stop Board	45 R.					P				
163 75	3 73	Horsehay & D.	40 F.	5 44		7 17	8 35	1 1	3 18	4 48	6 3	7 58
163 14	4 54	Doseley Halt	,,	5 47		7 20	8 38	1 5	3 21	4 51	6 6	8 1
162 24?	5 44	Lightmoor Jct.	50 F.			X						
162 19	5 49	Lightmoor Pl.	,,	5 51		7 23	8 42	1 11	3 25	4 55	6 10	8 5
161 43	6 25	Green Bk. Hlt.	50 F.	5 54		7 26	8 45	1 14	3 28	4 58	6 13	8 8
160 72	6 76	Coalbrookdale	50 F.	5 57		7 29	8 48	1 20	3 31	5 0	6 16	8 11
160 23	8 9	Buildwas { arr.	6 1		7 33	8X52	1 30	3 35	5 5	6 20	8 15
		{ dep.	40 R.			7 45	8 55	1 30	3 50		6 25	8 20
162 33	10 29?	Farley Halt	40 R.			7 55	9 4	1 39	3 50?		6 34	8 29
163 43?	11 30	MUCH WENLOCK { arr.	,,			8 2	9 11	1 44	3 56			8 34
		{ dep.	40 R.		6 30		9 23		3 59			
165 18	13 4?	Westwood Halt	48 R.		6 38		9 35?		4 4			
166 39	14 25	Presthope	48 R.		6 38		9 35		4 9			
168 30	16 16	Easthope Halt	150 F.				9 38		4 13?			
170 17	18 3	Longville	100 F.		6 45		9 44		4 18			
172 34	20 20	Rushbury	100 F.		6 50		9 49		4 23			
174 69	22 55	Harton Road	100 F.				9 55		4 28			
177 42	25 28	Marsh Farm J.	170 R.			C:R			4 33			
— 26 79?		Wistanstow H.	170 R.				10 4		4 37			
— 28 44		CRAVEN ARMS arr.	106 R.		7 5		10 7		4 40			

Up Trains. — Week Days only.

STATIONS	Ruling Gradient 1 in	B Pass. (Workmen).	B Pass.	B Pass.	B Pass. K	D Engine and Van SO	B Pass.	B Pass.	D Empty C'ches
		a.m.	a.m.	a.m.	a.m.	p.m.	p.m.	p.m.	p.m.
CRAVEN ARMS dep.	—			7 50	11 10			5 0	
Wistanstow Halt ,,	106 R.				11 14				
Marsh Farm Jct. ,,	170 F.			7 56	11 17?			5 6	
Harton Road ,,	200 R.			8 2	11 23			5 12	
Rushbury ,,	100 R.			8 7	11 28			5 17	
Longville ,,	100 R.			8 14	11 33			5 23	
Easthope Halt ,,	150 R.			8 18	11 36			C5 27	
Presthope ,,	100 R.			8 23	11 41			5 32	
Westwood Halt ,,	48 F.			8 27	11 45			5 36	
MUCH WENLOCK { arr.	—			8 31	11 49			5 40	
{ dep.	43 F.		7 0	8 34	11 51	1 50		5 43	
Farley Halt ,,	40 F.		7 4	8 38	11 55			5 47	
Buildwas { arr.	—		7 9	8X43	12X 0	2 0		5 52	
{ dep.	40 F.	6 10	7 10	8 53	12 12		4 55	6 2	7† 0
Coalbrookdale ,,	50 R.	6 15	7 15	8 58	12 17		5C7 0	6 7	—
Green Bank Halt ,,	50 R.	6 18	7 18	9 1	12 20		5 3	6 10	—
Lightmoor Platform ,,	50 R.	6 21	7 21	9 4	12 23		5 6	6 13	—
Lightmoor Junction arr.	50 R.		X						
Doseley Halt dep.	,,	6 25	7 25	9 8	12 27		5 10	6 17	—
Horsehay and Dawley ,,	40 R.	6 29	7 29	9 12	12 31		5 14	6 21	—
Lawley Bank ,,	45 F.	6 33	7 33	9 16	12 35		5 18	6 25	—
New Dale Halt ,,	45 F.	6 35	7 35	9 18	12 37		5 20	6 27	—
Ketley Town Halt ,,	45 F.		7 38	9 21	12 40		C5 23	C6 30	—
Ketley ,,		6 39	7 40	9 23	12 42		5 25	6 32	—
Ketley Junction ,,	50 F.	6 41	7 42	9*27	12*47		5 27	6 34	7* 48 7†51
WELLINGTON arr.	132 F.	6 44	7 45	9 30	12 50		5 30	6 37	7†51

§—Mixed Train Buildwas to Much Wenlock.
:—Calls to set down passengers only. Guard to collect tickets of passengers alighting.
¶—See No. 12.
C—Trains call during daylight only.
K—If branch train to time, working between Ketley and Wellington to be regulated according to the running of the 9.10 a.m. ex Paddington.
R—London mileage via Oxford, Worcester and Severn Valley applies to stations on Severn Junction Branch.

Extract from the Working Timetable of 1942.

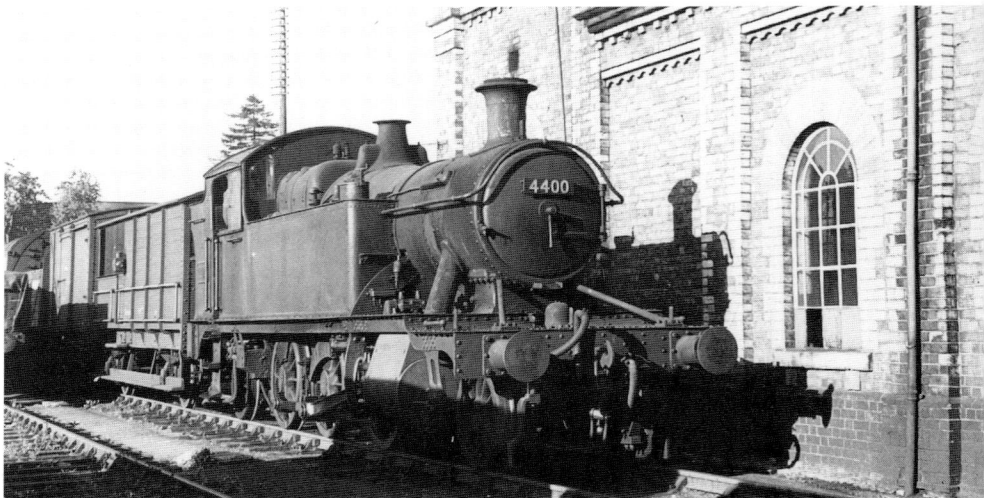

Above: Shunting operations being carried out in Wenlock goods yard by '44XX' class 2-6-2T No. 4400 on 10th September, 1949. After finishing shunting the yard the train would form the 3.45 pm goods to Wellington via the Madeley branch.

H.C. Casserley

Right: The 8.20 am ex-Wenlock goods to Craven Arms, between Much Wenlock and Presthope hauled by '57XX' class 0-6-0PT No. 3732. Note the vacuum pipe hanging free from the stopper, the purpose of this was to enable the driver during shunting to operate the engine with the steam brake only. This saved having to use the ejector to create a vacuum during each shunting movement. *Author's Collection*

The Wrekin Foundry sidings, Ketley. In 1924 James Clay (Wellington) Ltd moved their agricultural implement works from Wellington to this site on the branch between Ketley and Ketley Junction. In 1929 it became a subsidiary of the Allied Ironfounders and by 1960 it had been taken over by Aga Heat, another Allied Ironfounders' subsidiary. *Ironbridge Gorge Museum*

easy access to the mines of these areas. Slack trains from mines in the Midlands were routed via Oxley Sidings and over the Madeley branch to Buildwas, also trains from South Wales were coming from Shrewsbury over the Severn Valley line. In addition, from the Shropshire coalfield came slack from the Lilleshall Company's Granville Colliery via Hollinswood sidings to Madeley Jn, thence over the Madeley branch. The opening of the open cast mining site on Horsehay Common in 1942 brought about increased activity in the goods yard at Horsehay, with a slack train leaving there daily for Buildwas.

In addition to the daily slack trains into the power station at Buildwas, for the last 20 years of the branch's existence there were five goods trains daily operating between Wellington and Wenlock, two of these being routed over the Madeley branch. From Wenlock to Wellington there were two goods trains each day, one from Buildwas to Hollinswood over the Madeley branch, and one from Horsehay to Wellington.

The 8.20 am goods from Wenlock to Craven Arms during the latter years was very seldom seen to be hauling more than two wagons and the guard's van, and on many days it would be just engine and van.

After World War II passenger traffic dropped dramatically, but goods traffic remained buoyant on the branch, due no doubt to the industrial concerns along its route: the Sinclair Iron Company, and the Wrekin Foundry at Ketley, the bridge building works of the Horsehay Company, the brick and tile works at Lightmoor, the Coalbrookdale Company's foundry, and the coal traffic from the Kemberton Colliery on the Madeley branch.

The Madeley Branch

Although this branch was not on the direct route from Wellington to Craven Arms, it is an integral part of the Much Wenlock branch line story.

The Madeley branch is of an undulating character, on leaving Madeley Jn the ruling gradient is 1 in 150, rising and then falling to 1 in 92 to Madeley Court station. It then changes to 1 in 94 falling, and afterwards remains practically level to Lightmoor Jn.

Although in 1864 the Madeley Wood Company had opened its Kemberton Colliery, which was quite close to the Madeley branch being situated between Madeley Jn and Madeley Court station, no sidings were provided until 1870. From the outset no GWR locomotives were allowed into the colliery sidings, all wagons both in and out being moved by an endless rope. In the early days goods trains were only booked to call as and when required at Kemberton sidings, not until the mid-1880s were there booked goods trains working from the sidings. The siding accommodation was as follows:

No. 1 Siding	38 wagons
No. 2 Siding	17 wagons
No. 3 Siding	17 wagons
No. 4 Siding	18 wagons

The empties for the colliery were conveyed by the 9.30 am ex-Hollinswood; on arrival at Madeley Jn it would then propel the empties to Kemberton Colliery. The porter from Madeley station would meet the train at the colliery sidings to work the ground frame, which was unlocked by the Madeley Jn to Lightmoor Jn train staff. The Madeley station master was required to notify Hollinswood the previous night if the 9.30 am would be required to call at the colliery on the following morning. In the event of further empties being required at Kemberton Colliery the 1.50 pm Hollinswood to Oxley would convey them to Madeley Jn, from where they would be picked up by the 2.45 pm Shifnal to Buildwas and propelled to the colliery.

On leaving the colliery the line was dominated on either side by pennystone clay mounds, created by the considerable coal and ironstone mining carried out in this area providing these essential ingredients for iron smelting in the nearby Court furnaces.

WELLINGTON AND SEVERN JUNCTION,
And Madeley Branch Railway.

BRANCH LINE TIME TABLE

DOWN. — Week Days / Sundays

STATIONS	1	2	3	4	5	6	7	8	9	10	11	12	13	14	15	Sun 14	Sun 15
		Pass.	Pass.	Goods	Goods	Pass.	Pass.	Goods		Pass.	Goods	Goods	Goods	Goods	Goods	Pass.	Pass.
	A. M.	On Mondays only. a.m.	This Train will not run on Mondays. A.M.	A. M.	A. M.	A. M.	P. M.	P. M.	P. M.	P. M.	P. M.	P. M.	When required only. a. m.	When required only. a. m.	When required only. a.m.	A. M.	P. M.
Shiffnal	...			...	11 0	...	12 50	...	...	6 45	...	...		...	...	7 55	3 20
Madeley Junction	...			...	...	To run on Thursdays only.	...	...	...	...	...	...				...	...
Madeley	...	6 55	7 5		11 25	11 40	1 8	...	...	7 3	9 15	...				8 13	3 37
Lightmoor	...	7 5	7 15		11 30	11 45	1 13	3 30	...	7 8	9 20	..				8 18	3 42
L'moor Rd. Siding	...	...	...		...	...	...	3 37		...	...	...				...	...
Horsehay	..	7 15	7 25	9 0	...	11 55	1 23	8 50	...	7 21	9 35	11 10	12 40	2 15	3 40	8 28	3 52
Lawley Bank	...	7 20	7 30	...	..	12 0	1 28	...	...	7 26	...	...				8 33	3 57
Ketley Works	...	...	...	9 15		...	...	4 5	...	...	9 50	...				...	...
Ketley Station	..	7 25	7 35		...	12 5	1 33	5..	...	7 32	..	...				8 40	4 3
Wellington arr.	...	7 33	7 43	9 25	...	12 15	1 40	4 15	...	7 40	10 0	11 30	1 0	2 35	4 10	8 50	4 12

UP. — Week Days / Sundays

STATIONS	16	17	18	19	20	21	22	23	24	25	26	27	28	29	30	Sun 29	Sun 30
	Goods		Goods	Pass.	Goods	Goods		Pass.		Pass.	Goods	Goods	Pass.	Goods	Goods	Pass.	Pass.
	A. M.		A. M.	A. M.	A. M.	P. M.		P. M.		P. M.	Mid-night.	Mid-night.		A. M.	A. M.	A. M.	P. M.
Wellington	5 0	...	8 10	10 0	...	2 15		5 10	...	8 40	10 20	12 0	12 20	1 20	2 55	9 0	6 30
Ketley Junction	5 10	...	8 25	...		2 25		...	...	...	10 30	12 10		...	...		
Ketley Station	...	...	...	10 10		...		5 20		8 50	...	...		..	...	9 10	6 40
Ketley Works	5 25	...	8 35	...		2 35		...		...	10 40	...		...			
Lawley Bank	A	...	...	10 15	This Train will not run on Thursdays.	...		5 25		8 55	...	...				9 15	6 45
Horsehay	5 35	...	8 43	10 20		2 50		5 30		9 0	10 55	12 25		1 55	3 25	9 20	6 50
L'moor Rd. Siding	5 50	...	...	...		3 10		...		...							
Lightmoor	5 55	...		10 30	12 5	3 15		5 40		9 10	When required only.	When required only.	When required only.			9 25	7 0
Madeley	6 50	...		10 35	12 10	...		5 45		9 15						9 30	7 5
Shiffnal arr.	...			10 50	12 30	...		6 0		...			12 35			9 45	7 20

The Gradients on the Line being heavy, and there being several level crossings, great care will be required in working these Branches, and two Guards will accompany every Train, with two Break Vans or Break Carriages, one to be placed next the Engine, and the other last on the Train.

When a Goods Train consists of more than Eight Wagons and two Vans, it must be brought to a stand at the summit of the Incline, (both on the Up and Down Journeys,) in order that the Guards may pin down the necessary number of Breaks, before descending the Incline in either direction, which must be done with extreme Caution.——If a Passenger Train consists of more than eight Carriages and two Break Vans, additional Break Vans must be placed on the Train, namely, one Break for every four Carriages.

Goods may be sent by any Passenger Train, but not Minerals, or Timber, or Timber Trucks, or Mineral Wagons.

A. This Train to return from Lightmoor or Lightmoor Road Siding to Horsehay, when required.

Extract from the Working Timetable of 1863.

Shifnal station and staff *c*. 1892. Notice the lifting jack attached to the tender of the locomotive.
Lens of Sutton

Madeley station staff *c*. 1908 with an unidentified saddle tank. Note the station porter on the right holding the Lightmoor Junction to Madeley Junction electric train staff.
Keith Beddoes Collection

The area surrounding the station at Madeley was once the scene of considerable industrial activity. It was here that the Stourbridge ironmaster James Foster set up his Madeley Court furnaces in 1845-6, adjacent to the newly opened mines on his Madeley Court estate. The ironworks ceased in 1902 but in 1912 they were taken over by Thomas Parker, an electrical engineer. With his son H.C. Parker they established the Court Works Ltd which were engaged in the making of iron castings for the electrical industry.

The station was Madeley (Salop) from 1897, but often referred to as Madeley Court, due no doubt to its proximity to the nearby Court house, and also to distinguish it from the former LNWR station at Madeley, known as Madeley Market. The station was closed to passenger traffic in 1915. However, following requests from local inhabitants who were backed by the Madeley District Committee of the Wenlock Borough Council, the GWR opened the branch to passengers once again in July 1925. After only three months' operation of the renewed passenger service the GWR had certain misgivings about the service, and rumours abounded that it would have to be withdrawn. The Madeley District Committee were obviously concerned about these rumours after having fought so hard to get the passenger service renewed. The following item appears in the minutes of their meeting held on 12th August, 1925:

> The Town Clerk read certain correspondence which he had received from the GWR stating that owing to the disappointing traffic results it had been decided to withdraw the service. It was resolved that the Town Clerk be instructed to point out - that the service had not been given a fair chance - not been advertised adequately - little been done to encourage traffic - no facilities had been provided for the conveyance of milk.

Despite this protestation, and the fact that one councillor stated that he could ensure the carriage of 100 gallons of milk per day over the line, the railway company went ahead and closed the line to passenger traffic on 21st September, 1925.

Although closed once again to passenger traffic, Madeley remained a busy station for both goods (principally the traffic from the Court Works) and parcels traffic. In 1925 it served the village of Madeley with its population of 8,100 and it also served the village of Stirchley with a population of 1,500. There was only one platform which was situated on the up side of the line. The station buildings comprised a booking office, general waiting room, ladies' waiting room and gentlemen's toilets. There was also a station master's house, situated on the drive from the road into the goods yard, for which he paid a rental of six shillings per week.

The goods yard was on the up side, the facilities consisting of a warehouse and a truck weighbridge, and a crane of 1½ tons capacity. Both the station and the yard were lit by oil lamps, and this form of lighting continued until the yard closed to traffic in 1964. On the up side (the goods yard) there were two sidings, both of which held 10 wagons, access to which was controlled by the East ground frame; on the down side there were also two sidings controlled by the West ground frame; No. 1 siding held 57 wagons, and No. 2 siding held 29 wagons. Access into the Madeley Court works was by way of No. 2 siding. There was no signal box, and the ground frames were unlocked by the key on the electric train staff.

The staff in 1924 consisted of a station master, a goods clerk, one shunter, one goods porter, and one porter, grade 2. Despite the fact that there was no passenger traffic Madeley retained its station master until 1934. The parcels traffic destined for Madeley station was collected together at Shifnal, and was conveyed daily in the guard's van of the 6.15 am Oxley to Buildwas freight service. The parcels were then delivered in the Madeley area by the carting agent who worked jointly for the GWR and the LMS.

On leaving Madeley Court station for Lightmoor the line passed under the bridge which carried the line of the former LNWR branch from Wellington to Coalport. About 200 yards after passing under the bridge on the right-hand side of the line, the site of the quarry where the S&B Railway quarried the stone for the building of Madeley Court station could be seen. The line continued on the level before approaching the slight falling gradient to Lightmoor Jn.

Chapter Seven

Locomotives

The Directors of the Wgton&SJR agreed prior to the opening of the line between Ketley and Horsehay in February 1857, that the cost of operating such a short line for freight traffic only would not be economically viable. It was therefore agreed that the Great Western should operate the line with its locomotives and stock, although there was no formal agreement entered into with the GWR until September 1861.

The goods trains were hauled by a Beyer, Peacock 0-4-0 side tank engine purchased specifically for the branch. This was the same locomotive on which Captain Tyler the Board of Trade Inspector had ridden on a trial run between Horsehay and Ketley, and of which he was far from complimentary with regards to its suitability for working on the line. The name of Joseph Armstrong was indelibly engraved on the locomotives operating on the Northern division of the GWR; Armstrong became locomotive superintendent of the Shrewsbury and Chester Railway, later becoming superintendent of the joint Shrewsbury and Chester and Shrewsbury and Birmingham companies, the latter being run by a joint managing committee. In 1854 these two companies were amalgamated into the GWR and Armstrong became superintendent of the Northern division, based at Stafford Road, Wolverhampton. Upon the retirement of Daniel Gooch in 1864 he became locomotive superintendent of the GWR.

A note book bearing the name of Joseph Armstrong reveals that GWR locomotives were working goods traffic over the Wgton&SJR from May 1857, between Ketley and Horsehay, covering an average of 70 miles per week. These locomotives were undoubtedly privately built, two of them having been constructed by Beyer, Peacock. In 1861 Beyer, Peacock introduced 0-4-0 inside frame tank engines for branch line work, with 5 ft coupled wheels, 15 in. x 20 in. cylinders and a steam pressure of 120 lb. per sq. in. Two of these engines were working between Wellington, Lightmoor Jn and Shifnal between 1862 and 1865. These engines would have been based at the Waterloo Sidings, Ketley, and not at Wellington, for, as already mentioned, the goods shed at Wellington was not converted to an engine shed until late 1867.

The first recorded engine to be built by the GWR to operate on the Wgton&SJR was No. 1A built in 1864 at Wolverhampton, and by mid-1865, by which time it had been re-numbered 17, it was operating on the branch. This was a 2-4-0 well tank engine, with inside frames and a domeless boiler. By 1868 a further two engines of this class had been allocated to Wellington, although by then they had been fitted with saddle tanks. In 1867 No. 17 was found to be working from the Croes Newydd shed at Wrexham.

Very little documentary evidence has come to light concerning the first locomotives to operate on the Wen&SJR. When the line opened from Wenlock to Buildwas in February 1862 all that is known is that it was a West Midland 0-4-2 tank engine in use, and until the line was extended to Craven Arms this was the only engine stationed at Wenlock. By the late 1860s, two Wolverhampton-built 0-6-0 saddle tanks, Nos. 1033 and 1038, were working both passenger and goods between Wellington and Wenlock.

In 1881 the Wolverhampton-built '645' class 0-6-0 saddle tanks appeared at Wellington together with 0-6-0 '655' class, and until the turn of the century these classes covered both passenger and goods work. In 1902 No. 2076 of the '2021' class was allocated to Wellington: built at Wolverhampton in 1900 as a saddle tank, the occasional engine of this class was to be found at Wellington throughout the years up to and including World War II.

The popular branch line engine of the GWR was the '517' class of 0-4-2 tanks. From the building of the first engine of this class in 1868 to the last in 1885 various and many were the modifications and improvements carried out. These developments evolved not only during the building, but also during rebuilding both at Swindon and Wolverhampton, which

Built at Wolverhampton in 1868, '517' class 0-4-2T No. 521 was stationed at Wenlock between 1913 and 1921 and was finally withdrawn in April 1930.   *Author's Collection*

'2721' class 0-6-0T No. 2778 worked both passenger and goods trains over the Wenlock branch for many years. Built at Wolverhampton in October 1900 as a saddle tank, pannier tanks were fitted in April 1917, and it was withdrawn from service at Wellington in July 1947. Travelling over the branch bunker first in the early hours of a cold winter's morning was an experience never to be forgotten by both Wellington and Wenlock men.   *RAS Marketing*

continued until 1915. Although these engines were operating on many of the branch lines of the Northern division of the GWR, they did not find their way on to the Wenlock branch until 1907 when No. 521 was based at Wellington. This engine was built at Wolverhampton as a saddle tank in 1868; but when it was reboiled in 1889 side tanks were fitted, and a weather board with eye glasses was also fitted to the bunker. For many years this engine retained its brass dome and brass safety valve cover.

In the years following 1907 the '517s' were found working over the branch, and by 1912 there were three stationed at Wellington and two at Wenlock. From 1912 to 1931 these engines tended to dominate the passenger working both from Wellington and Wenlock, with the '645' and '655' classes carrying out most of the goods working.

With a blaze of local press publicity, steam rail cars were introduced on the branch on 1st May, 1906, together with trailers (*see Appendix Eleven*). These were stationed at Wenlock. The timetable for that year shows that all the passenger trains were worked by the steam rail cars. The Wenlock unit worked the first train of the day from Wenlock to Craven Arms. The rail cars also worked two trains each way between Wenlock and Shifnal via Lightmoor Jn and Madeley Jn. As previously mentioned, the gradients proved too severe for these units with trailers attached, so by early 1907 passenger services had reverted to locomotive haulage.

Immediately after World War I, the revised version of the '517' class, 0-4-2T No. 1424, was working at Wellington. This '1421' series was distinctive, with its tall brass dome, and rolled copper-topped chimney. Throughout the 1920s and into the early 1930s engines of the '1421' series tended to work most of the passenger trains.

The 1930s witnessed a great change in motive power working. The year 1934 saw the demise of the '517' class on the passenger trains, in fact engine No. 517, the first of the class built at Wolverhampton in 1868, was withdrawn at Wenlock in February 1934. In August 1933 one of the '58XX' series of 0-4-2T was allocated to Wellington. The appearance of No. 5810 on the branch passenger trains, with its gleaming paint work, enclosed cab and sleek lines created a great deal of attention. Engines straight from the workshops at Swindon or Wolverhampton were a sight very rarely seen on the Wenlock branch. In February 1934 a further engine of this class, No. 5811, was allocated to Wenlock, to replace No. 517. Later in 1934 No. 5809 was also allocated to Wellington.

Although this class had been designed for branch work, their slightly extended wheelbase compared with the '517' class, gave rise to difficulties on the gradients, especially in the up direction when getting away from Doseley Halt and Horsehay. By the end of 1934 the '58XX' class had been withdrawn from Wellington. That summer there appeared an engine which was to dominate both passenger and goods work over the branch for the next 20 years. This was the 2-6-2 '44XX' outside cylinder tank engine, which proved to be the ideal workhorses for this roller coaster branch. Although these engines were built between 1904 and 1906, they did not find their way into the Northern division of the GWR until 1934. Until then most of their work had been confined to the West Country branches. Eleven of these engines were built, of which five were to be found stationed at either Wellington or Wenlock between 1934 and 1936. These were Nos. 4400/1/3/6/9, their 4 ft 1½ in. radius wheels proving to be ideal when negotiating the steep gradients between Buildwas and Horsehay, and Buildwas and Wenlock.

The early days of the '44XX' class were not without problems, complaints from the passengers being numerous due to the rough ride they were experiencing. The contents of shopping baskets were strewn about the compartment floor, luggage descended from the racks on to the luckless passengers below, a scene which could equal any Hollywood comedy. To alleviate this problem the wheels were rebalanced. Another cause of this excessive vibration was that the engine shackle was being wound up too tightly when coupled to the coach.

In March 1936 trials were carried out with the new AEC diesel railcars between Wellington and Craven Arms. Again the severity of the gradients proved to be their

'58XX' class 0-4-2T No. 5811 was allocated to Much Wenlock Shed in February 1934. By the end of that year this class had been removed from the Wenlock branch its wheelbase giving rise to difficulties when getting away on the severe gradients of the branch.   *RAS Marketing*

'44XX' class 2-6-2T No. 4401 about to enter the Crewe platform at Wellington on 3rd August, 1935. No. 4401 was transferred from Plymouth to Wellington in September 1934. *R. Carpenter*

No. 4400 stands alongside Wenlock Shed in September 1949.   *Photomatic*

No. 4409 is seen standing in No. 3 bay at Wellington on 10th September, 1949. This locomotive came to Wellington in April 1935. After their early teething troubles were dealt with they proved to be ideally suited for both goods and passenger work over the Wenlock branch.

H.C. Casserley

Ivatt 2-6-2T No. 41241 and '51XX' class 2-6-2T No. 4158 are seen on shed at Wellington in 1961.
R. Carpenter

'51XX' class 2-6-2T No. 4120 stands beside the new coal stage at Wellington *c.* 1958. These locomotives were introduced to Wellington in the early part of World War II to work over the Wenlock branch to Much Wenlock, and also to Crewe, Shrewsbury and Leamington. Following the building of the new coal stage an electric winch was introduced for coaling the engines.
R. Carpenter

downfall. This new form of transport, which for the branch was ultra modern, caused a great deal of excitement amongst both passengers and staff. The excitement was however short lived, the railcars being withdrawn after running light for a period of less than a month.

At the commencement of World War II in 1939 the branch from Ketley Jn to Wenlock was upgraded from a 'yellow' to a 'blue' route. This colour classification, indicating the routes over which locomotives could work, was indicated by a letter superimposed upon a coloured disc on the cab side of the engine. Following slight adjustments to the platforms at the signal box end at both Ketley and Horsehay, this allowed the '41XX' and '51XX' class 2-6-2T to carry out the passenger work over the branch between Ketley Jn and Wenlock. This class of engine had been at Wellington since 1933, but had only been working from there to Wolverhampton and Crewe.

When the engine shed at Wenlock closed on 31st December, 1951, the '44XX' class returned to the West Country, with the exception of No. 4400 which was withdrawn from service at Wellington in April 1951. Nos. 4401 and 4406 went to Newton Abbot, and 4403 and 4409 to Laira. Following the departure of the '44XX' class from Wellington the branch line working for both passenger and goods was mainly in the hands of the '5700' class in the '36XX', '37XX', '57XX' and '97XX' series. At the end of the 1950s an LMS class '2', 2-6-2T No. 41201, was regularly seen working passenger trains over the branch.

By 1961 single car diesel units in the W55000 series were allocated to Wellington, one of these being No. W55009, and the units took over a number of the daily workings. In addition to the diesel units, two auto-fitted pannier 0-6-0 tanks, Nos. 6421 and 6429, were sent to Wellington in the same year; these two locomotives operated with a push-and-pull set over the branch. With the diesels and the push-pull working there was no longer a need for the gravity shunting spur at the north end of Nos. 3 and 4 Bays at Wellington and this was removed, so ending a feature that had been unique to the Wenlock branch. Most of the goods workings continued to be worked by the '57XX' class.

An interesting locomotive at Wellington was No. 92 built by Beyer, Peacock in 1857 as an 0-4-2 saddle tank; whilst this engine never worked over the branch it spent its declining years in the shed at Wellington. In December 1878 No. 92 was reconstructed at Chester as an 0-4-0 saddle tank. Most of its working life was spent in the Northern division of the GWR. It came to Wellington in 1939 where it was used as a stationary boiler until, in July 1942, it was withdrawn after giving 84 years of service, during which period it had covered 785,000 miles. After withdrawal its 50-year-old boiler was retained at Wellington for steam raising for a few more years.

An unusual engine at Wellington in September 1960 was an LMS '2P' 0-4-4T No. 41900 which had been working between Ashchurch and Upton-on-Severn. It proved to be unsuitable for the Wenlock branch, and for 18 months it languished outside the shed at Wellington until it was finally withdrawn in March 1962.

Following the closure of Wellington Shed in 1964, a variety of locomotives could be seen hauling the coal trains over the Madeley branch into the power station at Buildwas. These were '94XX' 0-6-0 tanks, and '56XX' 0-6-2 tanks together with LMS class '8F' 2-8-0 and BR Standard class '4' 2-6-0s. These engines were stationed at Oxley Shed.

The early part of 1967 witnessed the demise of steam-hauled coal trains into the Ironbridge Power Station. The first type of diesel power to be used on these trains was the Brush type 4s (later class '47s'), though there were rare appearances of class '50s' when this type was allocated to Crewe depot. The heavier class '56' freight diesel began to appear on the coal trains soon after their introduction in the late 1970s. Oil trains were hauled by type '2' locomotives (later class '24' and '25') with occasional sightings of class '40s' demoted from main line passenger work. Double-headers, using combinations of all three types were more common than single locomotives on oil trains. Most coal reached the branch from the Warwickshire and Staffordshire coalfields and from Shropshire's last remaining pit, the Granville Colliery, which closed in August 1979.

A view of '57XX' class 0-6-0PT No. 5745 standing on the middle road at Wellington in the late 1950s. The batch Nos. 5700-5749 were built by the North British Locomotive Company. The house in the background was once the residence of the Wellington station master. *R. Carpenter*

'57XX' class 0-6-0PT No. 3732 is seen standing at Wellington's No. 2 bay platform and it is about to leave with the 11.20 am to Much Wenlock *c.* 1960.   *R. Carpenter*

Ivatt class '2' 2-6-2T No. 41201 stands in the down platform at Wellington in 1961 having just arrived on a passenger train from Much Wenlock. Four members of this class were stationed at Wellington at this time, having been transferred from the Somerset & Dorset line. *R. Carpenter*

BR Standard class '2' 2-6-2T No. 82006 on Wellington Shed in 1959. There were three of this class at Wellington, working over both Crewe and Wenlock branches. This class was much favoured by Western men due to the space and comfort on the footplate, also they had many standard Great Western footplate fittings. *R. Carpenter*

Wellington three-road engine shed. On the right are the carriage sidings, pump house and water tank *c.* 1960.   *R. Carpenter*

Wellington coal stage on 13th December, 1958 showing '57XX' class 0-6-0PT No. 3732 being coaled using the electric crane.   *M. Mensing*

An early 1930s view of Wellington Shed, the wooden panelling and grill at the front end of the shed was removed in the mid-1930s. The engine is a 'Barnum' class 4-4-0 which is waiting to leave the shed to work a stopping train to Crewe. *R. Carpenter*

Wenlock Shed designed by Joseph Fogerty, with the pumping house and water tank at the rear. Water for the tank was pumped from a reservoir situated on the down side of the line just south of Westwood Halt. *R. Carpenter*

Craven Arms four-road shed in the early 1950s; seen standing outside is ex-LMS Fowler class '4MT' 2-6-4T No. 42305. *J.A. Peden*

Craven Arms Shed on 20th February, 1955 showing an ex-LNWR 'Coal Tank' 0-6-2T No. 58904 and ex-Midland Railway '2F' class 0-6-0 No. 58213. *F.W. Shuttleworth*

Temporary cessation of rail traffic was brought about by the miners' strike of 1984-5, and on resumption it was rather surprising to find most coal trains were being hauled by the ageing class '20' locomotives, working from the Bescot depot. This type was to dominate the scene for the rest of the decade, the '47s' and '56s' disappearing almost totally. Later the class '58s' were to be seen making their way over the Madeley branch into Buildwas, these were based at Toton depot in Nottinghamshire. One of this class - No. 58 042 - was officially named *Ironbridge Power Station* at an open day at Buildwas in September 1986, though it was rarely seen on local coal trains afterwards. When the majority of the class '20s' were withdrawn in the early 1990s, most coal trains reverted to class '56' haulage, though another new type, the class '60', made regular visits depending on where the coal was coming from.

Return slack train empties from the Ironbridge Power Station passing Cherry Tree Hill between Coalbrookdale and Lightmoor. It is hauled by an unidentified Transrail Class '56'.

Ironbridge Gorge Museum

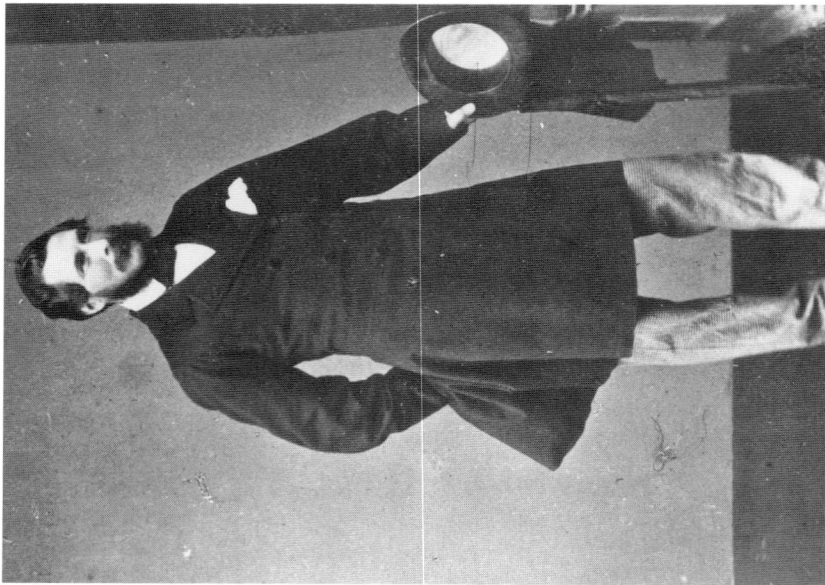

R.C. Blakeaway, Town Clerk of the Borough of Wenlock and Secretary to the Wenlock & Severn Junction Railway and the Wenlock & Craven Arms Company.

Shropshire Records & Research

George Adney, Mayor of Much Wenlock 1852-1853 and owner of the tannery in the town, who called a meeting in the Library of the Corn Exchange on 5th September, 1853 to discuss the building of a railway between Wenlock and Buildwas, which was later to become the Wenlock & Severn Junction Railway.

Shropshire Records & Research

Chapter Eight

People of the Line

The popular romance of railways centres around their locomotives, rolling stock and their operation, and there is a tendency to forget the people who built it, and the staff who ran it. Doubtless the people who had the vision to build the line did so to serve their economic interests, but in so doing they benefited the miners and their families between Ketley and Coalbrookdale, and the agricultural labourers similarly between Much Wenlock and Craven Arms. To these people, who could not afford the luxury of a pony and trap, it opened up the markets of Wellington and Much Wenlock, and if they wanted to be a little more venturesome, Shrewsbury!

It was Alfred Darby (I), when he walked the tramways linking Ketley with Coalbrookdale with his superintendent of mines, who had a vision that one day a standard gauge railway would be laid, over which passengers would be carried. Alfred commenced work in 1828 in the Horsehay works of the Coalbrookdale Company, and joined his brother, Abraham (IV), as joint manager of the Coalbrookdale Company's affairs. Under this joint managership almost revolutionary changes were brought about in the fortunes of the company. Unfortunately Alfred died in 1852 at the young age of 45, never seeing his vision come to fruition.

From the outset the influence of the Coalbrookdale Company was very much in evidence in influencing the affairs of the Wgton&SJR company. The first Chairman of the company was Henry Dickinson, a Director and son of Barnard Dickinson a manager of the company from 1810-1827, and a grandson of Abraham Darby (III) the builder of the first iron bridge. Dickinson would also have been well aware of the workings of the GWR, as his Aunt Hannah Darby married William Tothill, a Bristol merchant, who was one of the original Directors of the GWR Bristol Committee, and its first Secretary. Henry Dickinson remained Chairman of the Wgton&SJR until his death in 1886. He was succeeded by another Quaker Director of the Coalbrookdale Company, William Gregory Norris. Norris was a complex person, he had interests in many coal mines in South Wales, was Chairman of the West Somerset Mineral Railway, and Director of the Swansea and Mumbles Railway. He also played an active part in local affairs, being a governor of many local schools, a member of the Madeley Poor Law Board, and for many years its Chairman. He was also Chairman of the Severn Tow Path Commissioners and Clerk to the local Quaker Society in Coalbrookdale. He remained Chairman of the Wgton&SJR until it was absorbed into the GWR in 1892.

Another member of the Darby family, William Henry Darby, was also a Director of the Wgton&SJR and also a grandson of Abraham (III); and a Quaker. Upon leaving school he went into the family business at Coalbrookdale, however, in 1841, he joined the Robertson family, the pioneers of the railway industry in North Wales, and took over the Brymbo Iron Works which specialised in the making of iron rails and locomotive boilers. Although living in Brymbo, he still continued to play an active rôle in the affairs of Coalbrookdale and the surrounding area.

Thomas Campbell Eyton of the 'Vineyard' Wellington was another Director of the Wgton&SJR. He was a well known naturalist and author of many books on ornithology. He was an active magistrate and held a commission in the Shropshire Yeomanry. Eyton sprang to prominence during the miners' riots in the Coalbrookdale coalfield in 1842, when he acted as the representative of the Deputy Lord Lieutenant of Shropshire, the Earl of Powis. In this capacity it was his duty to endeavour to quell the riots, which he did by August of that year, doubtless because he had the Yeomanry at his command. Eyton wrote to the Earl of Powis informing him of the end of the riots and concluded: 'Having now no colliers to wage war against, I shall set to work in good earnest at the partridges'. The letter is a poignant reminder of the great divide that existed between the aristocracy and the miners of that day.

Andrew Goode Brookes, Chairman of the Wenlock & Severn Junction Railway 1862-1894.
Shropshire Records & Research

Charles Milnes Gaskell, Chairman of the Wenlock & Severn Junction Railway 1894-1896.
Shropshire Records & Research

Joseph Fogerty, Assistant Engineer to the Wenlock & Severn Junction Railway and the Wenlock & Craven Arms Railway. Fogerty's influence can be seen in the design of the station buildings between Coalbrookdale and Harton Road.
Shropshire Records & Research

Ralph Augustus Benson, who chaired the meeting held in the Corn Exchange in Much Wenlock on 1st March, 1860 to discuss the proposed extension of the railway from Much Wenlock to Craven Arms. He was later to play a considerable part in the development of the line. *Shropshire Records & Research*

The Wgton&SJR appointed William Newill as its solicitor in 1853; he died in 1886, and was succeeded by his son Robert, who remained with the company until it was absorbed in 1892.

As mentioned earlier, Henry Robertson was appointed Engineer to the company, no doubt it was Robertson's close association with William Henry Darby that prompted the Directors to appoint him. He had been Engineer to the Shrewsbury and Chester and later the Shrewsbury and Birmingham railway companies. It was agreed to pay Robertson the sum of £1,050 for his services, which were to include the preparation of working plans and sections, and all engineering assistance up to the opening of the line. Robertson agreed to take up £700 on account in shares in the company.

The Wenlock companies were greatly influenced by the Brookes' brothers. Andrew Goode Brookes was appointed Chairman of the Wen&SJR on its inception in 1859. He qualified as a surgeon in 1832, and first practised at Cressage, a village near Much Wenlock; he moved to Shrewsbury in 1867, becoming Chairman of the Shrewsbury Gas Company and a Director of the Shrewsbury Kingsland Bridge Company. Although living in Shrewsbury, he still retained close links with Wenlock, and remained Chairman of the Wen&SJR until his death in December 1894.

Following the death of Andrew Goode Brookes, Charles Milnes Gaskell was appointed Chairman. The Milnes Gaskells were substantial land owners in the Wenlock area.

William Penny Brookes, brother of Andrew, was appointed Chairman of the Wenlock Railway Company. William was indeed a remarkable man, and very often referred to as the 'King' of Wenlock. He took over his father's medical practice in the town in 1830 and remained as the town's medical practitioner until he retired in 1891. He introduced gas lighting into Wenlock, and was also instrumental in setting up a library and reading room. However, his chief claim to fame was that in 1850 he set up the Wenlock Olympian Society, and from that year annual Olympian Games were held at Wenlock. He became a member of the National Olympian Association founded in 1865, this became the germ of the International Olympian Society. Dr Brookes's dedication to athletics and physical education undoubtedly gives the small town of Much Wenlock the right to lay claim to being the birthplace of the modern Olympic Games. William Penny Brookes died at Much Wenlock on 10th December, 1895.

John Fowler was the Engineer responsible for the construction of the Wenlock Railways, and the Coalbrookdale extension. However, it was his assistant, Joseph Fogerty, whose influence can be seen from Coalbrookdale to Marsh Farm Junction. Fogerty was also engaged by the GWR as Resident Engineer in the construction of the Lightmoor extension. A lasting memorial to him is the great 26-arch viaduct at the north end of the Coalbrookdale valley. In the late 1860s he was also engaged by the famous Shropshire Iron Company, the Lilleshall Company, as a consulting engineer on the construction of the extensions to its considerable private rail network.

Fogerty was born in Limerick on 7th April, 1831, he came to England in 1856, and immediately took up an appointment in John Fowler's London office. Before coming to England he had been in business on his own in Ireland, mainly engaged in the construction of steam- and water-powered mills. He was admitted to the Institution of Civil Engineers on 14th April, 1863. Fogerty first came to Shropshire in 1861 when he was appointed by Fowler on the construction of the Severn Valley Railway, taking up residence in Coalbrookdale and later moving to Shrewsbury. He also became a member of RIBA, and in 1865 he began to practise on his own, preparing designs for an elevated railway system in Vienna, for example.

In later life Fogerty devoted his life to writing novels, his first work being *Lauterdale* in which he gives an insight into life in the Coalbrookdale valley in the 1850s. In this novel Fogerty describes Lightmoor station, and gives his impressions of the surrounding area, when he first set foot on the platform with his family at what he calls 'Brightmoor':

When railways had penetrated the northern counties of England there existed on the summit of a large cinder-mount, close to some outlying furnaces of a great iron company in a north-western

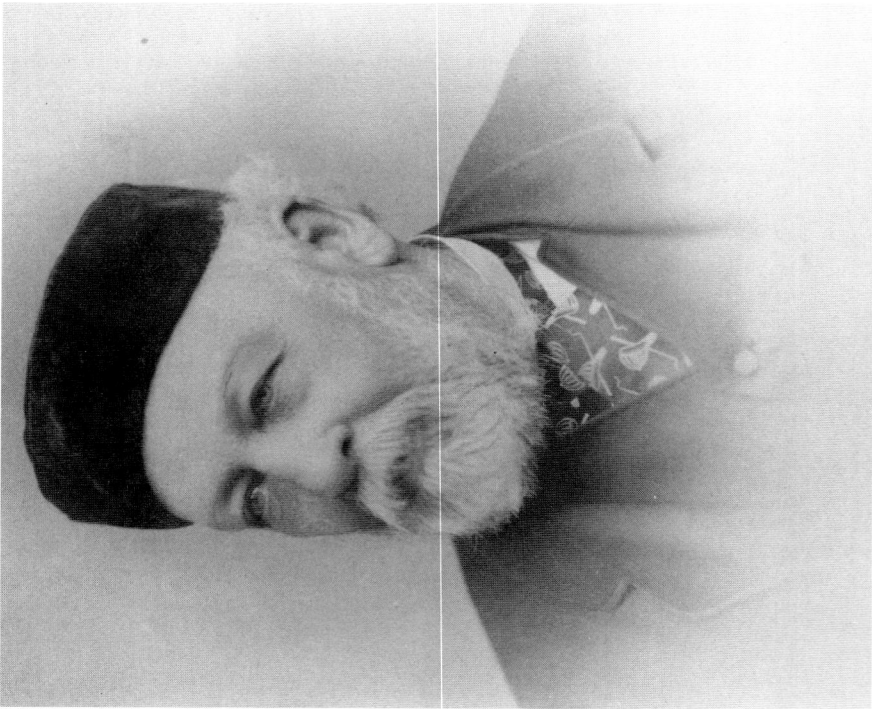

John Fox, Manager of the Coalbrookdale Company's Bradley limestone quarry at Farley. He claimed to be the first passenger to board the train at Coalbrookdale station on the day of its opening on 1st November, 1864.

Shropshire Records & Research

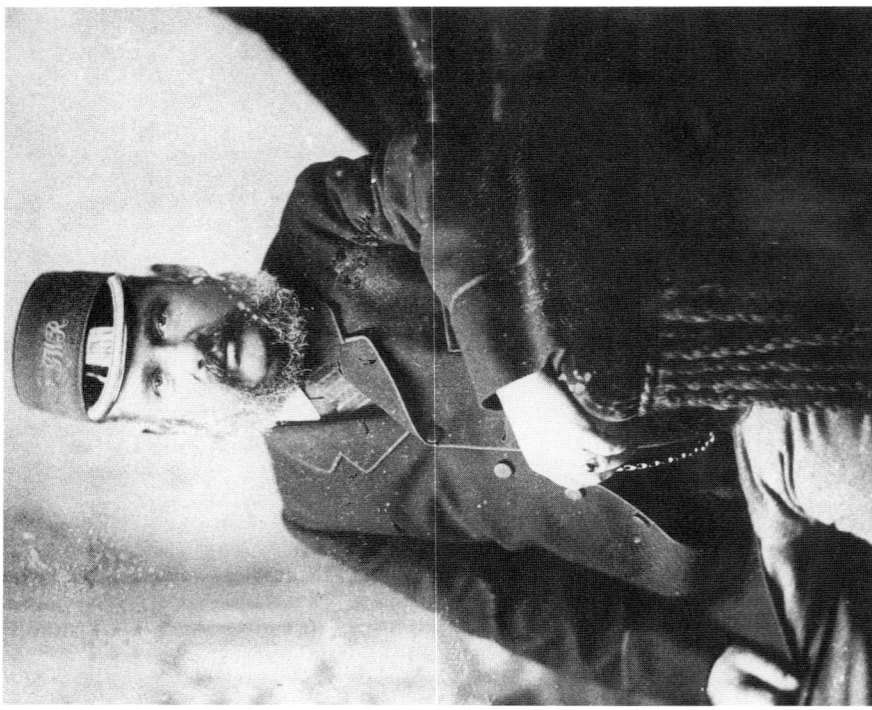

William Ruscoe, the first station master at Coalbrookdale when the station opened for traffic on 1st November, 1864. This photograph was taken when he was station master at Oakengates.

Ironbridge Gorge Museum

county, the most forlorn and dismal looking railway station which the ingenuity of an unskilful engineer, sadly deficient in taste, and equally at a loss for funds, could possibly have contrived.

Previous to his operations it was a bleak, desolate spot, where the scoriae and cinders of the centuries of iron manufacture had been piled in huge heaps, bearing witness to the industry of bygone generations; but the erection of a rickety platform and an unsightly passenger shed, both painted a sombre hue, and fast settling down amidst the surrounding chaos together with an uncanny aspect of the place, marked it out as the *ultima thule* of railway progress and the end of all things, so far as locomotion by steam in that quarter was concerned.

The waste tip mounds of numerous 'pit workings' with hideous engine-sheds and blackened head gear, lay scattered around, lit up by the flame of a solitary blast furnace at full work, which shed a fitful glare over the cinder heaps and the bleak moorland beyond. On a board which hung flapping from a shaky fence some local artist had inscribed the word 'Brightmoor,' in crooked straggling letters . . .

The branch railway which came to a undignified end at Brightmoor was private property, and was worked on economic principles - its chief passengers being rough miners and colliers willing to ride on anything, no matter how hard and uncomfortable, so long as the fare was only a few pence.

Twice on each weekday a clumsy composite carriage, having one first-class compartment, was attached to the tail of a mineral train, drawn at an average speed of six miles an hour to and from the junction with the great railway from Birmingham to the north.

Fogerty's abilities as an engineer are evidenced by the number of occasions he was congratulated by the Directors for his design and construction of their respective lines. Joseph Fogerty died at his residence at Sydenham on 2nd September, 1899.

Into the villages and hamlets along the branch from Wellington to Craven Arms came a new breed of men, men in uniform; a striking contrast to the moleskin trousers and cloth caps of the men in the coalfield, and the smocks and corduroys of the farm workers in the Ape Dale. Men descended into the area from strange sounding places like Llanfyllin, Llansillin, Drws-Y-Nant and Trawsfynydd, men fluent in Welsh as well as English. Into Wellington and Much Wenlock came the drivers and firemen from all quarters of the GWR system.

The first recorded evidence of personnel on the branch is that of William Parton, not in fact employed by the GWR, he was an employee of the Ketley Iron Company at its offices situated a little below Ketley station. He worked as a tally clerk, and each day had to walk from Ketley to the Waterloo Sidings to take a tally of the coal bound for the ironworks. It is from William Parton that an insight into the activities at the sidings and the engine shed is gleaned. This shed was no doubt built by Dickson to house the locomotive which he operated on his private line linking the Waterloo Sidings with the Ketley Ironworks.

The elite of the uniformed staff of the traffic department was the station master, a man of considerable standing in the community, his importance noted by every passenger, as he stood with watch in hand on the arrival of every train. Albeit only a branch line station, his standing locally equalled that of the station master at the greater main line stations.

On the opening of the Lightmoor extension on 1st November, 1864, William Ruscoe was appointed the first station master at Coalbrookdale. He had commenced his career with the GWR in 1855; in 1867 he moved to Much Wenlock, later to Ruabon, and was finally, in 1893, appointed station master at Oakengates (where he died in 1895). However, it was not until the early 1890s that the designation of station master appears at the branch stations. Prior to this they were designated 'station inspector', this form of designation applied to many of the smaller stations on the GWR system.

Whilst many of the station masters at main line stations progressed through the clerical grades to that post, a number of those at branch line stations came from the uniform grades. Most of them had been signalmen, rising to the position of first class relief signalmen. A typical example on the Wenlock branch was Ted Davies, who was appointed station master at Ketley in 1907. Ted was a native of Bala, and began his railway career as a lad porter on 1st October, 1881 at Llanuwchllyn. He moved to various stations in North Wales, eventually moving to Shifnal in 1905 as signalman. In 1906 he was appointed station master at Arenig

Thomas Davies (1837-1933), the author's great-grandfather who in 1863-1864 worked as a navvy during the building of the Lightmoor extension from Lightmoor Junction to Coalbrookdale.

Author's Collection

Alfred Strange, station master at Rushbury 1901-1910. *Author's Collection*

Station staff at Much Wenlock in 1904. The only member that can be identified is William Norry standing next to the boy. By this time ivy had completely taken over the frontage of the station and appears to have obliterated the station master's bedroom and lounge windows.   *Mr Leek*

The station staff at Coalbrookdale pose for this photograph after winning the best kept garden competition in the Chester division in 1925. The photograph gives an indication of the number of staff employed there, due no doubt to the traffic engendered, both passengers and goods, by the Coalbrookdale Company.   *Author's Collection*

William Winsley, Wellington Shed foreman (1928-1936) standing alongside 'Barnum' class 2-4-0 No. 3210 on Wellington Shed on 3rd August, 1935.   *R. Carpenter*

Wellington Shed football team in 1932 on the Bucks Head football ground in Wellington.
                                                                    Don Houlston

(on the Bala to Blaenau Festiniog branch), moving to Ketley the following year. His wage in 1907 was 27s. per week. He remained at Ketley for 25 years, retiring in January 1931.

Ketley was well served by station masters from the Welsh Hills. John William Jones, a Welsh Calvinistic Methodist, started his railway career at Bala as a lad porter in 1910, moving to Carrog as a signal porter in 1915; in 1918 he moved to Corwen as a signalman, 2nd class. In 1940 he crossed over the border into Shropshire and took up the position as station master at Coalbrookdale, a class 5 station. Two years later he moved to Ketley for promotion, by this time Ketley had been regraded to class 4 due to Horsehay and Lawley Bank coming under the control of Ketley. In 1948 John William returned to his native Wales upon his appointment as station master at Dolgelly.

Up to World War I the staff at Lawley Bank consisted of just one, the station master, although during the day he would be assisted by a signal porter from Horsehay. In 1888 Henry Rickard was appointed station inspector at Lawley Bank and he remained there for many years. The last station master there was John Evans, who left in 1927 to become station master at a small station in the London division; by this time there were two signal porters, these now under the control of the Ketley station master. The Wgton&SJR acquired a cottage close to the station at Lawley Bank for the purpose of housing the station master. Later a house, No. 14 Clares Lane, about three miles from the station, was let to the station master, this being his residence until the departure of John Evans in 1927.

The station master at Horsehay at the turn of the century was William Rickard, the brother of Henry at Lawley Bank. William's wage in 1901 was 32s. per week. The station master occupied the station house which was situated some 300 yards north of the station, and in the early 1920s he was paying a rental of 6s. 6d. per week for the house. Upon the retirement of the last resident station master at Horsehay, Thomas Phillips in 1932, Horsehay also came under the control of Ketley.

The station master at Coalbrookdale in 1898 was William Marshall; in that year his weekly wage was 28s. but by 1901 his wage had been increased to 30s. His staff consisted of two porter-signalmen and two grade 1 porters. The Coalbrookdale station master was also responsible for the two signalmen and two porters at Lightmoor Junction. On many of the GWR branch line stations where porter-signalmen were employed, when the latter were employed on other station duties, the station master would take over the operating of the signal box.

Another signalman who eventually became station master at Coalbrookdale was George Guy. He began his railway career at Codsall as a lad porter in 1910, later moving to Hodnet on the Crewe branch as a porter in 1914. In 1919 he moved to Horsehay as a signalman, and in 1923 returned to the Crewe branch when he became signalman at Crudgington. In 1925 George was transferred to the signal box at Ketley Junction, moving to Coalbrookdale as station master in 1946.

The crossing keeper at Chunes Crossing between Coalbrookdale and Buildwas was also on the Coalbrookdale staff. In 1924 a woman crossing keeper was being paid 5s. per week plus a bonus of 3s. 6d., the rent of the crossing house at this time was 4s. 3d. per week.

Until 1923 most of the staff in the traffic department between Buildwas and Harton Road had begun their railway careers in the Worcester division. After this date this section of the branch was transferred to the Chester division.

The station master at Much Wenlock was graded class 3, and under his charge was one booking clerk, three passenger guards, one goods guard, one porter-guard, two signalmen, one porter, one male crossing keeper and one gate woman (part time). The station master lived in the station house situated on the platform and in 1924 he was paying a rental of 7s. 8d. per week. The crossing keeper was in charge of the Bradley Crossing, in 1924 he was paid a wage of 46s. per week out of which he paid a rental of 3s. 1d. per week for the crossing cottage. He was required to attend at the Bradley Sidings during shunting operations and whilst he was away from the crossing relief was provided by his wife, who was paid a wage of 4s. per week plus a bonus of 3s. 6d.

Longville station in 1932. Standing by the booking office door is the station master, Bill Tarver, and an unknown porter.

Mary Tarver

A well known station master on the branch was Bill Tarver. He joined the GWR at Honeybourne as a lad porter in 1898, later moving to Droitwich as a porter. Bill came on to the branch as a signal porter at Presthope in 1903, later moving to Bridgnorth, where he was placed in charge of the goods loading deck. In 1920 he was appointed station master at Rushbury; there was no station house at Rushbury, so he went to reside with his family in part of the old Manor House in the village. In 1927 Harton Road and Longville, like many other stations on the branch, lost their station masters, in consequence both stations were placed under the control of Rushbury. Following these additional responsibilities, Bill moved from the village of Rushbury into Coates Crossing house, situated between Longville and Rushbury. Upon taking up residence at the crossing house, Bill's wife became the crossing keeper.

The sphere of influence of the railway company's Agents did not extend out to the branch line stations, in consequence it was left to the village station master to promote the services of the company. Bill was a typical example of the unpaid railway agent, who after finishing his station duties would tour the farms of Ape Dale in an endeavour to encourage farmers to send their stock and milk by rail. In addition, he would visit local schools, to promote an excursion for the scholars to some well known beauty spot, or place of historical interest. His promotional duties not having finished here, he would then have the task of negotiating with the divisional office at Chester the rates and fares to be charged; this would often prove to be a frustrating exercise. This unpaid work was being carried out by Bill in the late 1920s and throughout the 1930s, when fierce competition was being experienced by the railways from road haulage organisations.

Bill retired in 1948 after having served the company for 50 years, 25 of which he spent on the Wenlock branch. Mary Tarver, Bill's daughter, recalling her memories in Christopher Magner's book *South Shropshire Railway Memories* sums up the importance of the village station master, as seen through the eyes of a little girl: 'My own introduction to the railway was at the age of four when my father was appointed station master at Rushbury station. At that time some 76 years ago, the title 'Master' really meant something in my young life, and to see him in his uniform with his gold braided hat was the joy of my life'.

Turning now to the 'uniform staff' on the branch as the signalmen, porters and guards were usually known. The men responsible for operating the signals at the branch stations prior to the mid-1880s were designated as 'policeman' (this nomenclature remained with the signalmen for many years for in railway parlance they were often referred to as 'bobbies'). At the junctions they were designated 'pointsmen' (*see Appendix Ten*). Most signalmen started their railway careers as lad porters, progressing to senior porters, then to porter-signalmen, before taking charge of a signal box. The signal boxes were graded according to the number of lever movements made during an eight-hour shift, the lowest grade being 'six' rising to 'one' which was allocated to the top main line signal boxes. From these top main line boxes the avenue of promotion would then be to a second class relief signalman, rising eventually to that of a first class relief man. Most of the boxes on the Wenlock branch were either grade four or five, with the exception of Buildwas which was grade three.

In August 1909 the signalman at Ketley was Jack Clay, he having moved from Horsehay a little earlier in that year. Jack was a local lad and commenced his railway career at Oakengates as a lad porter in 1904. He eventually moved to Llangollen as a signalman in 1911, returning to his native heath in 1919 when he was appointed signalman at Hollinswood Sidings, where he remained until his retirement. Another signalman at Ketley was Percy Griffiths who eventually became the Chester district inspector. Percy started at Llangollen in 1908, later moving to Cefn, and afterwards Acrefair. He was appointed signalman at Ketley in 1914, later moving to various other signal boxes in the Chester division. In the late 1930s he became a passenger guard at Shrewsbury, becoming district inspector in 1943.

The Ketley signal box was class five until 1924 when it was regraded to class four. No doubt the signalmen were successful in bringing about this regrading due to the number of lever movements made, and the opening and closing of the crossing gates during shunting operations into the Wrekin Foundry sidings. It was during the opening of these crossing

Above: Station staff at Horsehay in 1920. *From left to right*, Jack Davies who ended his railway career as a signalman at Shifnal, Cecil Jones who finished as a signalman at Lightmoor Junction in 1960, Algernon Henly who left the railway in the mid-1920s and Griffith Lewis who finished his railway career at West Ealing. *Author's Collection*

Right: Henry Davies in Stretford Bridge Junction signal box on Sunday 21st February, 1937. This was the day on which the demolition train brought in to Craven Arms the last load of lifted rails off the Bishop's Castle Railway.
Author's Collection

gates on the busy A5 in 1937 that signalman George Chidlow received very serious injuries due to a vehicle failing to stop as he was opening the gates. Many attempts had been made by the staff over the years to have a wheel placed in the signal box for the purpose of opening and closing the gates, but the railway company would never accede to these requests, due, it was said, to the volume of traffic on the road and lack of distant visibility from the signal box on either side of the crossing gates.

Another signalman at Ketley was Cis Jones who spent most of his railway career on the Wenlock branch. It is appropriate here that Cis should tell his own story:

I joined the Great Western Railway on 10th May, 1915. I remember seeing a Mr Martin who was the district inspector at Wellington, he set me on as a lad porter at Oakengates station. My duties there were to attend to the passenger trains when they came into the station, and collect tickets. After a time I transferred into the Goods Department. I well remember Oakengates was a busy station both for goods and passenger traffic. Goods were delivered from the goods yard on drays drawn by horses, also horses were used in the yard for shunting purposes.

From Oakengates I went to Peplow on the Crewe branch, at the end of 1915, as a signal porter; there was one signalman there but when he was off duty, and a train arrived to put off or pick up wagons, the signal porter was required to open up the signal box. From Peplow I went to Hodnet which was also on the Crewe branch, I only had a very short stay there, from there I went to Lightmoor Platform; 'platform' was printed on the tickets, in fact it was never called a station. Whilst I was at Lightmoor I had to assist with the shunting in the yard, for at that time Lightmoor tile works was in operation. The ticket office for the platform was by the railway bridge, close to the road at the bottom of the steps leading on to the platform. From Lightmoor I went to Madeley Court station at the end of 1916 at this time only goods traffic was dealt with. Passenger traffic on the Madeley branch ceased in the early part of 1915. There was a station master there together with a shunter who dealt with the goods traffic at the Madeley Court works, and the coal traffic at the nearby Kemberton Colliery. After leaving Madeley Court I went to relieve the crossing keepers at Doseley, and Dawley Parva crossings, on the Wenlock branch. At this time it was a 10-hour day on the railways, but at the crossings I was doing 14 hours a day, with no question of overtime pay.

After relieving at the crossings I returned to the Crewe branch, in fact to Market Drayton. Drayton was a busy junction for not only were you dealing with the Great Western trains, but you had also to deal with the North Stafford trains, or the 'Knotty' as they were called, as they came in from Stoke. I was only at Market Drayton for a short while, early in 1917 I was moved to Rednal & West Felton, which was on the main line from Shrewsbury to Chester. This move meant that I was now a fully fledged signal-porter.

I left Rednal and returned to the Wenlock branch in May 1919 when I was appointed signalman at Horsehay. The Armistice had just been signed, and the railways were being handed back from the Government to the railway companies. Following this return the railwaymen experienced a considerable drop in wages. The companies introduced a marks system [for the grading of signal boxes, marks being allocated on the basis of lever movements made], and I well remember that at Horsehay I dropped from £3 15s. per week to £2 10s. which was a considerable drop. During my first year at Horsehay I took part in my first railway strike. This strike was brought about by the fact that the railway companies wanted to reduce the wage of the platform porter to £2 per week. We were out for about 10 days, this strike brought the railways to a complete standstill.

Shortly after the signing of the Armistice in November 1918, the eight-hour day was introduced in January 1919.

Horsehay was a class five signal box, and to gain promotion I moved to Ketley in May 1927, a class four box, which enabled me to receive the large increase of 2s. per week. At Ketley the signal box was attached to the booking office, and when the station master was not on duty the signalman had also to see to the booking of tickets. The hours of duty at Ketley were 5.15 am to 1.15 pm. and the late turn was 1.15 pm to 8.15 pm, on a Saturday night it was 10.15 pm. On a Saturday night before World War II you had to remain on duty for the Wolverhampton & Birmingham excursion, which ran to Buildwas, and returned empty stock. This meant that you did not book off until 12.45 am on the Sunday morning.

I left Ketley on 2nd October, 1950 and moved to Lightmoor Jn as a signalman, whilst this was not promotion as far as wages were concerned the working conditions were much better. At

Above: Bill Pearce, signalman at Buildwas Junction with his wife. This photograph was taken outside their cottage at Burnt Houses, Buildwas.   *R. Evans*

Right: George Evans, passenger guard at Wenlock (1915-1949) taken on the day of his retirement. Note the flower in the buttonhole, this was worn by most GWR passenger guards.   *D. Davies*

Ketley the big heavy crossing gates had to be pulled back and to across the line for each train, and during shunting operations into Clay's Sidings you were a veritable 'Jack in the Box'. At Lightmoor it was purely signal box work.

I retired in 1960, after serving the railways for 45 years, on my mantelpiece is my presentation clock to prove it.

A well known signalman on the branch was Bill Pearce, who started as a lad porter at Ironbridge station in 1898 earning 15s. per week, and was fortunate in obtaining rapid promotion for, by 1906, he was a signalman at Buildwas Station and Buildwas Junction signal boxes. The signalmen at Buildwas at this time worked on a rota basis spending two weeks at each box on the early and late shift. Bill was a native of Broseley and had to walk a distance of 10 miles each day. However, in 1913, he moved to the Burnt Houses, a row of eight cottages which were in sight of the signal box at Buildwas. In 1923 the Station and Junction signal boxes were demolished and replaced by one central box. Bill was one of the signalmen appointed to this newly erected box.

Due to retire at the age of 65 in 1939, with the commencement of World War II he was required to continue his duties in the signal box until 1942, when he retired aged 68. His three sons followed in his footsteps on to the railway: William was a platelayer on the Cressage to Buildwas length, Cyril was a goods guard at Crewe, and Victor was a platelayer at Buildwas. Victor was eventually promoted to permanent way inspector at Machynlleth on the Cambrian Coast line.

The goods and passenger guards who worked over the Wenlock branch were stationed at Wellington and Much Wenlock. From the middle of the 1920s to the commencement of World War II there were two passenger guards and six goods guards stationed at Wellington, and three passenger guards, one goods guard and one porter-guard at Much Wenlock.

The passenger guards on the GWR were usually resplendent in their gold braid and polished brass buttons, and invariably to add that extra touch of refinement to their calling they wore a flower in their buttonhole. From their smart and well groomed appearance it was evident that they saw themselves as the direct link between the railway company and its travelling public. A passenger guard at Wellington for many years was Bill Weatherby. He commenced his railway career at Ruabon as a lad porter in 1911, becoming a goods guard at Shrewsbury Coton Hill in 1920 and moving to Wellington as a passenger guard in 1923, where he remained until he retired in 1957. The Wellington passenger guards worked between Birmingham (Snow Hill), Chester, Crewe and Much Wenlock.

Another passenger guard at Wellington for many years was Fred Bentley. Fred started as a lad porter at Codsall in September 1914, moving to Coalbrookdale as a grade 1 porter in 1923. In 1930 he was promoted to passenger guard at Wellington where he remained until he retired. Emrys Matthews was another passenger guard at Wellington; commencing his work on the railway in the goods shed at Bala in 1925, he later became a porter-guard working on that lonely outpost of the Great Western system, the single line branch between Bala and Blaenau Festiniog. In the late 1930s he came to Much Wenlock as a porter-guard; as the name of the post implies he was required to carry out platform duties at Wenlock, and also work as a passenger guard as required. He was later promoted to signalman at Much Wenlock. In 1945 he moved to Wellington as a passenger guard, finally, in 1955, moving to South Wales as a station master where he remained for the rest of his railway career.

Of the three passenger guards at Much Wenlock, the two longest serving in that capacity were Harry Johnson and George Evans. In 1914 George was serving as a conductor on the road vehicles at Plymouth Millbay station, these early GWR buses serving the rural villages in the Plymouth area. He came to Much Wenlock in 1915 and remained there until he retired in 1949. His gentlemanly manner and genial disposition endeared him to the travelling public between Wellington and Craven Arms. Harry Johnson started on the platform at Crudgington on the Crewe branch in 1911, and later worked at various stations in the Chester division. He volunteered for service in World War I in 1914, and remained in the army until 1920. In 1921 he returned to the railway as a passenger guard at Much Wenlock.

Another passenger guard at Wenlock before World War II was Tom Warburton. He started as a porter at Corwen in 1896 at the age of fourteen and after serving at various stations in North Wales he came to Wenlock as a porter-guard. Later moving to Ludlow as a passenger guard, from there Tom moved to Chester in the same capacity. It was whilst at Chester that he worked on the double-home turns between Chester and Paddington, but seeking lighter work due to failing health, he returned to branch work at Wenlock. Sadly he died in January 1933 at the early age of 51.

In the 1920s and up to World War II there were 10 goods guards stationed at Wellington. Most of their duties entailed working local goods trains between Wellington, Oxley, Market Drayton, Shrewsbury, and Much Wenlock. This meant shunting at each station; they were virtually travelling shunters, not experiencing the work of their main line counterparts, who, upon entering their van at some main line depot, did not have to touch their shunting poles again until they reached their distant destination. The only break which the Wellington men had was when they worked the occasional passenger train over the Wenlock and Crewe branches.

From lad porter to inspector was the career of one goods guard at Wellington, Albert Timmis, who began his railway life at Oakengates as a porter on 5th September, 1913, moving to Crewe as a shunter in 1919 for 24s. per week. In 1935 he came to Wellington as a goods guard, eventually in 1949 being promoted to inspector in the goods yard at Banbury.

Another native of North Wales, Harry Davies started at Trevor on the Ruabon to Dolgelley branch in 1911. Harry moved to Ruabon as a shunter in 1915 where he remained until April 1917, when he moved to Wellington as a goods guard. In 1946 Harry was promoted to yard foreman at Buildwas, where he remained until he retired in 1955.

William Fenn started his railway career at Oswestry in 1910, his wages at that time being 10s. per week. After seeing service at Brymbo, Baschurch and Ruabon, he came to Wellington as a goods guard in May 1931.

A goods guard at Wellington who always gave the impression that he was not prepared to be outdone by the passenger guards when it came to smartness of dress was Charlie Haycox. He always ensured that his uniform and cap buttons were highly polished and his button hole would always be adorned with a rose or carnation, or any other flower in season. Charlie was famed for his racing tips; before departing with the train he would come up to the engine on a winter's morning, with shunting pole and hand lamp under his arm, and from his wagon book he would quote the make up of the train; from the same page he would impart to the driver and fireman the hot favourite for the 2.30!

In addition to the two goods guards stationed at Wenlock between the late 1880s and 1910 there were also two brakesmen, they were no doubt required for braking duties for the heavy limestone traffic on the steep gradient between Presthope and Buildwas. However, by World War I there was one goods guard stationed at Wenlock, and his duty entailed the only goods to Craven Arms which was the 8.10 am returning from there at 12.15 pm for Wenlock. This post was occupied by Tom Hughes from 1937 until the line closed in 1951. Tom's career started on the road motors at Wrexham in 1915; he remained at Wrexham until 1920 when he was promoted to goods guard at Chester. In 1926 he came to Wellington as a goods guard, and finally to Wenlock in September 1937. Sadly after a long illness Tom died at Much Wenlock in 1954, at the age of only 54.

Buildwas Junction was without doubt the busiest station on the Wenlock branch. With its high and low level platforms serving the Wenlock branch and Severn Valley lines respectively, and its continuous stream of coal trains into the power station, a further impetus was given to the Junction with the opening up of the Farley oil terminal on the Wenlock branch at the commencement of World War II. There is no one better qualified to talk of life at this busy junction station than Ernest Dicken who worked both as a shunter and later yard foreman there. Ern was well grounded in railway matters for both his grandfather and father had been railwaymen.

My grandfather was goods yard foreman at Much Wenlock. I've been told by older railwaymen that I'm just like him. I believe that he used to go along to the 'Stork' at Much Wenlock and have rum and coffee every morning. My father was also on the railway, and his brother was chief inspector at Worcester Shrub Hill. My father started his career on the Wenlock branch as a lad porter at Longville, at that time the station master's name was Strange. From Longville he later moved to Ironbridge as a goods porter, later becoming signalman at Ironbridge on the Severn Valley line.

Ern followed in his father's footsteps and started his railway career as a lad porter at Longville in 1917.

They called them lad porters at that time because you weren't appointed until you were aged twenty-one. At Longville it was a heavy job for a young lad. I used to have to unload those big country lorries, which used to bring in wheat and barley in bags. At Longville there was a slaughterhouse nearby, and they used to send the raw meat away by train, it was a terrible job loading that and the smell was awful. The hours were 7.30 am until 6.30 pm. Another heavy job for a young lad was helping to load the milk churns on to the Craven Arms to Wellington train in a morning, which went every day to Wath's dairies at Birmingham. Then the empty churns would be brought back on the afternoon train to Craven Arms.

The first train was the 7.30 am which went to Craven Arms and back to Wellington. On a Monday morning the first train was 4.30 am, this was a cattle train which used to come from Salop to Buildwas down the Severn Valley, and it used to distribute the empty cattle wagons off at Wenlock, Presthope, Longville, Rushbury and Harton Road, and through to Craven Arms. Then it returned picking up the loaded cattle wagons at each station, and on to Wellington where the cattle market was held on a Monday.

From Longville I went to Bewdley lamping, this meant filling and taking out the signal lamps which would last about eight days before they needed refilling. I also had to relieve the ticket collector, and help out on the goods deck. My wages at Bewdley were one pound and three pence per week. I moved from Bewdley to Ironbridge as a mileage porter, this meant shunting in the yard, and loading the railway drays. There were seven horses kept at Ironbridge, five for hauling the delivery drays, and two were used for shunting at Jackfield.

Ern is typical of the railwayman of his era who had to move considerable distances on the Great Western system in order to earn an extra shilling or two per week. From Ironbridge he moved to Berrington on the Severn Valley line, then to Corwen, from Corwen to Wellington, eventually coming to Buildwas as a shunter in 1939. His wage was then 55s. per week.

The first train into Buildwas on a morning was the 5.20 am empty stock from Wellington, this returned as the workmen's train to Wellington. At this time a workman's ticket from Buildwas to Coalbrookdale was three ha'pence, Horsehay five pence, Ketley eight pence and Wellington ten pence. This of course was old money. The first train from Wenlock was the 7.00 am to Wellington. The first goods train into Buildwas was the 5.50 am ex-Wellington which went through to Presthope to pick up limestone for the Lilleshall Company.

Most of the men who worked over the Wenlock branch could relate hair-raising experiences which they had encountered on descending the 1 in 41 descent down Farley Dingle with a heavy goods train. These experiences were heightened with the introduction of the oil trains from the Farley terminal, hauled in many cases by 'Halls', 'Granges', 'Manors', '28XXs' and '72XXs', engines which were totally unsuitable for this precarious stretch of line. Ern Dicken relates one such experience:

We had no difficulty in getting Buildwas regraded with all these petrol trains coming in at all hours of the day and night. I remember one occasion with a petrol train running away, a nasty experience I can tell you. One night an engine and van came in from Salop to go up to Farley to bring out a load of petrol tanks. When it arrived there was a driver on it by the name of Perce Richards. He said to me, 'Are you coming up?'

I said 'No'.

'Well' he said, 'I aren't going'.

I said 'How's that?'

He said, 'The guard I've got in the back, he doesn't know the road. He doesn't know where Farley is, and I'm not going up with him.'

I said, 'I can't come, I've got the passengers to look after and the goods'.

So I fetched the station master out. He didn't care much about it but came out and did the work and I went up to Farley and did the shunting there. Good job I did, or we should have had the nastiest accident that ever was. The guard stopped in the van, I did the shunting off the two roads fetched 13 off one road, and 12 off another. This 'Grange' engine with the big wheels, of course, was no good for Farley bank. We used to have a stop board by the old mill. So I banged some brakes down as we came out of the sidings, ten or a dozen, then I went back on to the other road to pick up the brakes so that we could get them out of the sidings and drop them on to the tanks standing on the branch, hooked them all together about 25 or so. Then dropped the van on the rear of the train. I put down more brakes, I still thought he was going a bit sharp. Anyhow we got down to the mill, then the driver couldn't start them, so I had to ease a few more brakes. So of course when I eased another couple of brakes, away we went. So I run and jumped on the engine. He said, 'I haven't got them under control - I aren't going to hold them'. Of course he blowed his brake whistle all the way down, and the guard never assisted us one bit by putting his brake on the van. If he had done it would have been alright. I said to the driver, 'Ah well, when we get round by them rabbit berries, and the distant signal, there'll be one missing off the engine'. The fireman though, he was getting ready to jump off the engine straight away. But anyhow, when we got to the distant signal, the train started to pull up, so I got off and started to ease the brakes again. Oh I was thankful, because I was thinking about the passenger coming over the junction, that eight o'clock at night. I had visions of going straight through the middle of him.

Oh, that Farley Bank was a treacherous bit of line. I come down with Joe Watkins from Wenlock to Buildwas once on the passenger in 4½ minutes. I was never so frightened in all my life. Poor old George Evans the guard was trying to put his brake on in the van.

From the many stories related by the men who worked the trains over the undulating territory of the Wenlock branch, it was obvious that their skills in train operation were expended to the limit.

The other grade of men whose hours of work were not confined to an eight-hour shift were the crossing keepers. Their day began with the first train in a morning and ended with the last train at night. In the event of the crossing keeper requiring a break it was usually his wife who had to take over. The only two level crossings which employed crossing keepers full time were Doseley (between Doseley and Little Dawley) and Dawley Parva (between Little Dawley and Lightmoor).

Many of the crossing keepers on the GWR had previously been either shunters or guards who had had the misfortune to meet with a serious accident whilst carrying out these duties. This of course was in the days before large sums of compensation were paid to men who experienced this misfortune. In some ways they had to consider that they were fortunate in so far that they were given a job, in an age when many men seriously injured at work saw the end of their working lives.

The crossing keepers at Doseley and Dawley Parva between the wars were Fred Roberts and Charlie Flute. Fred came to Doseley in the early 1920s after having lost an arm in a shunting accident on the Ponkey branch (from Ruabon to Legacy). His wages in 1924 were 24s. per week out of which he paid 2s. 6d. per week for the rent of the crossing keeper's cottage. Fred was an ardent believer in the Co-operative movement, and took every opportunity to contact his fellow railwaymen by telephone from his crossing keeper's cabin about the advantages of membership. During the building of Doseley Halt in 1932, Fred saw fit to place (amongst the slag and furnace ash which was being used for the base of the platform) in a sealed container a time capsule containing three coins of the realm, a current copy of the *Wellington Journal & Shrewsbury News* and certain other artefacts that were appropriate to that period. The platform of the old Halt remains, now completely hidden by bushes; it is to be hoped that when the Halt gives way to a contractor's digger, that it will reveal to a future generation the contents of Fred's time capsule.

Charlie Flute joined the railway as a goods porter at Paddington on 8th January, 1901, unfortunately he lost a leg whilst shunting at Lord Hill's Yard, Paddington. In May 1915 he came as a crossing keeper to Chunes Crossing, Coalbrookdale, and on 27th January, 1919 he moved to Dawley Parva Crossing. The wages and the cottage rental were the same as that at Doseley.

One class of railwayman on whom the spotlight never fell were the platelayers - no smart uniform with brass buttons for them. They had to provide their own clothing, which in the main consisted of thick corduroy trousers, heavy steel capped boots, union shirt, red neckerchief, old jacket and waistcoat. They would set out from their cabin in a morning armed with pick and shovel, and the ganger with his key hammer, exposed to whatever the elements cared to provide that day. During fog or falling snow a platelayer would be stationed below the distant signal post crouched over an open brazier, ready to replace the detonators recently exploded by the last passing train. A hard, unenviable task on a bitter winter's night.

The permanent way sections on the branch were from Ketley Jn to Lightmoor Jn, Lightmoor Jn to Buildwas, Buildwas to Wenlock and Wenlock to Marsh Farm Jn. Each section had its own ganger and platelayers; after World war II these sections were merged, and in consequence the gangs had a larger section of branch to cover.

Bill Mills was a platelayer, firstly on the section between Buildwas and Wenlock, and later between Wenlock and Marsh Farm Jn. Bill was a native of Berriew in Montgomeryshire who went to work on the land on leaving school. In 1914 he joined the Army and saw service in the Dardenelles and France. Following his demobilisation in 1919 he returned to his job on the farm where his wages were 8s. per week and his keep. Eventually, in a endeavour to better his prospects, he came to live with his sister at Presthope in 1921, where he managed to get a job in the Wenlock platelaying gang. He remained as a platelayer in the Wenlock gang until he retired at the age of 65 in 1960.

Another platelayer was Landy Edwards, following in his father's footsteps. Here Landy tells his own story:

My father was a platelayer on the branch for 45 years. When we lived at Longville the P. Way length from Marsh Farm Jn to Wenlock was split into three. In 1932 he moved to Much Wenlock because the three lengths were merged into one gang, and made into a trolley gang. The trolley in the early days was pumped by hand by two men on each side of the trolley, a rod was connected from the pumping arm to a ratchet on the axle of the trolley to give the necessary propulsion. The trolley men have the token to authorise them to go into the section exactly the same as the driver on the train.

I have heard my father tell the story many times about when they had to do relaying work on a Sunday on the main line, they would pump the trolley from Wenlock to Marsh Farm Jn. Then they would join the P. Way train which would take them to the section which they had to relay, which could be anywhere between Shrewsbury and Hereford. Before they could have their breakfast they would have to remove the old track for a distance of one mile and put in the new section. They would leave Wenlock at four in the morning and get back between six and seven at night, and for this he would have been paid 6s. 4d.

I started as a platelayer at Much Wenlock in 1948 working between Wenlock and Marsh Farm Jn, my father's old length. I have many happy memories of working on that length. By this time of course we had a motorised trolley. I also on a Sunday would be required to work on the main line relaying. We used the motorised trolley to take us to Marsh Farm Jn, the trolley would take 10 of us. When I started with the gang there were no mechanical aids for relaying the track it was all done by pick, shovel and muscle power. Some of the winters on the branch were really grim, especially between Presthope and Longville where you were so exposed to all the elements, at this point you were on top of Wenlock Edge where there was no protection. As you emerged from Presthope tunnel the snow drifts had to be seen to be believed.

We booked on in the goods yard at Wenlock, we were given our orders for the day by the ganger. We would be instructed to do either track maintenance, hedgeing, ditching or 'quick

Job Price, platelayer on the Madeley branch, operating the three-wheeled hand-operated platelayer's trolley *c.* 1910.   *Keith Beddoes*

A posed photograph of the staff at Madeley at the turn of the century. The station was known as Madeley Court due to its close proximity to the nearby Madeley Court House.
                                                                            Author's Collection

Enoch Langford, who was a platelayer in the gang that operated on the line between Much Wenlock and Buildwas. However, Enoch was better known as the Wenlock Borough town crier announcing both joyous and sad news to the residents of the ancient borough. Enoch took over the position as town crier from his father in 1919.   *Author's Collection*

The once luxurious accommodation provided for the loco staff at Wellington, a former broad gauge coach. It was replaced after World War II by a more substantial brick building.

R. Carpenter

Fireman Don Houlston (*left*) and driver Joe Watkins (*right*) are seen at Wellington in 1957. Joe was a driver at Wenlock until the shed closed in December 1951 when he was transferred to Wellington. The former clerestory coach in the background is the carriage cleaners' cabin.

Don Houlston

digging' this meant digging a ditch between the hedges and the embankment along the side of the track to avoid the risk of fire caused by a spark from a passing engine.

After a few years in the platelaying gang Landy transferred to the traffic department, eventually becoming a porter-guard at Much Wenlock.

The Train Crews

In the Passenger Department there was an influx of staff from North Wales on to the branch, but the same situation did not apply so far as the Motive Power Department was concerned. With the train crews on the GWR it was an 'all-line' system of promotion, in consequence they did not move for promotion in just their own division, which in the case of Much Wenlock and Wellington sheds was in the Wolverhampton division extending from Banbury to Birkenhead. When a driver, or fireman's, registered number came to the top of the promotion list they would be required to move to any shed on the GWR system where a vacancy existed.

With the opening of the Wen&SJR on 1st February, 1862 the engine shed was nearing completion in the goods yard at Wenlock. In the case of Wellington Shed, as already mentioned, this was a former joint goods shed, and was not purchased by the GWR for use as an engine shed until September 1867. Therefore between 1857 and 1867 the engine shed built by Dickson at the Waterloo Sidings, Ketley was used to house the locomotives operating on the branch between Ketley, Horsehay and Shifnal.

From the GWR staff records it appears that a James Jones was stationed at Ketley in 1862, transferring to Wellington in 1867 upon the opening of the shed there. Also at Ketley was Edmund Connell, who was transferred from Shrewsbury as a fireman in 1862, Connell eventually moved to Wenlock as a driver in 1867. Whilst he was at Wenlock he had the misfortune to demolish the gates at Farley Crossing, for which he was fined one shilling, in October 1871. In the following year whilst working a passenger train from Wenlock to Craven Arms the pistons failed at Marsh Farm Jn due to lack of oil. For this lack of attention to the engine he was suspended for two days.

Thomas Lambert was a driver at Ketley in 1865 who moved to Wellington in 1867, where it is recorded that he was a first class driver earning 8s. per day.

Another driver who moved into Wellington upon the opening of the shed in 1867 was Thomas Smith, who had been appointed a driver at Market Drayton in 1863 when an engine shed was built there following the opening of the Nantwich & Market Drayton Railway on 20th October, 1863. When the railway to the south of Market Drayton was opened by the Market Drayton & Wellington Railway on 16th October, 1867 the shed closed, and the men moved to Wellington. Another early engineman at Wellington was William Jones who came from Shrewsbury in 1867. From the records we learn that he was fined the sum of 5s. for allowing his fireman to move the engine at Presthope, resulting in damage to the engine. There were also two cleaners at Ketley in the early 1860s who both moved to Wellington upon the opening of the shed there.

Many of the footplatemen started their railway careers as greasers in the goods yard; these were the boys who would walk the full length of a line of wagons armed with a broad bladed piece of wood with a handle, and a metal grease box, lifting each axle box lid as they progressed putting a plentiful supply of grease into each box for lubrication purposes. They would commence this work at the age of 13 or 14, then at the age of 16 they would hope to progress into the engine shed and start their footplate career as a cleaner.

One such boy who commenced his railway career in this way was John Harper, who joined as a greaser at Wellington in 1885, and by 1887 he had moved into the shed at Wellington as a cleaner. Up until the end of World War I the drivers and the firemen on the GWR were graded third, second or first class, and they had to move to attain each of these grades. John Harper moved from Wellington to Wolverhampton to become a third class fireman in 1889 at the rate of 3s. per day. To become a second class fireman it was necessary for him to move to Leamington in 1891, thereby commanding a further 6d. per day. In 1895 he was required to move again, this time to Plymouth as a first class fireman at the rate of 4s. 6d. per day. After two years he was on the move again, this time to Chester to become a third class driver at the rate of 5s. 6d. per day. In 1902 he eventually got back to his home station at Wellington as a second class driver, and it was to be a further 10 years before he was promoted to a first class driver at Wellington at a rate of 7s. per day. In 1927, due to ill health, John was given a regular day turn working the 8.00 am goods from Wellington to Hollinswood, and then on to the Stirchley branch to the Randlay brickworks and the Stirchley chemical works. He retired in 1932.

The career of John Harper was typical of the careers of the majority of GWR footplatemen who, until 1919, had to move compulsorily three times as a fireman, and three times as driver, each move bringing with it earnings of only a few additional pence per day. John Hellon, a driver at Wellington in 1906 had a complicated turn of duty. He would work the 9.00 pm passenger from Wellington to Crewe at night, returning with the 11.45 pm Crewe to Worcester goods. He would book off at Worcester, and return at night with the 8.25 pm Worcester to Crewe goods, leave the engine on the shed at Crewe, and travel back to Wellington as a passenger. This turn he worked regularly for a number of years. William Roden started as a cleaner at Wellington in 1877, after moving to various depots on the system he eventually became a driver at Wellington in 1897. His three sons followed in their father's footsteps; Horace and Walter became drivers at Wellington and William became a driver at Oxley and Stafford Road, Wolverhampton.

The shed foremen at Wellington were responsible also for the engine sheds at Crewe and Much Wenlock. The shed foreman at Wellington in 1906 was George Hogg who had recently moved from Corwen. He was followed in 1921 by Ernest Winsley who started his railway career as a cleaner at Newport (Mon) in 1894, later moving to Pontypool Road and Old Oak Common as a fireman, finally becoming a driver at Tyseley in 1911 before moving to Wellington. Ernest Winsley retired in 1931, and he was followed by Joseph Holloway who had also been a driver at Tyseley. Joseph Holloway remained at Wellington until 1943 when he also retired and was succeeded by Harry Griffiths who had been a driver at Shrewsbury. Unfortunately Harry died in 1949 and in his place came Frank Sumner, a Crewe driver, who remained at Wellington until the shed closed in 1964.

The first recorded drivers at Much Wenlock were Giles Bullock, Edmund Connel and Thomas Rogers, and their firemen were Joseph Moreton, John Rodgers and John Hill. The career of Edmund Connel has already been referred to. Giles Bullock had been a fireman at Shrewsbury transferring to Wenlock in 1865, his wage following his appointment at Wenlock being 5s. 6d. per day. It is evident when examining the accidents and misfortunes which befell many of these early enginemen that their expertise in railway operation was sadly lacking. In the early days, there was no question of a driver or fireman having to progress through three stages before they became a top driver or fireman. Many of them within five years of starting their careers would be in charge of a locomotive. In the case of Giles Bullock he was reprimanded for being late off the shed due to the fact that he had failed to see that the engine was lit up in time. Later he had the engine derailed at Wellington, for which he was fined two shillings. Also at Wellington a few days later he experienced the greatest ignominy which could befall any engineman, he dropped a lead plug; this meant that the water level had dropped below the lead plug, in consequence the remaining water left in the boiler would flow through the melted lead plug immediately putting out the fire. This cost him one week's suspension.

In the 1860s the moves of the locomotive men working on the branch seemed to be confined to Wellington, Shrewsbury and Much Wenlock. However, in the 1870s the 'all-line' system of promotion began to appear; for instance, Thomas Rogers came from Shrewsbury as a driver to Wenlock, for promotion he had to move to Aberdare in 1873. Mention has been made of Joseph Moreton who, as a fireman at Wenlock in 1868 was earning 3s. per day; for promotion he had moved to Birkenhead in 1871.

In 1888 Sydney Rowles came to Wenlock as a driver; he had started his career as a cleaner at Newport (Mon) in 1873. For causing unnecessary delay to his train at Wenlock on Christmas Day he was fined 2s.; the cause for the delay is not given, one can only assume that not having the opportunity to celebrate the festive day at home, he was determined not to let the day pass without some form of recognition, despite the rigours of the railway timetable!

It was every boy's dream as he clambered around an engine with an oily rag, that one day he would be driving a gleaming locomotive at the head of an express train. However, life is not built on dreams, but on hard facts, and sadly these were experienced by many locomotive men. After spending a long apprenticeship, cleaning and shovelling hundreds of tons of coal, their career could be blighted by ill health or failing eyesight. A man on the footplate had to have the stamina of a horse, the agility of an entrant in the Olympic Games, and these qualities had to remain with him throughout his career. Failure to meet these requirements could mean that he would be reduced to shunting engine duties, or worse still, some menial task in the engine shed. One such driver who had to face up the hard realities of footplate life was Harry Lipscombe. Harry started his railway career at Shrewsbury as a cleaner, moving to various sheds as a fireman and eventually moving to Wenlock as a driver in February 1894. His days at Wenlock were blighted by misfortune: firstly he was fined one shilling for leaving Wellington with a passenger train with the tail lamp still on the engine. Then it was found that he failed to give proper attention to the brake gear on the engine at Craven Arms, resulting in it suffering serious damage, for which he was fined two shillings. Later he failed to enter the correct times on his daily record sheet, resulting in suspension. His footplate career ended at Longville when he was working engine No. 1702; he slipped off the footplate and received serious injuries. Harry is next heard of on the shed staff at Shrewsbury, boilerwashing. A sad end for a man who had spent so little time at the top of his profession.

Up until World War I drivers on the GWR were paid a bonus based on the amount of fuel and oil they had used over a monthly period. In the event of any fines being imposed on the driver, as in the case of Harry Lipscombe, the amount of the fine was deducted from the bonus. In consequence drivers were bonus orientated, which could make life difficult for the fireman, for every shovelful of coal was closely checked by the driver. However, if you had a munificent driver he would be prepared to share the bonus with his fireman. The fines could be imposed on enginemen on the slightest pretext, such as emission of too much smoke whilst standing in a station, or allowing steam to escape from the safety valve whilst standing. Something which all drivers feared was the 'registered caution' which was issued for any serious misdemeanour, such as passing signals at danger, or demolishing level crossing gates. Three such cautions could mean the driver being removed from main line work and put on shunting engines or shed work.

Another driver at Wenlock who was accident prone was Roland Cope who came to Wenlock as a driver in 1898. On 30th December, 1899, whilst working a passenger train to Craven Arms, he failed to notice a faulty draw bar on the engine, for which he was cautioned, but it may be added not a registered caution. In 1901 he passed a signal at danger at Wenlock and for this error his promotion was suspended for one month. At Wellington he allowed a steam railcar to run off the line causing considerable damage to the car, for which his promotion was suspended for six months. Despite all these misfortunes Roland Cope was eventually moved to Llanelly in 1907 as a first class driver.

Until 1919 Wenlock shed had its own cleaners, after this the engines were cleaned at Wellington. Many of the cleaners started in the yard at Wenlock as carriage cleaners, including Albert Perks who started as a carriage cleaner in 1917, becoming an engine cleaner in 1918. He became a fireman at Wenlock in 1921 and for the next 20 years fired on the branch; for most of that time his driver was Fred Clinton.

Another carriage cleaner at Wenlock who later went on to the footplate was Bill Jones, Bill started on the railway in 1919, and here takes up his own story:

A Mr Hall who was a driver at Wenlock met me in the street one day, and asked me if I would like to go carriage cleaning. I immediately said I would. Up until then my only connection with the railway was when I used to go and visit my aunt at Presthope on a Saturday, and the fare was three halfpence. The coaches I used to clean were the four-wheelers with the straight back seats. When I started first it was a 10-hour day, but I had not been on the railway long when they introduced the eight-hour day. In those days they were gas-lit carriages, and we used to have to gas them once a week. The gas truck came from Wellington, the tanks on the gas truck were connected by a pipe to the gas cylinder under each coach. In 1920 I went to Wellington as an engine cleaner, by this time the engine cleaning was no longer done at Wenlock shed. I was eventually made a fireman and sent to Tyseley. In 1923 I returned to Wellington as a fireman, and remained there for the rest of my railway career both as fireman and a driver.

The driver that Bill Jones refers to who was responsible for getting him his job, Jack Hall, was the senior driver at Wenlock, and as such he was in charge of the engine shed and the carriage cleaners. This was in the days when the carriage and engine cleaners could be hired by the shed chargeman (as in the case of Wenlock), or by the shed foreman (at Wellington). After 1921 all appointments had to be made through the divisional locomotive superintendent's office.

Another driver at Wenlock, Joe Watkins, was a legend, mainly for the speed which he attained on the passenger trains. Joe began his career at Wenlock as a cleaner in 1911, moving to Chester as a third class fireman in 1912, remaining there as both a second and first class fireman. He was promoted to driver at Chester in December 1923, returning to Wenlock as a driver in June 1932. It was always said that his penchant for speed was brought about by his experiences firing on the Birkenhead to Bournemouth and Birkenhead to Dover trains, which were worked each day by Chester men. Joe remained at Wenlock until the shed closed in December 1951, when he was transferred to Wellington.

The period of 'apprenticeship' as a cleaner and a fireman varied considerably, depending to a very large degree on the economic fortunes of the railway company. Men who were firing on the GWR system at the end of World War I were very soon promoted to drivers. The situation, however, was soon to change, and cleaners who started in the mid-1920s found that they were to be faced with a very long period of apprenticeship. A typical example was Eric Tipton who started as a cleaner at Wellington in 1924 and whose period of cleaning was to last for 11 years before promotion to fireman at Banbury. Ten years awaited him as a fireman before he was to be made a driver at Evesham. It was only when the war clouds began to appear on the horizon that the wheels of promotion began to turn again as far as Great Western locomen were concerned.

The talking point amongst the railwaymen on the branch, and no doubt men throughout the railway system, was the strikes in which they had been involved. The older men recalled the strike in 1911 in which they were successful in getting trade union recognition. The strike of 1919 brought about the eight-hour day, but the strike which proved to be a disaster for the railwaymen was the General Strike of 1926. This was the dispute in which they had no grievance with the railway companies, but came out in sympathy with the miners. The railwaymen were out from the 4th to 14th May, 1926, and at the end of that period they had to return on the terms laid down by the companies. In the case of the Great Western men the terms proved to be quite harsh. Felix J.C. Pole, the then General Manager of the Great Western, acting on behalf of the General Managers of all the railway companies, set out terms of settlement agreed between the companies and the railway trade unions; item one stated that:

Those employees of the Railway Companies who have gone out on strike to be taken back to work as soon as traffic offers, and work can be found for them. The principle to be followed in reinstating to be seniority in each grade at each station, depot or office.

One young fireman at Wenlock who experienced the harshness of this dictum was Cyril Northwood, who following the termination of the strike was out of work for three weeks. At the end of that period he had to travel to Wellington shed at his own expense, firstly working two days a week, and after a further three weeks he went on to three days per week. It was six weeks before he returned to his home shed at Wenlock to work a full week. If the trains were not convenient for the turns on which he was required to work at Wellington he had to cycle there. In addition to these impositions his privilege tickets and free passes were withdrawn for a period of 12 months. Bert Bostock, who was a cleaner at Wellington, recalls that after the strike it was his duty to take the notes round to the various drivers and firemen informing them of the day, or days, they would be required to work during the week. The youngest hands, both drivers and firemen, were the last to be recalled for duty. Bert mentions that when they opened their doors to him and he handed them their notes, there was always a look of relief on their faces.

Bert Bostock was eventually promoted to fireman in 1919 and was sent to Aberystwyth. A great deal of his work there entailed firing on the branch from Aberystwyth to Carmarthen and also on the narrow gauge line up the Rheidol valley. In the summer months he worked on the double-home excursion jobs between Aberystwyth and Birmingham (Snow Hill). Bert returned to Wellington as a fireman, and was later appointed driver at his home station. Bert recalls his memories of working the workmen's train from Wenlock to Wellington over that precarious stretch of the line through Farley Dingle:

> We used to work the 6.50 am from Wenlock to Wellington and on one occasion we left at 6.53. Before we left a fellow came up to the engine who worked at the Buildwas Power Station, and said, 'Do your best if we're late into work we have to lose an hour'. So I did my best we went down to Buildwas, stopping at Farley Halt, and we arrived at Buildwas at 6.59, which was right on time. As the passengers got off the train for the Power Station, this fellow came up to me and said, 'Well done driver at that speed theet have us in the b..... taiter field one a these mornins'.

The Wenlock branch certainly produced its characters. The station master at Harton Road each morning would arrive in his donkey cart, the donkey being allowed to graze in the field adjoining the station for the rest of the day. One signalman, when on duty on a Saturday afternoon, would leave his box to take his place in the local football team playing in the field adjacent to the box! This activity however came to the notice of the powers-that-be and he was duly suspended for one week. Then there was the signalman who carried on the lucrative business of cobbling shoes whilst on duty, and the porter who carried on a most successful mail order business. These activities took place despite the cardinal rule in the company's rule book to the effect 'that no member of staff should indulge in any business, or other activity that would impinge on his duties as a railwayman'.

The drivers, firemen and guards also knew where they could obtain a rabbit, or a dozen eggs, from stations between Presthope and Harton Road. During the gardening season the goods guard's van, and engine bunkers, would come back loaded with pea and bean sticks obtained from the platelayers along the line.

Before the power station was built at Buildwas, the station and yard was completely surrounded by fields and hedgerows. The peace and charm of this idyllic scene could soon be shattered by the loud report from the signalman's shotgun as he took aim from the box window at any luckless rabbit, or pheasant, which happened to be lurking within his range.

Despite the occasional flouting of the rule book, the fear of suspension, the issue of a registered caution, or a fine, the men on the branch took a pride in their work. A standard was required of them which was well above the standards required in many occupations open to working men. It would appear that the Revd J.W. Johnson, the vicar of Benthall, Shropshire, was well aware of the standards required by the GWR when he penned the following in support of Bill Pearce's application for the post of lad porter at Ironbridge:

Longville station in April 1954 with (*from left to right*) guard Fred Clarke, fireman unknown, driver Bert Bostock, checker Bill Jefferies, clerk Bryan Goode, porter Williams, ganger Alec Evans, Much Wenlock station master Fred James and his son Richard James.   *Richard James*

Wellington fireman John Hicks takes water on 0-6-0PT No. 3732 at Much Wenlock *c.* 1960.
    R. Carpenter

I certify that I have known Mr Wm. Pearce for the past 5 years, and that I can speak of his character in the highest terms in every respect:

His diligence
attentiveness
assiduity
obligingness
civility
sobriety
carefulness
thoroughness
punctuality
regularity
dependableness and
conscientiousness

are all deserving of the highest praise

J.W. Johnson M.A.
Vicar of Benthall, Shropshire.
July 15th, 1898

It has only been possible to detail the lives of a few of the people who contributed to making the Wenlock branch an institution. Many others who lived and died unknown made an equal contribution. To them it was just as important that the engine and two coaches on the branch should run safely and to time, as it was to their counterparts on the main line dealing with express trains.

Wellington Loco Horticultural Society annual show at the Station Hotel, Wellington in 1958. Back row: (*left to right*) Charles Lewis (driver), George Fewtrell (driver), Jack Hicks (fireman), John Evason (fireman), Walter Roden (driver) and Joe Burden (driver). The judges in the front row are unknown. *Don Houlston*

GREAT   WESTERN   RAILWAY.   (5718)

CHIEF MECHANICAL ENGINEER'S DEPARTMENT,

SWINDON,   3rd July, 19 40

Wilts.

Engine Cleaner K.B.Jones, Wellington

Please note that you are to go to Swindon by the first train on   Tuesday
next   9th   instant.

You should leave Swindon Station, and on arriving at the foot of the steps, turn
to the right, and enquire for Park House, where you will report yourself to the
Company's representative for examination. Wednesday, 10th July.

The Office at Park House is closed between 12.30 p.m. and 1.30 p.m.

You should be prepared to
1500—B.M./18 1940 (1).   spend the night at Swindon.

                                                                    (5718)

G.W.R.   CHIEF MECHANICAL ENGINEER'S DEPARTMENT,

SWINDON, Friday 10th December 194 8.
WILTS.

Fireman K. B. Jones, 25802, Wellington.

Please note that you are to go to Swindon by the first train on Monday
next   20th instant.

On leaving station turn sharply to the right and walk straight along Station Road,
Sheppard Street, London Street, and Bristol Street, turning to the left, near a high tank,
at the end of Bristol Street. Keeping the Park on the right proceed for about 200 yards
and enter Park House (which is on the left at the bottom of this road) where you
will report to the Company's representative for examination.

By the Inspector to take charge

The Office at Park House is closed between 12.30 p.m.
and 1.30 p.m.

3,000-LC.1947-(2)

Chapter Nine

Branch Line Days and Branch Line Ways: My Memories

I was born in the era when most schoolboys, when asked what they wished to do when they left school, would invariably reply, 'I want to be an engine driver'. For me this was not just a passing phase, but a goal which I wished to achieve, and one from which I never wavered. My father was a signalman on the Wenlock branch from 1919 to 1960, but I did not receive any encouragement from him to pursue my quest to join the Great Western Railway locomotive department. In fact, it was just the opposite, he did his best to dissuade me. He suggested that if I wished to take up a railway career, I should endeavour to become either a goods clerk or a station booking clerk. He always laid great stress on the fact that 'on the staff' I should get two weeks holiday a year and full pay when I was off sick. I am afraid that these inducements had not the least attraction for me, and the thought of sitting behind a desk grappling with figures paled into insignificance with my aspirations to be on the footplate of a steaming giant. In my youthful mind, how could one possibly compare the two in terms of job satisfaction?

My interest in railways, and especially the Wenlock branch, was aroused at an early age, when my grandmother related to me her experience on the branch. She lived at a little hamlet called The Stocking between Horsehay and Lightmoor and occasionally would go by train to Shrewsbury. This would necessitate catching the train at Horsehay, travelling to Buildwas and changing on to the Severn Valley line for the county town. On this particular return journey she alighted at Buildwas to change for Horsehay and walked up the steps from the Severn Valley low level platform on to the high level Wenlock branch platform. At Buildwas the Wellington-bound train would stand at the north end of the platform, whilst the train bound for Wenlock would come in from Wellington on the through road, proceed on to the single line and then reverse into the platform backing up to the train already standing in the platform bound for Wellington. The traveller in those days had to be fully aware of this situation as branch line stations did not have the luxury of station announcers. My grandmother, instead of getting into the Wellington train standing in the platform, got into the Wenlock portion. This may have been all right had it been earlier in the day, but unfortunately, these were the last trains of the day. She was quite oblivious to her mistake until in the dwindling light of the evening, she glanced from the compartment window and instead of crossing the Albert Edward bridge, she saw to her right the ruins of Buildwas Abbey. She knew then that she was bound for Much Wenlock. What was she to do? This was in the days before there was any bus service into Much Wenlock. For the rest of the journey her mind was occupied in trying to fathom out how best she could extricate herself from her predicament. The train eventually pulled into Wenlock platform, she alighted in fear and trepidation and explained the situation to the guard and platform porter, who at that stage were at a loss to know what advice to give her.

The working arrangement at this time was that the coaches remained at Wenlock, whilst the engine returned 'light' to Wellington. The coaches were duly disposed of in the yard and the engine returned to the platform to pick up the electric train staff for Buildwas. The Wenlock guard, George Evans, approached the Wellington driver to see if it was possible for my grandmother to be given a lift back to Horsehay on the footplate and the driver readily agreed. She climbed on to the footplate, shopping bag and all. Whenever I travel through Farley Dingle, I can still see the ghost of my grandmother clinging to the side of the cab of the engine as it came hurtling down the sharp descent of the Dingle into Buildwas. That story fired my imagination, and one day I hoped that I should find myself clinging to the side of a cab of a locomotive as it hurtled through this Shropshire beauty spot. The Wellington driver on that occasion was Bill Dudley to whom, many years later, I was to fire. Bill related the story to me and it matched every detail of the saga as related by my grandmother.

I was given my first second-hand bicycle at the age of 12, costing the princely sum of 15 shillings. My first journey on my new found transport was not to a nearby town or place of entertainment. No! It was to Wellington Shed, where from the road I could gaze through the broken wooden fencing panels and see the engine movements on the shed, and the cleaners clambering over the engines with their oily rags. Oh! how the day seemed so far off when I should have an oily rag in my hand under the roof of Wellington Shed.

I trust that I shall be forgiven for once again bringing my grandmother into my story, but each weekend after school I would spend with my grandparents at Chapel House, Gravel Leasows, a small hamlet between Doseley and Lightmoor. To me this was an idyllic spot, as it was only about 150 yards from the branch between Horsehay and Lightmoor. From here every movement on the line could be observed, and in wet weather from a seat in the kitchen window. The highlight of the weekend was Saturday night, when I insisted on staying up until midnight, and on certain occasions until the early hours of Sunday morning. The reason for this late vigil was that during the early and mid-1930s an evening excursion train ran from Coalbrookdale to Wolverhampton, the return fare being only 1s. 6d, and to Birmingham 2s. The return train would pass through Gravel Leasows at about 11.35 pm, always double-headed, the locomotives being a 'Dean Goods' and a '17XX' open cab tank engine. I was to learn later that the 'Dean Goods' had worked the 8.50 pm Crewe to Wellington passenger train, and the tank engine was the Wellington yard shunter.

After the train had passed, I was not content to retire to bed. No, I still insisted on waiting for the return empty stock. This to me was the most exciting part of the long wait. Standing by the back door gazing out into the black stillness of the night, my first indication of the returning train was the faint sound of the exhaust beats of both engines echoing in the Lightmoor valley as they tackled the 1 in 50 climb from Green Bank to Lightmoor. The exhaust beats began to grow louder like an approaching storm, then there was a momentary silence as the exhaust beats ceased, this easing off to give the fireman on the second engine time to take the staff from the Lightmoor box picking-up post. Soon the reverberating blasts were to be heard again bouncing off the pit banks north of Lightmoor Platform. This was my signal to crane my neck over a low brick wall in the backyard where I could get my first glimpse of the glare of the firebox lighting up the night sky, first from the leading engine, then from the train engine. If it was a clear night, the red glare would pierce the sky like the rays from a giant searchlight; if there was low-lying cloud the red rays would bounce back on to the smoke and hissing steam giving a ghostly reddish hue over the engines and coaches. As the train drew nearer my excitement intensified. The sight of this train of four coaches tackling this stiff climb double-headed created in my mind a sense of wonder and awe, and putting men on to the moon paled into insignificance when compared with this once-weekly scene of power.

On leaving school at the age of 14 I was successful in obtaining a job as an invoice clerk in the Sales Dept of the Wrekin Foundry at Ketley. Having found work, I did not consider this as any great achievement, but managed to persuade my father to register me at Wellington Shed with a view to being taken on as a cleaner when I attained the age of 16, if I passed the medical examination. In those days, especially on the GWR, preference was given to your application if your father was in the company's employ.

I well remember returning from my first day in the office at Wrekin Foundry, and I was asked by my parents the usual question, which was only natural. How had I got on? My very short reply was 'alright' and immediately, without giving time for further questioning, I was soon in full flow giving details of the railway operations at the Ketley sidings. Before getting to know my way around the office, and the people with whom I had to work, my first and greatest discovery was that my desk was situated in a window which gave me a full view of Ketley station and the Foundry sidings. A little later on I made another discovery, that when I was called upon to take messages into the Foundry, a slight detour through a side doorway gave me an excellent view of Ketley Junction and the Birkenhead main line. After a while I had the taking of these messages off to a fine art, I could time them to coincide with the passing of one of the Paddington to Birkenhead expresses headed by a 'Star', 'Saint', or 'Castle'.

My contribution to the fortunes of the Wrekin Foundry Ltd during my two year stay was questionable. However, their contribution to the furtherance of my railway career was considerable, and one for which I was eternally grateful. They had quite unknowingly given me the opportunity to watch the daily branch and main line operations at Ketley and Ketley Junction. Not being content with keeping a watchful eye on train operations during the day, after finishing work, when my father was on late turn at Ketley Station box, I would spend many evenings there with him watching every lever movement, and absorbing every bell code. Between the age of 14 and 16, I had to be patient for I knew that I could not be taken on in the engine shed until I became 16. However, on attaining that magical age, and for the ensuing weeks and months, I was continually questioning my father as to whether he had any word from Wellington Shed concerning my application.

To my delight, after three months of waiting (and I am sure to the delight of my parents, for living with me over this period could not have been easy), the letter arrived from the shed foreman at Wellington requesting me to attend at the shed at 11 am on 5th February, 1938 for a written and eyesight test.

The day arrived and I presented myself. I was ushered into the foreman's office to be greeted by a gentleman from the locomotive superintendent's office at Wolverhampton who gave me a spelling test, and a written test. Then he laid out on the desk various coloured woollens to test for colour blindness, then came the eyesight test. Obviously he was satisfied that I could write and spell, and with my colour vision, for he then informed me that I should be getting a letter within the next few weeks requesting me to attend for a medical examination at Swindon.

Within two weeks a letter arrived, with an enclosed free pass, requesting I attend Park House, Swindon for a medical examination at 10 am on 3rd March, 1938. I was informed that I should have to travel up the day before and stay the night at the home of a Miss Hunt, who provided accommodation for all locomen attending for examination who could not return to their home station the same day. I believe she was paid the sum of 3s. 6d. for bed and breakfast.

On arrival at Park House I found that there were five other boys there from various parts of the GW system who were taking the same test. I had to submit myself to a very stringent medical test, together with another eyesight test. However, to my great relief I was told that I had passed. I was then measured for my overalls; in those days cleaners were not issued with pilot jackets, overcoats, or even uniform hats. These were only issued when you were made a fireman. I well recall returning from Swindon full of the joys of spring, with my brown paper parcel containing my overalls under my arm, and what was all-important to me, they had firmly imprinted on them 'GWR'. I was told at Swindon that I should be notified as to where I eventually had to report, this could well be any shed in the Wolverhampton division between Banbury and Birkenhead.

After what seemed a very long wait, I was eventually told to report to the shed foreman at Oxley Shed, Wolverhampton, at 8 am on 6th April, 1938. This would entail going into lodgings; the thought of giving up my home comforts did not appeal to me very much but I was prepared for this, for there were only a few cleaners employed at Wellington.

Having reported to the shed foreman, I was taken to the cleaners' cabin where I met the foreman cleaner who told me my shifts would be 6.0 am to 2.0 pm. and 2.0 pm to 10.0 pm. There were 14 cleaners on each shift, split into two gangs of six with two spare to help the boiler washers, tube cleaners, or lighters-up. Oxley was the freight locomotive shed, where every conceivable type of GW engine was shedded with the exception of 'Castles' and 'Kings'. To me the shed was a wonderful place with a permanent haze of smoke and steam pierced by the rays of light from the large shed windows, the clanking and banging, and the deep thud of each engine as it moved on to the turntable. The acrid smell of burning coal which belched forth not only from the chimney, but also from the firebox door, the smell of warm oil, the condensation from steam all around you; to me, all this was the romance of steam.

As my first task I was introduced, together with another cleaner, to unload a 12 ton wagon of sand into the pen adjoining a large furnace which dried the sand for the locomotive sand boxes. After the first hour it did not appear that we had made any inroad into reducing the amount of sand in the wagon. My arms were aching, my back felt as if it was breaking, there were blisters on my hands which had only been used to handling a pen and a typewriter. Had I made the right decision in taking up a railway career? The romance of riding on the footplate of a steam locomotive was fading. Although we did not empty the wagon that day, I was delighted to find the next day that the wagon had been moved, I did not dare pose the question why. I was allowed to stay on the 8 am till 5 pm turn for the rest of the week, and thereby travel home each day, thus giving me the opportunity to find suitable lodgings. By the end of the week, I found lodgings in South Street, Bushbury which was quite close to the shed.

The following Monday I started on the 6 am shift and was placed in one of the gangs of six cleaners. The senior cleaner in the gang was issued with a large roll of cotton waste, a can of oil, and a tin of bath brick for scouring the brass. Then the senior cleaner would toss a coin to determine which part of the engine you would clean; two for the boiler and brass work, two for the wheels and motion, and two for the tender. The most favoured part was the wheels and motion, the part most disliked was the tender; on the high tenders of the 'Halls' you had to balance precariously on a small ledge with one arm outstretched clinging to the top of the tender, whilst cleaning with the other. When I first started I found my outstretched arm was aching so badly that I had to rest half way along the tender. However, after a few weeks, the initial shock of moving from an office desk into an engine shed passed, and I soon began to enjoy every moment of an achieved boyhood ambition.

The procedure at Wolverhampton was that the senior cleaner at Oxley moved up to the passenger shed at Stafford Road, and after just over two years my turn came to move. Stafford Road, although a passenger shed, was much older and more dilapidated than Oxley. In fact one part of it was known as the 'Broad Gauge shed', and from its appearance little had changed since the broad gauge days. Here, of course, you were involved in the cleaning of 'Castles' and 'Kings', the 'Castles' on the Chester, Bristol and Plymouth runs and the 'Kings' on the Wolverhampton to Paddington expresses.

All footplate crews had to be called if they were booking on between the hours of 12 midnight and 6 am. In many sheds this was one of the cleaners' duties, but at Stafford Road they had full time callers-up. If however a caller-up was off sick, or extra men had to be called for any special trains during these hours, it fell to the lot of the cleaner to carry out these duties. On many occasions, when on the night shift, I was required for calling-up, and I must admit that it was a task that did not appeal to me. By this time the war was on, and going down a strange street in the blackout on the old shed bike, its only illumination an oil lamp, looking for the appropriate house number at 2 am left a lot to be desired. On finding the number, and not wishing to raise all the neighbourhood, you would first of all give a gentle tap. Soon you learnt that this gentle approach had very little effect on some drivers and firemen. You usually had to bang on the door, and in many cases brought down on your head the wrath, not of the person you had gone to call, but that of the next door neighbour. I was always relieved when I could get through the night shift without having to go 'calling-up'.

Whilst at Stafford Road I had quite a number of firing turns on the various yard shunters. With the coming of the war, promotion within the footplate grades became very rapid; this was a good thing in many respects, for many men in their early forties were still firing and had not even reached the top links. My promotion was quite rapid, for when I booked on at Stafford Road Shed one Monday afternoon, I was handed a letter instructing me to report to the foreman at Banbury Shed on Monday next 22nd July, 1940 to take up my duties as a fireman.

After reporting to the foreman at Banbury I was given the rest of the morning off to look for a suitable lodgings. This fortunately did not take long; I was advised to see a driver who was just booking off, and he took me along to see his wife who readily agreed to take me in.

My first turn at Banbury was on the North End shunter. This was one of the many turns in the shunting link, another turn in the link being the Hump Yard shunter which I found to be a most boring job. Within the shunting link there were always spare turns, which generally involved moving engines from the coal stage into the shed, but on occasions you did get the opportunity to get a main line firing turn. I well remember my first firing turn on the main line was on a goods train to Didcot. The engine was an 'ROD' class 2-8-0 and I can't imagine a worse engine on which to commence one's first main line venture. The engine seemed to sway one way, and the tender the other, this rocking movement bringing the coal from the tender on to the footplate so that each time you went to fire you found that you were standing on coal. Later in my railway life, when booking on for a particular goods train, my heart would sink when I saw that we had an 'ROD' booked for the trip.

The first week at Banbury I put in for a transfer back to Wolverhampton; this was a concession you were given to enable you to get to a shed of your choice when a vacancy arose. Although I should have to be in lodgings if I returned, at least I would be a little nearer home. I was at Banbury for about 14 months, before moving back to Wolverhampton.

Regardless of your seniority, either as a driver or fireman, when you moved to Wolverhampton you had to start on the Wednesbury shunting engines, there being two sets of men on each of three turns. On each turn one of the engines would also act as banking engine assisting goods trains up the heavy gradient from Wednesbury through Swan Village to West Bromwich. I have vivid memories of these banking turns. Before entering West Bromwich station there was quite a lengthy tunnel, and after the train engine had gone through, it left behind a sulphurous acrid stench, which our engine added to, and emerging from that tunnel was always a welcome relief.

When your turn came you moved either to Stafford Road or Oxley, depending where there was a vacancy, and it was not long before I moved to Stafford Road into the shunting and preparing link. The preparation turns certainly gave a young fireman plenty of tuition in getting an engine ready for the road. Most of the preparation jobs at Stafford Road entailed getting the 'Kings' or 'Castles' ready. Preparing engines was hard, dirty work, building up the fire, breaking up the coal on the tender, carrying sand, cleaning the footplate, under what at Stafford Road were not always ideal conditions. You had to ensure that everything was in order when these top link drivers stepped on to the footplate. By the time you had prepared three of these engines, sometimes four, you could consider that you had done a good day's work.

A memorable event for me while at Stafford Road was when I booked on for the 3.45 am preparing turn. No sooner had I got on to the footplate than the shed foreman came up to the engine, and informed me that I had to go up to the enginemen's cabin where driver Albert Williams was waiting for me. I thought this would be a shunting job for me, and a welcome relief from preparation. Albert informed me that we had to walk up to Wolverhampton, Low Level, and catch the 4.18 am mail to Chester and bring back a light engine, No. 6908, which was required at Stafford Road. This was a real thrill for me, riding to Chester as a passenger on a beautiful July morning and the thought of coming back light engine over what I considered to be a great distance. I had only been as far as Oxley Sidings before, and that was only on a shunting engine. At Chester we walked across to the shed where we reported to the office, and were informed that No. 6908 was on the spare road and had been prepared. There she was; No. 6908 *Downham Hall* stood with her brass and copper glinting in the morning sun. Everything was ready, coal broken and pulled down on the tender towards the footplate, and the fire nicely made up with a good tump under the firehole door, a good head of steam. My excitement was growing at the thought of a 'luxury' trip back to Wolverhampton.

All was ready, and we moved up to the shed signal, I telephoned the signalman at Chester South box to say that we were light engine for Stafford Road. He informed me that we would not be going light engine, but that he was putting us into the bay to await the arrival of the 8.30 am Birkenhead to Paddington express to which we should go 'attached'. My heart sank, my only main line experience being on a slow goods at Banbury, and banking from Wednesbury to West Bromwich. I went back and informed Albert of the arrangements that had been made by the Control. Albert was not in the least perturbed. He assured me that everything would be all right and all I had to do to build up the fire with an even bigger tump under the firebox door, and when we got on the road fire little and often up each side of the firebox, with one over the tump, and occasionally one in each front corner. The shed signal came off and we proceeded into the bay platform, where, standing on the next road, was the engine and Stafford Road men booked to work the express back to Wolverhampton. When informed that we were assisting the fireman was quite pleased as this meant less work for him. The signal came off for the other engine, which pulled out over the points and reversed back on to us. It was obvious then that we were going to be the train engine.

All the time we were in the bay I was fidgeting about, first of all looking in the firebox, then testing the water in the gauge glass, then the injectors. I was hoping that when we started away the right-hand exhaust injector would work perfectly. The water from this injector is warmed by the exhaust steam, consequently warm water is fed into the boiler. This makes a vast difference to your steam pressure, but unfortunately these exhaust injectors could be very temperamental. If you had to rely solely on your left-hand injector this meant that you were putting cold water into the boiler, and in consequence you were having to work harder to maintain your steam pressure.

Dead on 9.08 am the train arrived from Birkenhead with its 12 coaches; it called at Wrexham, Ruabon, Gobowen, Shrewsbury and Wellington after leaving Chester. We pulled out over the points and reversed gently on to the train. As we were the train engine it was my duty to get down and hook on, my mind was in a whirl; if only I had been over the road before with a light engine it would not have been so bad, but here I was, on an express. However, all the questions I had been asking myself were soon obliterated from my mind, as I gazed back down the platform to see the platform inspector's arm raised indicating that all was ready. The guard waved his green flag and we were away, the twin exhausts of engines echoing through the station. The needle was on the red arrow on the pressure gauge, the water was just below the top nut on the gauge glass, everything was perfect, if only I could keep it like this.

Soon we were crossing the Dee and past the racecourse. Already a welcome sound was the steam billowing forth from the safety valve cover. To my relief the exhaust steam injector worked perfectly. By this time I was firing in accordance with Albert's instructions, and after about each six shovelfuls of coal I would glance through the eye glass, and to my relief a thick pall of black smoke would be issuing from the chimney, a sure indication that the coal was burning well, and that the fire was not blocked with too much coal in one spot. We were now flying through Rossett, and Albert shouted in my ear that we were approaching Gresford Bank, and that a bit extra would be necessary, but not to overdo it. To me everything so far was perfect; a tender of Welsh steam coal, the engine steaming perfectly, the exhaust injector maintaining the water level in the boiler, to me a fireman's dream. The engine was responding to every shovelful of coal, and there was no need to use the pricker to breathe life into an over-full part of the firebox.

As we passed quickly out of Wales into England I am afraid my mind was so taken up with my footplate duties as we rattled over the Chirk viaduct, that I had no time to gaze on to the grandeur unfolding below me. It was only occasionally that I turned the exhaust injector off and when I did it was not long before a wisp of steam was emerging from the safety valve cover. Between bursts of firing one's eyes were glued to the eye glass watching for every signal. As you gazed ahead, you were caught up in the thrill of riding on that great heaving, rolling monster, with the smoke and exhaust steam billowing away, the feather of steam issuing from the cylinders, and each blast of the exhaust echoing around the cab.

On passing through Rednal station, on a steady climb, in the distance I could see Haughton Road bridge. That was my signal to give a loud blast on the whistle to attract the attention of the signalman in the Haughton Sidings box, who was my uncle. I wanted to make sure that he was at the window to see me pass on an express. As we got to the box I went over to the driver's side and leant out from the cab waving frantically. The shrill long blast on the whistle had brought him to the window with his lever cloth in his hand. The look of surprise on his face seeing me on the 8.30 am Birkenhead to Paddington express was indeed a sight to behold. As we sped through Baschurch & Leaton I could hardly believe my good fortune. The needle had hardly moved off the red arrow on the steam pressure gauge since leaving Chester, No. 6908 was obviously an engine in prime condition. We were now at the top of Hencott Bank and Albert closed the regulator as we made our sharp descent through Coton Hill Sidings. By now I had shut off the exhaust injector, and put on the left-hand injector to stop the engine frantically blowing off as we entered Shrewsbury station. As we arrived I pulled out my English Lever watch; these watches were the pride and joy of all Western enginemen. My watch agreed with the station clock: dead on time, 10.33. We were due away again at 10.42. Albert came over to my side to watch the platform operations and this gave me the opportunity to break up some of the larger lumps of coal and shovel it towards the front of the tender. Just a little time left to sweep up the footplate, and turn the pet pipe on to the tender to dampen down the dust. The platform was thronged with people and one wondered how they would all cram into the train. Of course this was in the days when if you joined a train *en route* there was very little chance of finding a seat and you had either to sit or stand in the corridor.

We were soon away again from platform 4, and the bustling activity of Shrewsbury station, for Shrewsbury was the gateway to the North and West of England, Central and South Wales. As we left the platform on a sharp curve we were soon passing that great Severn Bridge Junction box, and out into Abbey Foregate. Soon after leaving Walcot we passed the sugar beet sidings at Allscott, and started on a steady climb up through Admaston. The blast of both engines must have reverberated for miles around as we tackled this climb and into the cutting through Admaston platform. On emerging from the cutting, the distant signal for Wellington No. 4 box came into view at caution, which meant that we should have to come to a halt before entering Wellington. Every distant so far had been in our favour. As we rounded the curve towards the Crewe branch, I could see that the outer home signal was off, that meant that we should have a clear run into Wellington.

Although I had not been on the footplate before between Chester and Wolverhampton, I knew from my boyhood days that we were now in for a stiff climb out of Wellington, with the regulator right across and the reversing gear well down. Glancing at the chimney there was plenty of black smoke, so I felt fairly confident, even more so when a good head of steam issued from the safety valve cover. We were now passing the Haybridge Iron Works and on past Ketley Junction; soon we were passing the Wrekin Foundry, and I looked out on to the back of the works where I had stood as an office boy watching this very express pounding by, dreaming that one day I might be on its footplate. However no time now for nostalgic indulgence, here was a roaring monster demanding every ounce of coal that I could swing through that firebox door.

On through Oakengates station into a deep cutting, and into the tunnel full of steam and smoke. The glow from the firebox hit the tunnel roof and bounced back on to the footplate giving a reddish, ghostly glow. On through Hollinswood Sidings, and the end of our stiff climb. Albert suggested that I get the pricker into the firebox and level the fire over, as most of the hard work was now done, and I could start to work the fire down. For the first time I was able to sit down; with the excitement of the trip and so much to be done on the run I had had no time to relax.

After passing Cosford, we were soon starting to ascend Albrighton Bank, and it was now time to close the firebox door. The large amount of fire would soon be reduced on this last stiff climb before reaching our destination. All that remained for me to do now was to flash the odd shovelful of coal all around the box, and not in the systematic way in which I had been firing previously on the journey. Having reached the top of the Bank, we were soon on the level again and flying through Codsall and then Oxley North Junction. I wanted to make sure that the engine was 'blowing off' as we charged through Oxley Sidings, for I was sure that some of my mates would be firing on the shunters and I wanted to draw their attention to the fact that I was firing on this express, and that I had more than enough steam at the end of the journey.

Dead on 11.27 am we were pulling into Wolverhampton (Low Level), where we uncoupled from the train and were soon on our way to Stafford Road Shed. Under the coal stage I glanced into the firebox; there was just a thin spread all over the box, I had worked it just right for the fire dropper. Walking to the office to book off, my mind was still going over the events of the last few hours. With all the goods and passenger work which was to follow in my railway career, this early and exciting experience was the one which was to remain most indelibly engraved on my mind.

I was soon to learn that not all engines on main line work were as easy to fire as No. 6908. Each engine had it own characteristics and whilst some would steam at the sight of a shovelful of coal, others had to be coaxed and cajoled, extending to the limit the skills of the fireman. Leaking tubes, fallen brick arches, coal that with every shovelful caused clinker over the fire bars, continuous use of the pricker and the dart, all these problems went to make up what was called in enginemen's terms a 'rough trip'.

I was soon back down to earth, and back on the routine shunting jobs, and engine preparation. Having being in lodgings from my first day on the railway, the urge for home comforts began to take over, and I decided to apply for a transfer to Wellington.

It may well have been that when preparing the 'Kings' and 'Castles' at Stafford Road, and building up the fires in their great fireboxes, I imagined that it would not require the same effort on my part to swing the coal down the front and sides of the '37XX' and '44XX' class which operated on the Wenlock branch. I must say that deep down I had a lurking desire to work over the branch where my boyhood longings for a railway career had been fostered.

I eventually moved to Wellington in June 1942, a shed which was vastly different both in size and work allocated to it to what I had been used to. Prior to World War II the shed had about 22 sets of men, however, during the early part of the war additional relief turns were allocated to the shed, together with three additional shunting turns, giving a total of 33 sets of men. Also, Much Wenlock, with its three sets of men, came under Wellington. The routes covered were Wellington to Craven Arms, Wellington to Crewe via Market Drayton, and, on the main line, Shrewsbury and Leamington. Up until the early 1930s the Wellington men also worked an early morning goods to Stoke via Market Drayton. Certain Wellington drivers also signed the road to Chester, so on odd occasions a fireman would be given the opportunity to fire over this route.

The engine shed at Wellington was originally a goods shed built by the Shrewsbury & Birmingham Railway Co. However, on 15th July, 1867 the LNWR and GWR Joint Committee requested its Engineer to convert the goods shed into an engine shed. This work must eventually have been carried out by the GWR, for on 3rd April, 1868 the latter submitted an account for the sum of £635 5s. 8d. to the Joint Committee in respect of the cost of conversion. The shed contained three roads, one being a through road on to a stop block at the rear of the shed. Attached to the shed was the stores, and a fitting shop, which was also shared by the boiler washers. Outside the shed and near the stores was a wooden building acting as an office for the shed foreman and his clerk. The enginemen's accommodation was very basic; it had in fact been a broad gauge coach, with a wash basin in the corner, and one cold water tap; not much hope of removing too much coal dust and grime accumulated after a hard day's slog. There was no room for personal lockers; these were housed in the shed and proved ideal receptacles for collecting the dirt and grease which abounds in an engine shed. This cabin was also used by the coalmen, tube cleaners and firedroppers.

It was not until after World War II that a substantial brick-built air raid shelter situated between the shed and the coal stage was taken over and utilised as the enginemen's cabin. This indeed was luxury itself, with hot and cold water laid on, large windows, plenty of space, and the personal lockers removed from the shed into the new cabin.

At Wellington there were only three links consisting of shunting, middle, and top links. The men in the shunting link worked in the Wellington goods yard, and Hollinswood Sidings. The middle link consisted of passenger and goods work, over the Wenlock branch, and to Crewe and Shrewsbury. The top link was all passenger work between Shrewsbury, Wolverhampton, Crewe and Leamington. The men at Much Wenlock worked the passenger trains over the Wenlock branch, and one morning goods train from Presthope to Craven Arms.

I found it quite a change coming to a shed with only three links, after being at Stafford Road and Oxley with literally dozens of links and so many jobs in each link. There was one link at Oxley, the spare link, which consisted of 53 turns, and, by the end the year, anyone working in this link could claim that they had booked on every half-hour around the clock.

I well recall my first turn at Wellington, my driver being Bill Bevan, who also acted as deputy shed foreman from time to time. I had to book on at 1.00 pm to prepare the engine, which this day was No. 5127. We were due off shed at 1.45 pm to act as station pilot until we worked the 2.55 pm local stopping train to Wolverhampton (Low Level), returning with the 4.40 ex-Wolverhampton and back into Wellington at 5.27 pm. An uneventful run was made, after which we put our coaches away into the carriage sidings. For our next job, we were out on to the main up through road and into No. 3 bay platform, and coupled-up to our two-coach train (one auto-trailer and one corridor coach) which was to form the 5.50 pm to Much Wenlock. To me this was the exciting part of the day for I was about to venture into territory which had fostered my interest in railways. Flashing through my mind was the thought of charging over Ketley crossing, changing staffs with the signalman at the platform, and following in the footsteps of my boyhood heroes on the branch, many of whom I had come to know so well on my visits to Ketley and Horsehay during school holidays.

So much for nostalgia and romantic memories, this was now the real thing. Leaving Wellington, our two coaches nearly full with shop assistants and office workers employed in the town, we were soon approaching Ketley Junction, and I could see the signalman descending the box steps, staff in hand, to take up his stance with staff held high. I was still quite a way above the extended staff, which meant that not only had I to reach out from the cab but I had also to bend down to catch the staff. In those few brief seconds the various movements and positions into which I tried to manoeuvre would have been the envy of any contortionist. Another quick decision I had to make was whether to catch it in the palm of my hand and close my fingers around it, or to put my arm through the loop of the staff. I chose the latter but this proved to be a rather painful decision, for at the speed at which we were travelling the staff went up into my arm pit and the metal end swung right round giving me a painful bang on the right shoulder. However, despite my less than welcoming introduction to the branch, I considered that I had to carry out to the letter the instructions of the rule book, and shouted out to my mate the wording on the staff, 'Ketley Jn to Ketley'.

We were now starting on a steep climb into Ketley, and after passing under a cast-iron footbridge Ketley's home signal came into view. Soon we were passing over the level crossing across the main A5 road with a stream of traffic on either side . Here we entered another staff section. This time the staff had to be exchanged with the Ketley signalman on the platform; whilst still running quite sharply into the platform I had to give up the Ketley Jn staff with one hand, and quickly take up the Horsehay staff in the other. Fortunately for me, my introduction into the art of staff exchanging was being carried out on a summer's evening. My experience on dark winter nights and early mornings was yet to come.

Leaving Ketley we were soon on a sharp climb of 1 in 45 as we approached Lawley Bank station and into a deep cutting, before plunging into Horsehay tunnel. Having travelled as a passenger over the line on many occasions, I was fully aware that as we emerged from the tunnel the gradient would change sharply. Little did I realise the impact this sudden change had on the engine. Bill had already warned me to keep the water in the gauge glass well near the top nut; as we made our sudden drop of 1 in 40 towards Horsehay station, I saw the reasoning behind Bill's warning, the water in the gauge falling well below the half-way level.

I realised over the days and weeks ahead that the switch-back landscape of this branch needed all the latent skills of the engineman and his fireman in the working of both passenger and goods trains.

Rounding the sharp curve towards Horsehay station, I saw looming up before me a staff catcher. Was I going to get the staff on to the protruding arm? Yes! I managed it, but before I had had time to congratulate myself the signalman was standing at the edge of the platform holding up the Lightmoor staff for me to take up. Rushing into the platform I sang out to Bill, 'Horsehay-Lightmoor staff'. We now seemed to be disgorging more passengers than we were picking up. Still on a sharp descent, our next stop was Doseley Halt. This particular section, as I was to learn later, could be a nightmare for a driver of a non-fitted vacuum goods after a shower of rain, especially if the distant signal was 'on' for Doseley Crossing, which meant that the crossing gates were across the line. Just a little over-application of the brakes, meant that the wheels on the engine would pick up and you would find yourself sliding like a toboggan perilously close to those closed gates.

On to Lightmoor, and here I was faced with another staff catcher. At this point we were travelling at a good speed, and instead of dropping the staff on to the arm, I let it go too quickly and caught the tip of the arm which flung the staff into the air and down the embankment towards the Madeley branch. I well recall that the signalman was standing at the box window, and to avoid his reactions I immediately turned and looked the other way.

Now, for a while, I could forget staff changing problems as we were on a double line from here into Buildwas. Many times, as a passenger, I had admired the view from the carriage window, but from the footplate as you emerged from the cutting below Cherry Tree Hill the scene took on an entirely new perspective, as the vista of the Coalbrookdale valley opens out before you.

With the engine steaming well, my only duties were to keep my eyes on the signals and the water level in the gauge glass. Soon we were crossing the Albert Edward Bridge and the River Severn below and running into the high level station at Buildwas Junction, where at the north end of the platform the 5.00 pm from Craven Arms was standing, ready to depart for Wellington. We had to run past the platform on the through road and then reverse back on to the Wellington train. Here I was informed by my mate to take water to enable us to have a little more time at Wenlock to 'brew up' and have something to eat. By now I was beginning to feel a little 'peckish', for since leaving Wellington at 2.55 pm for Wolverhampton, there had been no time for a break. After filling the tank with water, I started to build up my fire in readiness for the long 1 in 40 haul up through Farley Dingle. At 6.36 pm we were away with the regulator well across, and the reversing lever right down, to enable us to get a good start at this stiff climb. I am afraid on my first trip up this bank I had over prepared, the safety valve cover was nearly lifting off and the boiler was over full; with nowhere else to go the excess water was issuing from the chimney with each blast and descending on to the cab and eye glasses in a shower of hot, sooty water. This necessitated Bill opening the cylinder steam cocks to relieve them of this great volume of water. What a scene this would have presented to the people on the station drive below, and what a godsend for the lineside photographer.

We were soon charging up through the Dingle, the echoes from the engine blast rebounding first from one side, and then from the other side of the valley, giving anyone at a distance the impression that we were hauling seven or eight coaches up this incline. First the Farley Brook was on our right-hand side, then to our left, as it came pounding down the valley. On past the old mill and to Farley Halt with the Rock House public house towering above us; on leaving the Halt to our left were Farley Sidings with their long line of petrol tank wagons, filled from the hidden tanks in the lofty mounds of earth and rock rising above the sidings. This had once been the site of the Bradley limestone quarries.

Continuing our steep climb over Farley Crossing, and on past the former sidings of the South Wales and Cannock Chase limestone quarries, we were soon entering an avenue of conifer trees, and the approach to Much Wenlock station. On the opposite side to the single platform was the well laid out rock garden with its conifers and shrubs, and two fountains which sadly had long since ceased to operate. What a delightful spot to while away the time while waiting for the Wellington or Craven Arms train. In such idyllic surroundings, I am sure the passengers would be prepared to forgive the station master in the event of a train being a little overdue.

Standing on the platform, the signalman was waiting to accept the Buildwas-Wenlock staff from me. I was quickly down off the footplate and hooking off, aware that every minute gained here would add to our meal break.

From the station, we went out over the points towards the goods yard, and back around the loop and on to the other end of our coaches. I soon realised that my break was going to be very short, for I found that the coal in No. 5127's bunker was now well towards the back and getting further from my reach. I was fully aware that I should need a ready supply of coal for the long haul up from Buildwas to Horsehay tunnel on the return journey. Into the bunker I got, with coal pick and shovel to get the coal down to the bunker door to make life easier for the return journey.

We were away from Wenlock at 7.05 pm, 'right time' and I soon realised that the reason for our rapid descent down Farley Dingle was that we were due in Buildwas at 7.14 pm, and within that nine minutes we had also to make a stop at Farley Halt. After handing over the Wenlock staff we were soon away again crossing over the Severn Valley line and out over the Albert Edward Bridge, and starting our steep climb through the Coalbrookdale valley and on to Lightmoor; constant swinging of the shovel was necessary on this section. With the continual starting and stopping, I soon found that it was much more difficult to maintain the fire in a suitable condition than if I was on a continuous run. Soon we were leaving Lightmoor, and once again I faced the problem of picking up the staff from the picking-up post. I played safe and put my arm through the loop of the staff. If you miss putting a staff on to a 'catcher' you can continue on, but if you fail to pick up the staff from a picking-up post, this means stopping the train and going back for it. If this happened on a passenger train you would certainly not be popular with your driver, or the signalman.

On arrival at Doseley Halt, I found that the engine comes to a stand on the steepest part of the rise, and in consequence we had to set back with the train to the crossing keeper's cabin to enable us to get away. On my first trip on the branch I found that I was a little too anxious to start to work down my fire, for on leaving Doseley I got the pricker into the fire box to level the fire over, but had failed to take into account the punishment that the fire still had to take, on the last section of the rise to Horsehay. On arrival at Horsehay, I found that the needle on the pressure gauge was falling back, and the water in the glass was coming down. We were chimney first, and when we entered Horsehay tunnel we would be on a sharp descent into Lawley Bank; with half a glass of water now showing when we emerged from the tunnel the water in the gauge glass would be virtually out of sight. Fortunately for me, the driver could watch out for the guard's signal, which gave me the opportunity to swing a few shovelfuls of coal around the firebox, and with the blower hard on I was able to get more water into the boiler. Away from Horsehay on the last stretch of our climb, we were soon plunging into Horsehay tunnel. I opened the firebox door to shed some light on the gauge glass, and to my relief there was about two inches of water showing.

The going was now easy through Lawley Bank, Ketley and arrival back into Wellington, 'right time' at 7.52 pm. We were then used as station pilot for about an hour, going on to the shed about 9.15 pm. So ended my first trip over the branch, and I must say I had not found it particularly easy.

One thing that I missed at Wellington was that I did not get called for the early morning shifts, i.e. turns between 12 midnight and 6.00 am, and there were plenty of these turns here. This was because I was outside the three mile call limit. I had to rely entirely on my alarm clock, but fortunately for me, when the clock went off my mother always heard it and gave me no peace until I got out of bed.

Talking of early morning turns, I found when booking off on the Saturday night of my first week that I had to book on at 12.02 am on Monday morning. Men were not booked on at midnight otherwise they would have had to be paid Sunday rate. On this turn you prepared two engines and carried out certain shed duties helping out the shed chargeman. In addition to the foreman at Wellington, there was a chargeman on each of three shifts, who had formerly been a footplateman, but had been fetched off the footplate for medical reasons.

On the Tuesday morning we would book on at 3.05 am, leave the shed at 3.50 am after preparing the engine, and carry out shunting duties in the Wellington GW Yard. We would be relieved at 10.45 am, walk back to the shed and book off. We would then book on again at 11.50 pm on the Tuesday night, prepare the engine and then work the 12.50 am Wellington to Coleham (Shrewsbury) goods, from where, after shunting and putting away our train, we would go light engine to Coton Hill the main GW goods yard at Shrewsbury. From there we would work the 3.45 am goods to Market Drayton, the bulk of the traffic on this train consisted of vans loaded with cigarettes and tobacco from W.D. & H.O. Wills factory at Bristol for the Potteries. After working the train to Wellington we would take water, and run round, and work the train on to Market Drayton; where, at Silverdale Junction, it would be taken on by the LMS over the old North Stafford line ('The Knotty') to Stoke. We would then complete our duty by working the 8.00 am stopping passenger train back to Wellington.

On the Saturday night we would book on at 10.45 pm, walk over to the platform and relieve the men on the 9.35 pm passenger from Wolverhampton, put the coaches away in the carriage sidings, and then go down to the goods yard and work the 11.30 pm goods to Coton Hill, returning with a goods to Wellington, and booking off at about 5.00 am. The end of a very varied week. In the link in which I was placed there were about 17 turns so consequently it would take about four months to work through the link.

The first train from Wellington over the branch was the 5.20 am empty stock to Buildwas, returning from there at 6.05 am and picking up workmen for Sinclair's Iron Works and the Wrekin Foundry at Ketley, and for the Sankey's Castle Works at Hadley. On this particular turn we used to book on at 4.20 am and invariably would find that you had to get the engine ready inside the shed. Your first job was to check the tool box to see you had all the necessary tools, then open the smokebox door to check the baffle plate was secure; if necessary fill up the sand boxes, and start to build up the fire, breaking up any large lumps of coal and cleaning up the footplate. Most firemen endeavoured to get to work before their driver, thereby enabling them to collect the oil and cotton waste from the stores, fill the oil feeder and have it warmed for the driver to commence his duties.

On completion of preparation duties you moved down to the water column, then you would telephone the signalman in No. 3 box and inform him that you were ready to leave the shed. Very often in my early days in the link the engine would be No. 2778, an open cab tank engine, and after preparing this engine in the close confines of the shed the sweat would be pouring off you. More often than not you would go bunker first to Buildwas, speeding down from Horsehay to Lightmoor on a bitter cold winter's morning with the icy wind blowing around your ears, and the tears streaming from your eyes, and nothing else to hang on to but cold steel which froze your fingers at the very touch. On these occasions I often wondered if my boyhood visions of working on the footplate on this branch had been misguided!

As a boy I had often travelled with my parents to Much Wenlock by train to visit relatives, but I had never travelled beyond there, which to me was the unknown. I knew that the train continued on over Wenlock Edge to a place called Craven Arms. However, I was given the opportunity to explore that unknown when my turn came round in the link to work the 7.10 am Wellington to Much Wenlock passenger arriving in Wenlock at 8.05 am. After putting our coaches away, we shunted in the yard, and then worked the 8.45 am goods to Presthope. Leaving Wenlock we were still on a 1 in 40 climb up to Wenlock Edge and Westwood Sidings, and then we levelled out for the run into Presthope. I well remember this first trip was on another open cab engine, No. 2772. At Presthope we changed over with Wenlock men working the 8.17 am Wellington to Craven Arms passenger. The engine on the passenger was

Much Wenlock station in March 1943. The group standing alongside '44XX' class 2-6-2T No. 4403 from left to right are guard Ted Jones, fireman Ken Jones (author), driver Jack Edwards and Wenlock porter-guard Mrs Chadd.   *Author's Collection*

No. 4403, one of the '44XX' class which were the ideal workhorses for this branch. On leaving Presthope we were soon into a deep cutting and entering Presthope tunnel, and as I have mentioned elsewhere, the sight on emerging from that tunnel was breath-taking with Wenlock Edge towering above you, Ape Dale opening out before you, and a backcloth of the Stretton Hills: a sight which I am sure was one of the finest to be seen on any stretch of Shropshire railway track.

With a good fire in the firebox and the engine steaming well, I was able to drink in the rural delights of this most charming area. As we approached Marsh Farm Junction on the Shrewsbury to Hereford line, I was told by my mate Tom Pinches that at the Junction there was no staff catcher, and that I should hand the staff to the signalman. As we approached the box there was no sign of him standing at the foot of the box steps, and I was getting a little concerned. Suddenly out of the box window appeared what seemed to be a white cloth being waved, however, on closer scrutiny I could see that it was the old signalman's white flowing beard just wafting in the breeze as it rested on the ledge of the box window, and his arm extended from below this flowing mass to grasp the staff from my hand. A look of surprise was registered on my face, and as I gazed across at my mate I could see a wry smile on his face.

We were now on the main line and the small wheels of No. 4403 were eating up rapidly the remaining miles into Craven Arms. To me Craven Arms was an entirely new railway experience, with the North to West of England expresses flying through, coal trains from South Wales to Birkenhead Docks, and the Central Wales goods trains waiting to be banked up the steep climb towards Knighton by the former LMS '2F' 0-6-0 tender engines with their distinctive cab protectors for use when banking tender first. After arriving at the down platform I got down and hooked off, and we then proceeded to the water column at the far end of the platform, filled our tank, and then ran back on the up road to run round our two coaches.

I was soon to learn that there was quite a ritual to be performed with regards to the coupling up of the coaches; as we backed gently towards the coaches our guard, George Evans, was standing by the coach, and as I was informed by George that the screw shackle on the engine required to be turned eleven times. If it was any tighter, it was would cause undue oscillation, and the passengers in the front coach would experience a far from comfortable ride. Although I worked this turn many times during my time at Wellington, George never failed to carry out this procedure at Craven Arms; all other firemen vouched to this same experience.

The working of the 8.17 am Wellington to Craven Arms, together with other trains over the branch, brought into sharp focus the vast difference between the operations on a branch line and the main line. The branch line was an institution where you got to know each individual member of the station staff, the regular members of the travelling public, the farmer delivering his milk each morning, the pigeon-fancying miners at Ketley, Lawley Bank and Horsehay, the paper boy collecting his morning and evening papers. You got to know the signalman, porter, or ganger who could get you a rabbit, a dozen eggs, or a bundle of pea and bean sticks during the gardening season. Or if you required your shoes soleing and heeling, the signalman at Much Wenlock was always ready to oblige.

To those residing alongside the line their daily routine was governed by the passing of each branch train: when to get up, when to prepare meals, when to call the children in for bed. On this branch there was no summer service between June and September with its excursions and relief trains to disrupt the daily train routine. There could perhaps be the occasional Sunday School trip, or a Friendly Society outing, and the Saturday night excursion to Wolverhampton and Birmingham. Apart from these extras, life proceeded at a very leisurely pace. The only time that a little excitement could be detected was when a passenger train was running late, and passengers on board had to make a connection either at Wellington or Craven Arms. At each station they would be making known their concern to the guard, and he in turn would ask the station master or porter to contact Wellington or Craven Arms to hold back the connecting train.

On the main line, with its bustling activity, to be stopped was the cause of annoyance to all concerned. No time to drink in the delights, or otherwise, of the area through which you would be passing. No time to get to know the individual passengers or its staff. Speed was of the essence, and in consequence it lost the charm of the rural branch line.

Returning now to the branch, I well recall two instances highlighting the fact that the service offered to its passengers very often extended beyond the instructions laid down in the Rule Book. The first relates to the 9.23 am passenger train from Much Wenlock to Craven Arms. On a Wednesday morning this train always had to stop at Coates Crossing between Longville and Rushbury, and we had to make sure that we stopped the centre of the auto-coach on the crossing. The guard would then pull over a lever in the coach which released the steps and extended them out from the coach on to the crossing. The lady crossing keeper would then alight with her weekly shopping. Coates Crossing was the home of the Longville and Rushbury station master, and his wife was employed as the crossing keeper. This was purely an occupation crossing used mainly by farm tractors and wagons passing from the nearby Coates Farm to its adjoining fields under Wenlock Edge. The second instance, also on Wednesday morning, involved the 11.50 am Much Wenlock to Wellington. A lady from Farley would join the train at Much Wenlock with her weekly shopping and perambulator. The lady resided at a house in Farley Dingle, just below Farley Halt. She never alighted at the Halt, the obliging trainmen always bringing the train to a stand outside the house where the steps of the auto-coach would be extended and the lady would alight, followed by the guard gradually inching the perambulator down the extended steps. The welfare of our passengers was all important.

Whilst on the subject of breaking the rules, one event which still stands out clearly was a day when working the 3.50 pm goods from Much Wenlock to Wellington. After the completion of shunting operations in the yard at Wenlock, I was approached by the goods checker and asked to drop off some coal for him at Farley Crossing, his wife being the crossing keeper there. I said that I would, and I placed three very large lumps of coal by the cab door. Approaching the crossing, I pushed the first lump off with my foot, and it landed safely, but the second and third lumps hit the protective boards over the signal rodding, and on impact bounced back into the air and through the plate class windows of the crossing box.

I lived in fear and trepidation for the next 24 hours until I returned to Wenlock the next day. To my relief, I was assured by the checker that he had reported that the windows had been vandalised. Here I had committed two cardinal sins, firstly by smashing the windows, and secondly by providing the crossing keeper with loco coal. The dropping off of coal for any railway staff was an offence for which not only the fireman could be severely punished, but his driver also.

It was essential for every driver and fireman to keep a record of his forthcoming turns, for having to book on during virtually every one of the 24 hours it was necessary if he wanted to attend any social function to be aware of his turn in that week. Social life, however, for a footplate man was very limited, your whole life revolving around the job. You would be booking on when every one else was finishing work, or going out for their evening's entertainment. You would go for three or four weeks and not know what it was like to have a good night's sleep. In my early days at Stafford Road, I well recall that there was one link called the 'ticket link'. When you booked off duty all that would appear on the duty roster was 'to be notified'. After having eight hours rest, they could send the call man round with a ticket notifying the hour to book on, and the train to work. This could have been a local train or a double-home job to London or Bristol. Men in this link were virtual prisoners, for after booking off the men had to stay around their home and be available when that 'ticket' arrived. Fortunately, before the commencement of World War II, the Unions were successful in getting this method of working abolished.

Following that slight digression, I now return to the question of the keeping of a record of weekly turns. Whilst looking through some old papers recently I came across my diary for 1943, which made most interesting reading after a lapse of 50 years. The entries recalled the turn on which I was booked, the time of booking off, in many cases the engine booked to the particular job, and my driver if it was not my regular mate. The first entry records the following: 'Jan. 1st. 9.45 pm Hollinswood shunter Engine No. 1758.' On 25th January, the following entry appears: '9.00 pm Relief - Down to Coton Hill Shrewsbury to relieve Birkenhead Bordesley-Goods.'

As I mentioned earlier, quite a number of these relief jobs were introduced to Wellington at the commencement of the war, and the booking-on time usually coincided with the departure from Wellington for Shrewsbury of one of the fast trains. In the case of the 9.00 pm relief, if there was no train to be relieved at Wellington, Control instructed you to catch the 9.53 pm from Wellington, which was the 6.10 pm from Paddington, always referred to locally as the 'Zulu'. Likewise on the 4.00 am relief you would catch the 5.10 am to Shrewsbury; this train was the 12.05 am from Paddington, and after it left Wolverhampton, for reasons unknown to me it was always called the 'Continental'.

For Saturday 6th February appears the following: '6.00 am LMS Shunter with Bill Bennet'. I always detested this particular turn due mainly to the engine. It was an ex-Lancashire & Yorkshire 0-4-0 saddle tank with the coal stacked at the side of the boiler. To fire it you needed to be a contortionist, a teaspoon would have been more appropriate for firing it than a shovel. This engine had been shedded at the former Trench LMS shed, which was on the Stafford to Wellington line. When the shed closed in 1942, the engine and its two sets of men were transferred to Wellington. Firstly you would shunt the LMS yard at Wellington, and then the LMS yard at Trench.

At Wellington we had a number of passenger trains to Crewe and on 4th May, 1943 I was on the 5.55 pm to Crewe returning from Crewe at 8.55 pm. I always felt when running into Crewe that we were interlopers, encroaching on LMS territory. Also we seemed so insignificant as we ran in with our '51XX' class and four coaches, alongside a 'Princess', or 'Royal Scot' class on a Euston to Glasgow express. However, I was less discouraged after listening to some of the drivers recalling that when they were firemen running into Crewe they would very often be greeted on the platform by that celebrated architect of LMS locomotive design and development, William A. Stanier, who was a former GWR man. I was told that he loved to talk about GW locomotive performance, and his days at Swindon.

My diary for Sunday 11th July, 1943 has the following entry: 'Booked on at 5.10 am down to Shrewsbury as passengers. Worked the Cardiff to Birkenhead goods, relieved at Chester'. When working with a driver by the name of Eddy Bryan on relief turns I was fairly certain of getting a job to Chester, as Eddy signed the road there being a former fireman at Chester. These turns made a change from the Wenlock and Crewe branch work.

Many and varied were the problems that faced railwaymen during wartime, and enginemen had their share of these; relieving trains whose engines had been on the road for hours on end, and in some cases days; fires blocked with clinker, tubes leaking, and brick arches down in the firebox. When what they called the 'block' was on you would spend hours in some cold exposed loop, not knowing when your relief would arrive. When an air raid warning was given, you would be stopped at the next signal box, and if the raid was not imminent you would be instructed by the signalman to proceed with caution. If the raid was likely to take place, if on a goods you would be turned into a loop or sidings, but a passenger train would be held on the main line.

One other wartime problem facing enginemen was the shortage of tools. The fireman's first job before preparing the engine was to search the tool boxes of other engines. All tool boxes were supposed to be locked and the keys handed in to the stores when an engine was brought to shed, but unfortunately these keys had been lost and consequently you seldom could obtain your keys from the stores. It was usual for the fireman to have his own shovel and hand brush. When you booked off, you would put your hand brush in your locker, and you would have to sort out a spot somewhere around the shed in which to hide the shovel. To ensure that no one else who found the shovel would use it, it was usual to burn your initials on to the handle of the shovel. Of course, you would only use your own shovel if you were bringing the engine back on to the shed. If you were on a turn on which you were to be relieved, you would have to make do with any old shovel which you found on the engine.

One turn for which I had a particular dislike, and this applied to most of the firemen in the link, was the 10.00 pm Saturdays-only to Much Wenlock. With the closure of the section from Much Wenlock to Craven Arms to passenger traffic in December 1951, the three drivers at Much Wenlock were transferred to Wellington. Two of the firemen left the railway, and one was made a driver. This last train to Much Wenlock was worked by a former Wenlock driver, who although he had been transferred to Wellington, did not have to move his home from Wenlock. After arrival in Wenlock and putting the engine on the shed, the driver would book off and go home. It then became the duty of the fireman to drop the fire, clean out the smokebox ashes, and rake out the ash-pan. With no means of getting back to Wellington at that hour the fireman had to sleep on a bench in the shed cabin, and on the Sunday morning catch a Midland Red bus back to Wellington. Sleeping in that cabin on a winter's night left a lot to be desired. Whilst you were away from your home station, but not actually working, you were paid the princely sum of 3s. 6d. per hour.

Fortunately, to the relief of the Wellington firemen, this working did not last too long. This last train was later worked by a Wellington driver and the engine returned light to Wellington.

Knowing that firemen from other depots who had passed out as drivers, and whose seniority number was only just a little way ahead of mine, had been moved for promotion to other depots, I knew that my time for moving was near at hand. Having moved around quite a bit in my railway career, and having married and settled down in Wellington, the thought of moving to some far-flung depot on the Western Region did not appeal. In consequence, I left on 3rd December, 1954 and went back behind a desk in a local government office. I never regretted the move, but having said that, my memories seldom centre around my days in local government, but those of my footplate days are ever clear. The dirt, dust and grime, the booking-on at all times of the day and night in all weathers did not blur that ray of excitement as you mounted the footplate and backed on to your train, whether to speed through the countryside or to rumble along on local goods, the thrill was the same. Will the drivers of the diesel and electric locomotives be able to relate to their grandchildren that same thrill? I wonder.

Chapter Ten

Declining Years

Rumours of closure abounded in the early 1930s when the ever increasing competition of road transport began to take its toll. These rumours sprang not from the railway management but from the local populace who were witnessing less and less passengers boarding the trains. This, however, did not deter the majority of people from thinking that the line was an essential part of their daily lives, and if it got to the stage that Mr & Mrs Smith and family were the only users of the line to Wellington, it would still continue to run. The word 'economics' was never mentioned. The whole atmosphere of the branch throughout this period gave the impression of success: well maintained stations, no cut backs in train services and very little reduction in staff. The only small economy effected was the merger of two or three stations under one station master.

Following the end of World War II, it was obvious that the rapidly declining numbers of passengers between Wenlock and Craven Arms would bring about its inevitable closure. In 1951 notices appeared at all stations between Wenlock and Craven Arms announcing closure of the line to passenger traffic. The Wenlock Borough Council protested vigorously to British Railways, and the aid of neighbouring local authorities was sought, such as Church Stretton Urban District Council, Atcham Rural District Council and Ludlow Rural District Council, the line running through parts of these authorities. However, no support was forthcoming from them, and their feelings on the matter are best summed up by the following reply received from Ludlow R.D.C:

The Council do not feel justified in opposing the attempt of British Railways to effect economies by closing down an unremunerative service. The Council had noted the proposed services to be operated by the 'Midland Red' to replace the passenger rail services shortly to be withdrawn, and considered them satisfactory.

The last days of this section were recorded by Mrs Lilian Hayward of Ticklerton, a small hamlet near Harton Road station. She contributed regularly to local newspapers on matters relating to the Shropshire countryside. Writing in the *Shrewsbury Chronicle* in December 1951 she had the following to say:

I well remember being taken by my grandfather the Revd R.J. Buddicom to Harton Road station in the 1890s to see the engine of the train decorated with oak boughs on oak apple day, and the other occasion was to see flags attached to the engine on the occasion of Queen Victoria's Diamond Jubilee. To many of the older people in the district the closing of the line will be a matter of regret. All my life I have heard our little train's cheerful whistle, and its hiccoughing puffs as it left Harton Road station. The line of smoke seen from my window has been as good as a clock. When the train has made its last journey I shall feel as if a dear friend has passed away.

The Revd R.J. Buddicom, to whom Mrs Hayward refers, was a shareholder in the Wenlock Railway Company, and he fought a long and hard battle to ensure that the railway from Wenlock to Craven Arms was routed down Ape Dale, the route eventually taken, and not down the Corve Dale to Craven Arms.

When engine No. 4406 pulled out of the bay at Craven Arms on the night of 29th December, 1951 bound for Wellington, a 90 year-chapter in railway history was to close. On the footplate were Wenlock men, Joe Watkins the driver and fireman Tony Faulkner, for whom it was a sad occasion, not just because it was the last passenger train between Craven Arms and Wenlock, but the following Monday the shed at Wenlock would close, and they would have to travel each day to Wellington Shed to book on.

With the closure of this section, the railway passenger was to be denied the joy of witnessing one of the most scenic railway routes in Shropshire. The line remained open from Wenlock to Longville, mainly for the conveyance of Bibby's and Silcock's cattle feeds to their

A Stephenson Locomotive Society excursion headed by 'Dean Goods' 0-6-0 No. 2516 enters Farley Halt on 23rd April, 1955.   *Real Photographs*

A sad sight: Rushbury station looking towards Much Wenlock with the track removed and the station falling into decay.   *David Lawrence*

A scene all too common on our branch lines in the late 1950s and early 1960s. A scene of dereliction and decay at Presthope on 30th August, 1958 with the 9.35 am goods ex-Much Wenlock standing at the platform. Behind the signal box can be seen the former station master's house.   *Hugh Davies*

respective warehouses in the yard at Longville. In addition to this traffic, limestone was still being conveyed from Westwood Sidings. The whole of the goods work on this remaining section was worked by the 9.35 am ex-Wenlock goods.

Initially the section between Longville and Marsh Farm Jn (7¼ miles) was retained for wagon storage purposes, but in December 1955 it was cut back to a short half-mile section at the Marsh Farm Junction end. The purpose of leaving in this section of track was to enable the Royal Train to be stabled overnight during the visits of members of the Royal Family to Central Wales and the Borders. This section was used on a number of occasions, and as well may be imagined, it created a great deal of interest among the local inhabitants.

The sight of a 'Castle' or 'Hall' class locomotive backing a train of Royal saloon coaches on to this short section was a sight which lives on in the memories of the local residents.

In July and November 1961, British Railways took counts of passengers using the stations and halts between Ketley and Wenlock. The survey revealed that, except on Saturdays, fewer than 40 passengers a day used the intermediate stations, and no more than 60 used the terminus at Wenlock. It was stated by British Railways that the branch was being operated at a loss of £12,300 per year. The annual movement costs, after the introduction of diesel units, amounted to £9,000 which did not include costs of staff and maintenance. All these costs were set against a passenger revenue of £4,000 per year. This damning report was to sound the death knell for passenger train operation and by April 1962 notices were posted at each station and halt announcing the date of closure, and the notice of alternative road transport that would be available.

It was a glorious summer's evening on Saturday 21st July, 1962, but at Much Wenlock station it was a sad and sombre evening for the few hundred people, railway enthusiasts, local residents and passengers who thronged the platform to witness the passing of an institution. On the stroke of 7.50 pm, engine No. 4178 with its wreath of flowers adorning the smokebox door, would pull away from the platform for the last time. On the platform to witness the departure of this last train was George Matthews, the Town Clerk; it was ironic that 100 years previously his counterpart Richard Blakeway had welcomed the first train into Much Wenlock. The station master to start the train on its last journey was Frank Cole, who had long associations with the Wenlock branch, as had his father before him. The driver was Jack Darral, and his fireman was Terry Thorpe, both of Wellington Shed. The guard was Fred Clarke and the assistant guard was Bert Griffiths.

An inspection train at Longville *c.* 1960 with 0-6-0PT No. 5764. The staff are (*from left to right*) driver Jim Sergeant, fireman Cliff Gough, inspection train attendant unknown, guard Jack Johnson. Note the sleepers below the bridge denoting that Longville was the end of the line.

John Smout

Diesel railcar No. W55012 approaches Coalbrookdale viaduct on 9th June, 1962. To the left can be seen the Lower Works by this time part of the Glynwed Foundry Group. To the right above the works is the imposing Literary & Scientific Institute built by the Coalbrookdale Company in 1859.

M. Mensing

The 5.45 pm Wellington to Much Wenlock hauled by '51XX' class 2-6-2T No. 4178 emerging from Heath Hill tunnel on 21st July, 1962; this was to be the last outward passenger train on the branch. This is at the peak of the summit before taking the plunge down into the Lightmoor valley, as indicated by the gradient board to the left of the engine. *M. Mensing*

The end. Prairie tank No. 4178 comes slowly to a stand in the down platform at Wellington on the evening of Saturday 21st July, 1962. Crowds thronged the platform to pay their lasts respects, and to witness the final chapter of nearly 100 years of passenger rail travel between Wellington and Much Wenlock. *M. Mensing*

BRITISH RAILWAYS
(LONDON MIDLAND REGION)

PUBLIC NOTICE

The British Railways Board **hereby give notice in** accordance with Clause 54 of the Transport Act, 1962, that on and from Monday, 6th July, 1964 public freight facilities will be withdrawn from the following **goods** depots, which will be closed completely:—

COALBROOKDALE
DAWLEY AND STIRCHLEY
HORSEHAY AND DAWLEY
*KETLEY
LIGHTMOOR
MADELEY (Salop)
OAKENGATES (Market Street)

★ Parcels facilities to be withdrawn

Station to station wagon load traffic will be **dealt with** at Wellington (Salop).

Coal, coke and patent fuel traffic will be **dealt with at** Wellington (Salop).

Parcels traffic at present dealt with at Ketley station will be dealt with at Wellington (Salop).

The present arrangements for the collection and **delivery** of goods and parcels traffic in the area will continue.

Any further information in respect of these arrangements may be obtained on application to:—

Mr. E. R. WILLIAMS,
DIVISIONAL MANAGER,
LONDON MIDLAND REGION,
43 SMALLBROOK RINGWAY,
BIRMINGHAM, 5.
Telephone Midland 5050. Extension 302

Euston Station,
May, 1964

H. C. JOHNSON,
General Manager

The notice informing the public that freight facilities would be brought to an end between Ketley and Lightmoor Junction and also from stations on the former Coalport branch.

Author's Collection

As the train left, and slowly vanished from sight under the Linden Fields bridge, the remaining throng on the platform would doubtless be recounting their memories of Wenlock station and the line to Wellington: travelling to Coalbrookdale High School, visits to friends and relatives, annual holidays, the excitement of an excursion to distant places, or waiting on the platform with high hopes of a special parcel being brought in by the next train. The scene witnessed at Wenlock was repeated at all stations and halts to Ketley, also every lineside vantage point was taken up with people paying their last respects. If only the same enthusiasm could have been engendered over the previous years as was being witnessed on this July evening, the name of Dr Beeching need never have appeared in the annals of the Wenlock branch.

The first act following the closure of the line to passengers was to close the line between Ketley Jn and Ketley station, and by the end of 1962 the section of track between these two points had been removed. The closure of this section now meant that all freight for the Wenlock branch from Wellington went via the main line to Madeley Jn, then over the Madeley branch to Lightmoor Jn and so via Horsehay to Ketley.

The Wenlock branch followed the pattern of so many branch lines. Following the cessation of passenger traffic, freight trains continued to run for a short while, but it soon became obvious that the death knell was tolling for the remaining freight working. By December 1963 the freight working between Wenlock and Longville was withdrawn. On 19th January, 1964 goods working between Buildwas and Wenlock also ceased to operate, though for a short while afterwards a few hundred yards of this track remained *in situ* from Buildwas and acted as an engineer's siding.

The final blow, however, was to fall on 6th July, 1964, when all freight working ceased between Lightmoor Jn and Ketley. The track between Ketley and Horsehay was very soon lifted, but between Horsehay and Lightmoor Jn the track remained following an agreement between British Rail and Adamson Alliance, the bridge and crane builders, who had taken over the former Horsehay Company's works. The agreement allowed Adamson Alliance the use of this part of the track for the transportation of special girder work at a cost to them of £3,000 per annum. The motive power provided on these specials proved to be of great interest to the railway enthusiast, for never before had this section seen 'Halls', 'Granges', and 'Manors' traversing its tracks. By the late 1970s very little use was being made by Adamson Alliance of the track between Horsehay and Lightmoor Jn, and in May 1979 the last girders to be made at the Horsehay works for transport by rail left Horsehay yard bound for British Steel at Redcar.

The first standard gauge track to be laid by the former Shrewsbury and Birmingham Railway in 1854, the Madeley branch, still remains open. This section between Madeley Jn and Buildwas via Lightmoor still sees coal trains rumbling down the Coalbrookdale valley into Buildwas each day. Following the commissioning of the new Ironbridge 'B' Power Station this section became more heavily used than at any time in its history as 'merry-go-round' coal trains were introduced. Perhaps 'merry-go-round' is a slight misnomer in the case of Ironbridge, as the trains do not traverse a continuous curve of track, as in the case of most other large power stations, but proceed to a head-shunt adjacent to the Buildwas to Wenlock road, on the track bed of the former Severn Valley Railway, just west of Buildwas Jn (itself obliterated by the building of the 'B' station). Here locomotives run round their loaded train before hauling it back in the opposite direction through the discharge hoppers. A quantity of oil is also consumed by the station, and an oil siding was constructed at the east end of the power station site so that this traffic could also be brought in by rail.

In 1979, to celebrate the bicentenary of the building of the first cast-iron bridge in the world, which spans the River Severn at Ironbridge, a limited weekend service of diesel passenger trains was operated from Birmingham (New Street) to a new temporary station erected just south of the viaduct in Coalbrookdale. Sadly, this bold experiment was not an overwhelming success, but nevertheless British Rail were persuaded to repeat the exercise on a few more occasions in the mid-1980s. A number of full-length passenger trains, crowded with rail enthusiasts keen to traverse 'freight only' track, have also visited the branch in recent times, one notable train from Bescot on 6th May, 1990 having no fewer than four locomotives! Following privatisation, such sights are unlikely to be seen again.

A class '47' diesel locomotive hauling a 'merry-go-round' of coal empties from the Ironbridge Power Station on 10th March, 1979. On the right of the clock tower can be seen the tree-lined Brierly Hill where the Coalbrookdale Company in 1792 constructed a tunnel and shaft system to bring their supplies into the works, later replaced by an incline.   *Reg Stanley*

Appearing on the curve below the Captain's Coppice is a class '47'-hauled return empties from the Ironbridge Power Station bound for Bescot in 1979. To the right is the new Coalbrookdale station under construction to coincide with the opening of the Ironbridge Gorge Museum's Museum of Iron.   *Reg Stanley*

The first passenger train at the newly-built station at Coalbrookdale on 27th May, 1979. The station was built near to the Ironbridge Gorge Museum's Museum of Iron at Coalbrookdale. The passenger trains were a Sunday-only service running from Birmingham (New Street) calling at Wolverhampton and on to Coalbrookdale, there were three trains each way. The trains would run on the down line to Buildwas giving the passengers the opportunity to view the Severn valley. The train would then return on the up line when the passengers would alight at the station. *Reg Stanley*

Double-headed class '20s' Nos. 20 020 and 20 106 are seen hauling a 'mery-go-round' coal train to Ironbridge Power Station as it passes the Museum of Iron at Coalbrookdale., 4th July, 1989. *P.G. Barnes*

Preparing '56XX' class 0-6-2T No. 5619 for Telford Horsehay Steam Trust open day on 19th May, 1981 with Reg Stanley on the footplate in the yard at Horsehay. The local fire service have been brought in to provide water. *Reg Stanley*

The Steam Trust's yard at Horsehay with No. 5619 on its first day of steaming on 19th April, 1981. *Reg Stanley*

Chapter Eleven

The Future

The decline in the fortunes of the Wenlock branch, and its eventual closure should have been the end of the story, but fortunately a ray of hope was to shine through the gloom of the events of its later years. This came about in 1963 when the boundaries of the former Dawley Urban District Council were designated a New Town (later with the incorporation of Wellington, Oakengates and Donnington it was to become the New Town of Telford). The nucleus of staff to set up what was then known as Dawley New Town was housed (in 1963) in Hartfield House situated between Horsehay and Doseley. For 12 months the staff at Hartfield House witnessed each day from their office window a '37XX' class pannier tank with two wagons and a van passing on the embankment above them on its journey between Horsehay and Lightmoor Jn, before it was finally withdrawn on 6th July, 1964.

The New Town staff were charged with the task of transforming the scars of the industrial past of this part of the East Shropshire coalfield with its slag tips, and pennystone clay mounds, into a New Town. Amongst the staff was the chief legal and administrative officer, Emyr Thomas, who later became the General Manager of the New Town of Telford. Emyr was a railway enthusiast, and although his task was to take this area into the future, he was aware of the importance of its industrial heritage. From his office he was planning for the future, but from his window he was witnessing, as the goods train passed, the last few days of a link with the past. Emyr was determined that this link should not be broken, but a few years were to pass before his vision of steam traction being seen again between Horsehay and Lightmoor was partly brought to fruition, when Telford Development Corporation designated the Spring Village area of Horsehay as a Conservation Area early in 1972. Negotiations were entered into with Adamson Butterley, the then owners of the bridge and crane building works at Horsehay, for an exchange of land within the Conservation Area which included the Horsehay pool, and the former Horsehay Company's engine shed. This shed was last used in 1958 when the former Horsehay Company withdrew its steam locomotive from shunting operations.

Following the prospect of acquiring an engine shed, the Development Corporation approached the Ironbridge Gorge Museum Trust informing them that they would look with favour on the purchase of a locomotive to be housed in the former engine shed at Horsehay. The Museum Trust lost no time in contacting Woodham Bros at Barry for a suitable locomotive. Whilst they were not successful in obtaining a locomotive of the type that had worked between Ketley and Lightmoor Jn, they did manage to obtain '56XX' class 0-6-2T No. 5619 which had spent most of its working life hauling coal trains in the South Wales valleys. Although negotiations with regards to the exchange of land had not been completed, on 24th October, 1973 Adamsom Butterley gave the Development Corporation permission to house No. 5619 in its engine shed. With the locomotive safely installed in the shed in May 1974 the Ironbridge Gorge Museum Trust, together with Telford Development Corporation, set up a working party to restore the newly acquired locomotive. From this small group of volunteers sprang the Telford Horsehay Steam Trust which came into being on 1st March, 1976. The aims of the Trust were: 'To restore steam locomotives and rolling stock of the type which used to operate on the Wenlock branch, and to operate trains between Horsehay and Lightmoor'.

The services of the dedicated band of volunteers of the Steam Trust were soon in demand for, after completing their restoration work on No. 5619, they took into custody an LNWR 'G2' 0-8-0 No. 9395. This locomotive was part of the National Collection, and at this time it was in the custody of the National Railway Museum at York. After a cosmetic restoration by the Steam Trust it was transported to the Ironbridge Gorge Museum's open air site at Blists Hill as a static display. Further cosmetic work was carried out in 1978 on the Ironbridge Gorge Museum's locomotive No. 5, an engine built by the Coalbrookdale Company in 1865 as a

The Coalbrookdale Company's shunting engine No.5 built by the company in 1865 and sold in 1930. It returned to Coalbrookdale in 1959 as an exhibit in the Allied Ironfounders Museum. This photograph was taken at the Telford (Horsehay) Steam Trust yard awaiting restoration on 24th June, 1978. *Reg Stanley*

Sam Wooley on the footplate of No. 5 outside the Steam Trust's engine shed at Horsehay. Sam was formerly a fireman on the GWR at Stafford Road, Wolverhampton. He joined the Brazilian Railways as a driver in 1913, returning to Shropshire in 1921 when he became the driver on the Horsehay Company's yard shunter remaining there for the rest of his working life. *Reg Stanley*

shunting engine for its works, which continued in this capacity until it was withdrawn in 1932. This locomotive was eventually returned to the Museum in pristine condition, and now has pride of place in the Museum of Iron at Coalbrookdale. To bring a touch of realism to the work of the Trust, GWR auto-trailer No. 38 was purchased; these auto-trailers were a common sight on most of the passenger trains on the branch between the mid-1930s and the early 1950s.

In May 1983 the Horsehay goods yard was conveyed by British Rail to Telford Development Corporation, giving a welcome boost to the activities of the Steam Trust. A little time elapsed before (in July 1983) the Development Corporation leased the station buildings and yard to the Trust at a peppercorn rent. The dream of running trains once again between Horsehay and Lightmoor was coming a little nearer reality. However, the great stumbling block still remained, the purchase of the track between Horsehay and Lightmoor.

Despite protracted negotiations between Telford Development Corporation and British Rail with regards to the purchase price of the land and track between Horsehay and Lightmoor, no agreement could be reached. The Development Corporation insisted that the asking price of £40,000 should include the track, but British Rail was not prepared to meet this request. Consequently British Rail lifted and sold the track, and a little later the land between Horsehay and Lightmoor was purchased by the Development Corporation. This meant that the Horsehay Steam Trust was faced with the situation of having to lay new track at its own expense, a daunting task, but one which they were determined to overcome. The first objective is to lay the track from Horsehay to Doseley Halt and, when funds are available on to Lightmoor. In the meantime the Trust has to be content by operating the short length of track between the yard at Horsehay and Horsehay (Heath Hill tunnel) on certain weekends and Bank Holidays.

The members of the Trust have never viewed their role as simply restoring locomotives, their main aim has been steam operation of the line between Horsehay and Lightmoor. It is hoped that their efforts will be rewarded, and that once again passengers will have the experience of steam and smoke wafting past their carriage windows as they make their way down through Doseley and on to Lightmoor, and perhaps, who knows, at some future date, into Coalbrookdale?

The original station buildings which were situated in the goods yard at Much Wenlock and used by the Wenlock & Severn Junction Railway prior to the opening of the permanent station buildings. This wooden-structured building is now being used as a bowling green pavilion on the Linden Fields, Much Wenlock.   *Author's Collection*

Wellington & Severn Jn Railway Share Prospectus; October 1853

Directors

Henry Dickinson. Chairman	Coalbrookdale
Thomas Campbell Eyton	The Vineyard, Wellington
John Williams	Ketley Hill
Charles Emery	Burcott, Wellington
John Benson	Wellington
William Henry Darby	Brymbo Hall, Wrexham

Bankers

The Shropshire Banking Co. Wellington, Shifnal, & Coalbrookdale

Solicitors

Pritchards, Boycott, & Nicholas. Broseley & Bridgnorth

The Act incorporating this Company (obtained after a severe ordeal) in the session of Parliament just closed, authorises the making of a Railway from the Shrewsbury & Birmingham Railway near Wellington to Coalbrookdale. In the course of the investigation before the Committee of the House of Commons, the utility and importance of this line of Railway were proved by the most conclusive evidence.

By the powers obtained, the Company are entitled to the use of Wellington Station, to distribute traffic to the lines centring at that point, and also to make a junction with the Severn Valley Railway. Thus this Company will link together a continuous line of railway at both termini to all parts of the Kingdom.

A very large population will be directly accommodated by it embracing the following places:

Wellington, Ketley, Lawley, Horsehay, Dawley, Madeley, Coalbrookdale, Ironbridge and Broseley.

Also because of the extensive ironworks coal, and mineral fields, lime, brick and other works in the district a great part of the produce will pass over the railway.

The Company is quite independent of all other companies, but is in possession of facilities for exchanging traffic with the railways in the district. Its own resources are considered amply to remunerate the Shareholders for the cost of construction, which it is believed will be effective.

Seal of the Wellington & Severn Junction Railway showing the Iron Bridge indicating that when the line was incorporated in 1853 it was the intention that the line should be constructed to Ironbridge to connect with the Severn Valley Railway.   *GWR Museum Swindon*

William Penny Brookes' Papers

From the personal papers of William Penny Brookes we glean from the letters which passed between various members of the family, a day by day account of the progress of the building of the railway between Wenlock and Buildwas; and the excitement which prevailed at the prospect of the railway coming into the Town.

The following is a letter dated 8th July, 1859 from Mary, the mother of William Penny Brookes, to Anne, her daughter.

We are likely to have a railway from Ironbridge to Wenlock in the course of another year. Mr Brassey will undertake it, and will take shares to the amount of £18,000 himself, and the remaining £12,000 we hope will be raised next Monday at a meeting at Wenlock of the neighbouring landowners. It is expected to pay better than any line in England, it will be of great importance in this neighbourhood as the lime is so very good, if there were a cheap means of carrying it away, and we shall be supplied with coal cheaper and better than we now get.

On 22nd March, 1860 Maria, the sister of William Penny Brookes, wrote to her younger sister Anne (who was then residing at Bridgnorth) the following:

We hear that next Monday is fixed for cutting the first sod for our Wenlock Railway. Alfred and Edith will perform the ceremony, and all the school children of the town will have a tea at first with all the little boys in the Drum and Fife Band, who of course will play on this occasion, and Mr Wayne will address the children. The Directors will dine with us on that day.

Maria however was wrong in assuming that Alfred and Edith the son and daughter of Andrew Goode Brookes would perform the ceremony of cutting the first sod, the honour of performing this task was bestowed upon Mary, the elder daughter of William Penny Brookes.

Not long after the cutting of the first sod, Maria again wrote to Anne informing her of the progress of the building of the line:

The navvies are working away at the railway in the Shadwell Coppice, through which pretty little wood it passes. Many of the trees are already felled, and they are working a passage through the limestone rock, to the left of the little wood. It will be a change to the old remembered scenes of our childhood.

Mary Brookes again wrote to her daughter Anne on 30th March, 1860, bringing her up to date with the festivities in Wenlock on the day of the cutting of the first sod of the line:

. . . on Monday we had the providing of the cakes, buns, teas, etc., for the children, and after all was over, the Directors, Mr Adney, Mr Amphlett, Mr Horton, and Mr Benson dined with us. Also, the contractor, Mr Brassey's nephew a Mr Seacombe. The land agent Mr Ashdown, the secretary Mr Blakeway, and Mr Potts of Broseley (solicitor) and Burd of Wenlock. Maty has been out this morning giving the men building the line a trifle, there were not many at work but it will be interesting to watch their progress. I wish I could get out to see them. William [her son] bears all these things wonderfully for he was out nearly all Sunday night, had two journeys on Monday morning, and then had to arrange the procession, for if he did not do it, it would be at a standstill . . .

A further letter from Mary to Anne written in 1860 which is undated refers to an accident on the railway:

William has just returned from an accident. A poor man working at the railway in the Allotment Grounds slipped down and a cart went over him and killed him instantaneously.

A letter dated 9th May, 1860 from Adeline a daughter of William Penny Brookes to her Aunt Anne acquaints her with the progress of the building of the line:

. . . they are getting on nicely with the Railway, and will very soon be commencing the bridge across Sheinton Street. They have commenced in several places about Buildwas, we often go to look at it. It is quite interesting to watch its progression . . .

Wenlock Railway Share Prospectus

From the William Penny Brookes papers in the Wenlock Borough Records, the following share prospectus appears in respect of the Much Wenlock and Craven Arms Railway, together with the Coalbrookdale extension.

MUCH WENLOCK & CRAVEN ARMS AND COALBROOKDALE RAILWAY 1860

Share Capital £150,000 in 15,000 shares of £10 each. Deposit £1 per share.
The following noblemen and Gentlemen, locally interested as proprietors of land and otherwise signify their approval:

The Earl of Bradford	
Lord Forester	
Lord Wenlock	
The Mayor of Wenlock	
Sir George Harnage	Belswardine Hall
James Milnes Gaskell	Wenlock Abbey
Moses George Benson	Lutwyche Hall
St John Chiverton Charlton	Apley Castle
Henry Dickinson Esq.	Coalbrookdale Company
Joseph Robinson Esq.	Coalbrookdale Company
Charles Crookes Esq.	Coalbrookdale Company
Beriah Botfield	Decker Hill, Shifnal
R.H. Cheyny	Old Park Iron Works
John Jones	Birchills Works, Walsall
George Barker	Chillington Co.'s Ironworks
Jones & Murcott	Spring Vale Ironworks
Revd Raymond Smythies	Rector of Easthope
Revd Frederick Holtham	Rector of Rushbury
Richard Butcher	Longville
Revd E. Sandford	Rector, Eaton-Under-Heywood
Revd J. Buddicombe	Rector, Smethcote
Revd J. Wakefield	Rector, Hughley
T.B. Proctor	Marsh Farm
J.T. Horton Esq.	Lilleshall Company

Provisional Committee

Ralph August Benson	Director - Wen. & Sev. Jn Rly
William Penny Brookes	Director - Wen. & Sev. Jn Rly
Robert Horton Esq.	Director - Wen. & Sev. Jn Rly
T.Campbell-Eyton Esq.	Director - Wellington & Sev. Jn Rly
Earl Shelbourne	Chairman - Great Western Railway
Engineer	John Fowler
Solicitor	George Potts (Broseley)
Bankers	Cooper & Purton (Broseley)
Shropshire Banking Co.	

The proposed extension railway to Craven Arms will commence at Much Wenlock station, and pass through Wenlock Edge between the Five Chimneys and Presthope into Ape Dale. Thence past Easthope, Longville, Rushbury, Eaton, and Wolverton to the Shrewsbury and Hereford Railway, at a point between the Marsh Farm and Fellhampton in the parish of Wistanstow, and thence to Craven Arms.

The proposed line to Coalbrookdale commences at or near the junction of the Wenlock & Severn Jn Railway with the Severn Valley Railway crossing the River Severn near the Meadow Turnpike Gate, directly to a station at Coalbrookdale, and from thence, under arrangements with the Great Western and Wellington & Sev. Jn Railway Companies will be extended to Lightmoor, there uniting with the lines of those Companies.

The importance of connecting the immense field of limestone around Much Wenlock with the iron manufacture of Coalbrookdale, Horsehay, Madeley, Dawley, Ketley and Staffordshire has long been felt. The agricultural district south of Much Wenlock will be brought into direct communication with the manufacturing districts. Manufacturing districts will have speedy communication with South Wales.

The extension to Coalbrookdale will greatly afford increased facilities to the Coalbrookdale traffic to Shrewsbury, Gloucester, and Bristol. The proposed stations at Presthope, Easthope, Longville and Rushbury can be readily approached through the opening in the ridge west of Corve Dale at Bourton, Brockton and Millichope.

It is desired that the Coalbrookdale extension shall be made as free as possible to all railway companies having an interest in the locality, who place themselves in a position to use it: and for this purpose it is intended to invite each such company to subscribe, and that the use of the line shall be granted to each subscribing company on reasonable terms.

Brassey and Field have consented to construct the line under similar arrangements to those which they are now completing the Much Wenlock & Sev. Jn Railway.

An agreement has been entered into with the Directors of the Much Wenlock Railway, by which all traffic conveyed over any part of the proposed new railways, and the Much Wenlock Railway shall be charged at an equal mileage rate.

The seal of the Wenlock Railway Company which used the 'Wen and the Lock' as its insignia.
GWR Museum Swindon

Appendix Four

Inspector's Report for the
Wenlock & Severn Junction Railway, 1861

Railway Department
Board of Trade
30th September, 1861

Sir,

I have the honour to report for the information of the Lords Committee of the Privy Council for Trade that in obedience to your minute of the 19th inst. I have inspected the Wenlock & Severn Junction Railway from its junction with the Severn Valley Railway to Much Wenlock . . . the line is single throughout with sidings at the junction at Buildwas and at Much Wenlock stations, . . . The land has been taken and enclosed for the doubling of the line at a future period.

At present the underbridges and one of the overbridges of which there are two are only constructed for a single line . . .

The line is one of steep gradients and sharp curves and will be required to be worked with great care, and very moderate speed . . . The engine turntable at Much Wenlock has not yet been completed, the station buildings for the temporary station at Much Wenlock are not yet ready . . . The distant signals at Much Wenlock, and the junction are not yet in working order, and indicators are required for the facing points . . . I have not received the undertaking as to the mode of working to be adopted. I have therefore to report that by reason of the incompleteness of the works the opening of the Wenlock & Severn Junction Railway for traffic would be attended with danger to the public using the same.

Signed,

W. Yolland

Colonel, Royal Engineers

The seal of the Wenlock & Severn Junction Railway again showing the 'Wen and the Lock' as its insignia.   *GWR Museum Swindon*

Appendix Five

Inspector's Reports for the Lightmoor Extension, 1864

Whitehall
10th September, 1864

Sir,

I have the honour to report for the information of the Lords Committee of the Privy Council for Trade . . . in compliance with your instructions combined in Minute of the 2nd inst. I have inspected the line from Buildwas and Coalbrookdale to Lightmoor the opening of which notice has been given by the Great Western Railway Company.

This is a double line 2¼ miles long extending from an incline with the Severn Valley Railway at Buildwas to the junction of the Wellington & Severn Junction Railway with the Shifnal branch of the Great Western Railway.

The steepest gradient which extends over the greater part of the line is 1 in 51, and the sharpest curves have a radius of 10 chains. This line should be worked by the telegraph which is not yet completed . . .

The permanent way is laid with double-headed rails, weighing 70lb. to the lineal yard and fished at the joints. The chairs are of cast-iron and weigh 22 1b. each. I should have preferred them to be much heavier, the sleepers are laid transversely 2 ft 9 in. apart and are stated to measure 10 in. x 4 in. The ballast is light and sandy, and should have better material mixed with it.

The works are of an important character comprising a bridge of 200 feet span over the River Severn, a brick viaduct containing 25 openings, and nine other bridges under and over the railway . . . I should have preferred to see the cross girders of the wrought iron bridges under the railway somewhat stronger. I propose to test these different works with rolling loads on my next visit.

A waiting shed and conveniences are required on the second platform at the Coalbrookdale station. A tree should be removed which now obstructs the distant signal from that station towards Buildwas, and a lodge and signals are required at a public bridle road level crossing [Chunes Crossing].

I have to report in my opinion that the opening of this line, would, by reason of the incompleteness of the works, be attended with danger to the public using it.

Signed

H.W. Tyler

Captain, Royal Engineers

* * * * * * * * *

Birmingham
30th September, 1864

Sir,

I have the honour to report for the information of the Lord's Committee of the Privy Council for Trade . . .

I have inspected the Coalbrookdale and Lightmoor section of the Great Western Railway, and the Wenlock Railway from Buildwas to Coalbrookdale.

I find that the bridge which has been constructed over the River Severn to be a satisfactory structure. It has a span of 200 feet, with cast-iron arched ribs resting on masonry abutments. It yielded a deflection of about $\frac{9}{16}$ of an inch under a load of 400 tons distributed over two lines of rails.

The Great Western Company are undecided at present as to whether they will retain Lightmoor as a passenger station. If so it should be improved and a second platform added. If not the present platform should be removed.

At Lightmoor Junction the stages* and locking apparatus have been completed . . . The points marked No. 2 should be made to interlock with the signal from Shifnal.

At the Buildwas Junction stage the crossover road No. 6 should be interlocked with the signals from Much Wenlock . . .

At the Wenlock platform box the points between the single and double line should be interlocked with the signal from Buildwas Junction box. Telegraph communication should be supplied between these two boxes.

Waiting sheds are still wanted at Coalbrookdale, and Buildwas . . .

A layer of cinders are required on the existing light ballast; speaking telegraph instruments are required at the telegraph stations; and continuous brakes for the passenger carriages.

I am obliged to report by reason of their incompleteness the works cannot be opened without danger to the public using them.

Signed

H.W. Tyler

Captain, Royal Engineers

---

* At the opening of the line at junction stations 'stages' were erected about six feet above the ground to which were affixed the signal and point levers.

Appendix Six

Inspector's Reports for the Wenlock Railway, 1867

Board of Trade
23rd September, 1867

Sir,

I have the honour to report for the information of the Lord's Committee of the Privy Council for Trade . . .

The new line commences at Much Wenlock and extends to Marsh Farm Junction where it joins the Shrewsbury and Hereford Railway. It is 13 miles 67 chains long and is single throughout with sidings. The overbridges and underbridges have been constructed for double line.

The permanent way consists of double-headed rails which weigh 71 lb. per linear yard and is laid in lengths of 24 feet. It is fished and fixed with wooden keys in cast-iron chairs that weigh 21 and 22lb. each. The chairs are spiked to sleepers laid transversely 3 feet apart . . .

The line is ballasted with gravel and broken stones. The greatest gradient is 1 in 45 and the sharpest curve is a 10 chains curve at the [Marsh Farm] junction.

Engine turntables are provided at Much Wenlock and Craven Arms.

The works consist of five masonry underbridges and five overbridges, that have stone abutments and cast-iron girders . . .

Two underbridges have wrought iron girders and eight have cast-iron girders carried on stone abutments. Five others have brick arches . . .

There is a tunnel 176 yards long west of Presthope station . . .

The sidings at all stations should be guarded by blind sidings where they fall towards the main line. Locked chock blocks should be provided in other cases.

The sidings leading to the goods yard at Much Wenlock should be controlled by a signal worked from the station platform in connection with the distant signals. A blind siding is required to be put in. The points of this siding should be locked with the siding signal . . .

The mineral sidings between Much Wenlock station and Buildwas Junction on the section which was opened some years since should be furnished with locked signals and catch points . . .

Rushbury station is on an incline of 1 in 100 this should be altered to 1 in 300. Also a second line of signals should be put in, and catch points placed below the station to catch any vehicle that may run away. A second platform will be required at this station, and at such others as are intended to be passing places . . .

The east mouth of the tunnel at Presthope should have a parapet wall across the front to prevent stones and rubbish falling on the line . . . The brick lining inside the tunnel should be extended to where the rock becomes firm and solid.

Lodges are required at both the public crossings . . . clocks are required at the stations.

The cast-iron chairs on this line are too light. One intermediate chair, and the chairs next to the rail joints should be removed and replaced with others weighing 20 to 30lb. each.

I submit that the Craven Arms extension of the Wenlock Railway cannot be opened for passenger traffic without danger to the public using the same, by reason of the incompleteness of the works.

Signed

F.W. Rich

Lt Colonel, Royal Engineers.

I have received no undertaking as to the proposed mode of working.

* * * * * * * *

Board of Trade
7th December, 1867

Sir,

I have the honour to report to the Lords Committee of the Privy Council for Trade . . .

I have inspected the Wenlock Railway

The works reported incomplete in my letter of the 12th ultimo have been done, except the lodges at the two public level crossings, which are now being roofed, and the signalman's box at Much Wenlock station . . .

I submit that the line may be opened for passenger traffic so soon as a satisfactory undertaking as to the proposed mode of working is received.

The company propose to work the line on the Train Staff system, staff stations being at each end of the railway.

Signed

F.W. Rich

Lt Colonel, Royal Engineers.

Appendix Seven

W.G. Norris' Report to the
Coalbrookdale Company's Directors, 1876

Sir,

The operations of last year have been attended with difficulty, and directly owing to the depression in the iron trade and decline in price. As far as practicable work was realised in some measure to meet the diminished demand, but orders were not sufficiently numerous to take off the product and a considerable increase of stocks has resulted.

The forge has not worked more than ¾ of its time, the decline in trade is also evident at the rolling mill, which has produced only 10,429 tons compared with 14,516 tons in the previous year.

Sales of bar iron have been 9,914 tons producing £94,890 as against 14,207 tons producing £147,575 in 1875.

The foundry has had a good supply of work, but owing to the decline in prices of coke and pig iron in other districts the price of general castings has fallen, and subjected us to increased competition. This has had an effect on the returns and net results, although the quantity of work has increased. Many matters which cause concern, shorter working hours, the employment of smiths, and need for keeping larger stocks of goods needing increased accommodation.

The lease from Mr Slaney of the mines in Dawley will require resolvement at the 25th March next. If Mr Slaney's resolve to purchase the unworked minerals is carried out, these will result in the discontinuance of colliery operations in the Dawley area, the stoppage of the furnaces at the Castle and restriction of the works at Horsehay.

W.G. Norris
Manager

William Gregory Norris, the Quaker Director of the Coalbrookdale Company and Chairman of the Wellington & Severn Junction Railway from 1886 to 1896. *Ironbridge Gorge Museum*

Locomotives Stationed at
Wellington and Wenlock at Various Dates

Year	No.	Type	Class	Built	Shed	W'drawn
1902	1530	0-6-0	'645'	Wolverhampton 1879	Wellington	12.1938
	1502	0-6-0	'645'	Wolverhampton 1878	Wenlock	7.1935
	1772	0-6-0	'655'	Wolverhampton 1892	Wellington	3.1929
	1803	0-6-0	'645'	Wolverhampton 1881	Wellington	12.1944
	2076	0-6-0	'2021'	Wolverhampton 1900	Wellington	12.1951
	1802	0-6-0	'645'	Wolverhampton 1881	Wenlock	10.1951
1905	1548	0-6-0	'645'	Wolverhampton 1880	Wellington	12.1937
	1559	0-6-0	'645'	Wolverhampton 1880	Wellington	8.1929
	2108	0-6-0	'2021'	Wolverhampton 1902	Wellington	12.1954
	1790	0-6-0	'655'	Wolverhampton 1894	Wenlock	6.1946
	1541	0-6-0	'645'	Wolverhampton 1880	Wenlock	12.1937
	1801	0-6-0	'645'	Wolverhampton 1881	Wenlock	9.1938
1907	521	0-4-2	'517'	Wolverhampton 1868	Wellington	4.1930
	1515	0-6-0	'645'	Wolverhampton 1878	Wellington	6.1929
	1541	0-6-0	'645'	Wolverhampton 1880	Wellington	12.1937
	1554	0-6-0	'645'	Wolverhampton 1880	Wellington	11.1944
	2108	0-6-0	'2021'	Wolverhampton 1902	Wellington	12.1954
1913	842	0-4-2	'517'	Wolverhampton 1874	Wellington	9.1930
	1478	0-4-2	'517'	Wolverhampton 1884	Wellington	5.1936
	1483	0-4-2	'517'	Wolverhampton 1885	Wellington	8.1932
	1535	0-6-0	'645'	Wolverhampton 1879	Wellington	8.1934
	1547	0-6-0	'645'	Wolverhampton 1880	Wellington	11.1934
	1750	0-6-0	'655'	Wolverhampton 1892	Wellington	6.1946
	1787	0-6-0	'655'	Wolverhampton 1893	Wellington	1.1947
	2005	0-6-0	'2021'	Wolverhampton 1892	Wellington	12.1944
	521	0-4-2	'517'	Wolverhampton 1868	Wenlock	4.1930
	1479	0-4-2	'517'	Wolverhampton 1884	Wenlock	4.1932
1921	759	0-6-0	'645'	Wolverhampton 1872	Wellington	9.1925
	842	0-4-2	'517'	Wolverhampton 1874	Wellington	9.1930
	1424	0-4-2	'517'	Wolverhampton 1877	Wellington	9.1933
	1485	0-4-2	'517'	Wolverhampton 1885	Wellington	12.1936
	1510	0-6-0	'645'	Wolverhampton 1878	Wellington	10.1938
	1554	0-6-0	'645'	Wolverhampton 1880	Wellington	8.1929
	1748	0-6-0	'655'	Wolverhampton 1892	Wellington	2.1946
	1778	0-6-0	'655'	Wolverhampton 1893	Wellington	10.1928
	1787	0-6-0	'655'	Wolverhampton 1893	Wellington	1.1947
	1914	0-6-0	'850'	Wolverhampton 1882	Wellington	6.1931
	2710	0-6-0	'655'	Wolverhampton 1896	Wellington	11.1945
	557	0-4-2	'517'	Wolverhampton 1896	Wenlock	5.1933
	1531	0-6-0	'645'	Wolverhampton 1879	Wenlock	12.1949
1934	768	0-6-0	'645'	Wolverhampton 1873	Wellington	9.1935
	1514	0-6-0	'645'	Wolverhampton 1878	Wellington	12.1934
	1524	0-6-0	'645'	Wolverhampton 1879	Wellington	5.1939
	1787	0-6-0	'655'	Wolverhampton 1893	Wellington	1.1947
	2706	0-6-0	'655'	Wolverhampton 1896	Wellington	10.1948
	2716	0-6-0	'655'	Wolverhampton 1896	Wellington	9.1950
	2717	0-6-0	'655'	Wolverhampton 1896	Wellington	10.1948
	2720	0-6-0	'655'	Wolverhampton 1897	Wellington	11.1950
	5810	0-4-2	'5800'	Swindon 1933	Wellington	1.1959
	1779	0-6-0	'655'	Wolverhampton 1893	Wenlock	1.1945
	5811	0-4-2	'5800'	Swindon 1933	Wenlock	5.1957

Signal Boxes

Wellington to Craven Arms

Signal Box	Opened	Closed	Type *	Frame No. of levers	Remarks
Wellington No. 1	1881	9.1967	LNW/GW2	22	
Wellington No. 2	1881	3.1953	LNW/GW2	?	
No. 2	3.1953		GW15	†71	Renamed Wellington 30.9.1973
Wellington No. 3	1881	9.1973	LNW/GW2	58	
Wellington No. 4	1881	9.1973	LNW/GW2	46	
Haybridge Sdgs	c. 1880	12.1932	?	?	Used as ground frame from 1924. Three lever ground frame at entrance to sidings in 1932.
Ketley Jn	c. 1875	9.1967	GW2	18	
Ketley	1893	7.1968	GW6	15	Not interlocked in 1881.
Lawley Bank	1893	?	?	6	Not interlocked in 1881. Ground frame by 1924.
Horsehay	1890	1893	?		Not interlocked in 1881.
	1893	7.1968	GW6	9	Not blocked until 1909.
Lightmoor Jn	1875	1951	McKenzie & Holland	25	26 levers by 1907.
	1951		GW15	†31	
Coalbrookdale	1890	1893	?	?	Not interlocked in 1881.
	1893	1958	GW5	15	
Buildwas Jn	c. 1888	11.1923	?	32	Interlocked by 1881.
Buildwas Stn	c. 1888	11.1923	?	49	Interlocked by 1881.
Buildwas	11.1923	3.1964	GW7D	113	In 1931 Box extended to provide for power station sidings.
Wenlock	1864	1893	Lane	?	One of the earliest locking frame boxes on the GW system. Designed by Michael Lane the GW chief engineer. Installed in 1864, the frame was covered in 1867.
	1893	12.1963	GW5	31	
Presthope	By 1886	1893	?	?	Interlocked by 1881.
	1893	10.1954	GW5	31	
Longville	7.1892	?	GW6	15	Interlocked by 1881.
Rushbury	7.1892	12.1951	GW6	15	Interlocked by 1881. Not blocked until 1907.
Harton Road	7.1892	?	GW6	?	Interlocked by 1881.
Marsh Farm Jn	?	9.1903	?	?	
	9.1903	5.1972	LNW4	36	
Wistanstow	By 1901	1933	?	10	This was an intermediate box. No sidings

Signal Box	Opened	Closed	Type *	Frame No. of levers	Remarks
Bishop's Castle Jn	1865	6.1901	Saxby & Farmer	15	
	6.1901	3.1937	LNW4	25	Renamed Stretford Bridge Jn.
Long Lane Crossing	By 1878	3.1931	?	21	
	3.1931		GW28B	†30	Craven Arms Crossing from 3.1936.
Craven Arms Sta.	By 1878	3.1956	LNW/GW1	33	
Central Wales Jn	c. 1872	12.1965	LNW/GW1	55	Craven Arms Jn. From 3.1936

Madeley Branch

Signal Box	Opened	Closed	Type *	Frame No. of levers	Remarks
Madeley Court	8.1892	1899	?	19	Frame to Dinas Isa signal box on the Penycraig to Toneyrefail branch
Madeley Jn	?	10.1969	McKenzie & Holland	34	Ex-Newport, Mon.
	10.1969		LMR 1943	†40	

Notes

*   Taken from the Signalling Record Society classification.
†   Frame still in use.

Details regarding the interlocking are taken from a letter from E.G. Saunders General Manager of the GWR to the Railway Department of the Board of Trade dated January 1881.

A Stephenson Locomotive Society excursion on 23rd April, 1955 coming off the Madeley branch at Madeley Junction headed by a 'Dean Goods'. The fields surrounding the line at this point are now covered by the buildings of the Stafford Park Industrial Estate of the new town of Telford.

Real Photographs

Early Signal Box Staff Appointments
on the Wenlock Branch

Name	Station	Date of Appt	Grade	Weekly Wage
Edward Ferrington	Ketley Jn	17.9.1873	Pointsman	22s.
Thomas Lewis	Ketley Jn	10.12.1881	Pointsman	22s.
John Vyse*	Ketley Jn	9.7.1895	Pointsman	20s.
Richard Jones	Ketley Jn	4.12.1896	Pointsman	22s.
Edward Diggory	Ketley Jn	16.1899	Signalman	22s.
John Delves	Ketley	2.1860	Policeman	15s.
Edward Hall	Ketley	18.12.1873	Policeman	16s.
George Shelton	Ketley	3.10.1879	Policeman	18s.
Herbert Davenport	Ketley	19.7.1892	Signalman	18s.
Charles Millington	Ketley	16.8.1893	Signalman	18s.
John Roberts	Ketley	23.5.1894	Signalman	20s.
Harry Morris	Ketley	10.11.1900	Signalman	18s.
Walter Truelove	Ketley	29.7.1901	Signalman	18s.
John Delves	Lightmoor Jn	1864	Pointsman	20s.
Charles Barlow	Madeley Jn	8.1858	Policeman	18s.

* On John Vyse's record there is a note to the effect that bonus was discontinued from 18th February, 1900 owing to the introduction of the through electric train staff. Pointsmen, later designated signalmen, up to the late 1890s had been paid a yearly bonus based on good conduct and the general efficiency in the working of their boxes.

The following shows the progression of William Garbet from porter to station master.

Date	Station	Grade	Weekly Wage
3.12.1877	Ketley	Porter	15s.
7.11.1878	Codsall	Pointsman	18s.
9.10.1880	Llangollen Road	Pointsman	18s.
1.5.1893	Plas Power	Station inspector	23s.
1.12.1898	Rednal	Station inspector	27s.
1.12.1899	Rednal	Station master	28s.

Appendix Eleven

Travelling Transformation:
By Motor Train from Wellington to Craven Arms

(Extract from the *Wellington Journal* 28th April, 1906)

People who live in very populous places are as familiar with rail-motor transit as their forefathers were with the old fashioned 'bus', but in those scattered villages where the inhabitants are comparatively few the former means of locomotion is almost entirely unknown. That is especially so in Shropshire and there are many places in the county where the introduction of such a system would be an inestimable boon. Happily the railway companies are beginning to recognise not only the public needs in the matter, but also the prospect of increased revenue from such provision for them. Among the first to benefit are those who live along the Great Western Railway from Wellington to Much Wenlock and Craven Arms, and others whose dwellings stand in close proximity to the branch line which leads from Shifnal to Madeley Court and Coalbrookdale. The company who control these routes have determined to inaugurate a rail-motor service which, so far as frequency and excellence are concerned, will be equal to any in the country, and that will commence on the 1st May. All the trains will call at existing intermediary stations and, if necessary, accommodation for booking or alighting will be made at newly erected platforms.

The greatest care has been taken to ensure the safety as well as the convenience of the project. The company's chief engineers and other trustworthy officials weeks ago thoroughly inspected the route, and yesterday morning a trial trip was made. The 'train' consisted of a motor-car and a trailer. The portions for the use of the passengers are built on the same principle as the ordinary Pullman cars, with corridors and separated seats running from end to end. The sides of the cars are filled in almost entirely with glass so that the outlook is greatly increased. They are luxuriously upholstered, and the sensation of travelling in them is extremely pleasant. The coaches used yesterday would seat about 150 people, but it is probable on most of the journeys the trailer would be detached, and only the single car would be brought into requisition. Steam for the engine is generated by coal, and the engine is compact and powerful.

A steam railmotor passing over the Coalbrookdale viaducts in May 1906. To the right is the Green Bank Farm, above the farm can be seen the Coalbrookdale Company's row of workers cottages with the unusual name of 'Tea Kettle Row', above the cottages can be seen the boundary wall of the Quaker burial ground. *Ironbridge Gorge Museum*

The journey was from Dunstall Park (Wolverhampton) to Shifnal, where the train was driven on to the branch line through Madeley Court to Coalbrookdale, whence it proceeded along the branch line to Craven Arms, calling at the intermediary stations. The return journey was straight from Craven Arms to Wellington, and the whole was completed in excellent time, considering the fact that stoppages were frequently made for further engineering inspection. The officials in attendance were: Mr Hitchcock (assistant superintendent for the Northern Division), Mr Robinson (locomotive superintendent), Mr Wood (divisional engineer), Messrs Snell, Noble and Eaton (locomotive department), chief inspector Thomas (Chester), inspectors Lockley (Wellington), Davies, Steene and Skinner. All of them discharged their individual duties with marked ability. A number of invited guests were present, and were apparently enraptured with the day's experiences.

This is a general outline of the more practical part of the scheme, but a 'trial trip' which proved to be of such a delightful nature deserves more than a passing reference to facilities for travelling, rapidity of transport, and commercial enterprise. Nobody could have been carried in yesterday's cars without being enchanted with the scenic splendour of the whole of the country through which the line has been laid. There was nothing to detract from an undisturbed contemplation of it. The train was running with the utmost smoothness - there was no jolting, nor jarring; and all that could be heard was the gentle throbbing of the engine's heart, and the rhythm of the revolving wheels. To those who had not been there before, Coalbrookdale first awakened admiration, and probably the place never looked more lovely than it did at that moment, despite those useful industries which do not contribute to the pictorial features of the locality.

The sun was effulgent during the whole of the day, and shed lustre on the bursting blossoms, and the verdant foliage which form the garment of the cliffs, while down below the Severn scintillated as it slowly flowed through the valley. The rest was one long panorama of unrivalled grandeur. Wenlock, with its ancient Abbey - 'majestic though in ruins' - elicited unbounded appreciation: but probably the consummation of ecstatic feeling found expression just after Presthope was passed. A narrow and unlighted tunnel momentarily caused an unpleasant effect, but every vestige of that died away as the train slowly moved along the activity on which the track has been built. There was then to be seen one vast and glorious expanse of undulating landscape. On the right the Wrekin could be plainly descried, and rising to the left were the summits of the Stretton Hills.. but in the more immediate distance rivulet and lake, green pastures and wooded eminences, constituted a scene whose charm could not be exaggerated in words.

WELLINGTON, MUCH WENLOCK AND CRAVEN ARMS. RAIL MOTOR CAR. ONE CLASS ONLY.																			Sun	
Wellingt'n	..	8 30	8 54	9 50	..	1029	1115	12 25	1 35	1	12 48	3 19	4 25	40	...	7	6	9 10	9 45	9 35
Ketley	..	8 35	N	9 55		N	1120	1227	1 40	N	2 53	N	4 35	6 45	...	7	10	9 15	9 50	9 40
Lawley B'k	..	8 40	..	10 0		..	1125	1231	1 45		2 58		4 35	5 60	...	7	15	9 20	9 55	9 44
Horsehay	..	8 43	..	10 3		..	1128	1254	1 48		3 1		4 3	5 53	W	7	18	9 23	9 58	9 49
Shifnal	..	..	9 25	..	11 0	..		..	..	2 10	...	4 10	...	...	5 47	..	..	..	..	..
Madeley	..	..	9 36	..	1112	..		..	..	2 22	...	4 22	...	...	6 0	..	..	..	..	..
C'brok D'l	..	8 51	9 41	1011		1118	1135	1242	1 56	2 26	9 4	28	4 46	16	1	7	26	9 31	10 8	10 0
Buildwasa	..	8 54	9 44	1015		1122	1138	12 5	2 0	2 31	13	4 31	4 50	6	6	18	30	9 35	1011	10 5
Buildwasd	..	9 16	9 47	..	1055	..	12 3	1248	..	2 19	3 16	4 35	4 53		6	22	7	50	9 37	1012	10 7
Wenlook	6 45	9 23	9 57	..	11 6	..	1211	1257	..	2 47	3 47	4 48	5 4	...	6	30	7	58	9 45	1020	1017
Presthope	6 53	..	10 5	..	1113	..	..	1 5	..	...	3 35	4 52	5 12	...	...	..	..			a.m
Longville	7 2	..	1013	..	...	..	..	1 13	..	...	...	...	5 21	...	...	..	..			W
Rushbury	7 8	..	1019	..	...	..	..	1 19	..	...	...	...	5 27	...	...	..	..			
Harton	7 15	..	1026	..	...	..	..	1 26	..	...	...	...	5 34	...	...	..	..			
Crvn Arms	7 28	..	1039	...	...	..	..	1 38	..	...	...	...	5 47	...	...					
Crvn Arms	a.m	..	8 5	..	..	..	1135	..	...	1 55	...	..	..	...	...	6 35	...			Sun
Harton	..	...	8 19	..	..	..	1149	..	...	2 9	...	..	..	...	...	6 49	...			p.m
Rushbury	..	...	8 26	..	..	..	1156	...	...	2 16	...	..	..	...	...	6 56	...			
Longville..	..	...	8 32	..	..	..	12 2	..	...	2 22	...	..	..	...	...	7 2	...			W
Presthope	..	...	8 41	..	..	1120	1212	..	...	2 31	...	3 35	..	...	...	7 11	...			
Wenlook	7 35	8 20	8 51	1010	..	1127	122	1233	..	2 50	3 32	4 5	..	...	5 38	7 21	8 30			6 35
Buildwasa	7 42	8 27	8 58	1 17	..	1136	..	1227	1245	..	2 57	3 39	4 12	...	5 46	7 28	8 37			6 43
C'brok D'l	7 47	8 34	9 17	1023	1032	..	1149	1234	1255	2	9 3	14	3 46	...	4 40	6	47	7 49	8 53	6 47
Madeley	..	8 41	..	1030	..	..	..	1 6	..	3 21	...	...	...	6 11	..	...	..			6 52
Shifnal	..	8 52	..	1042	..	..	..	1 18	..	3 32	...	...	...	6 22	..	...	..			
Horsehay	7 56	..	9 26	..	1041	...	1158	1245	..	2 18	...	3 55	..	4 53	...	8 0	9			7
Lawly B'k	7 59	..	9 29	..	10 4	...	12 1	1249	..	2 21	...	3	..	4 56	...	8 4	9			7
Ketley	..	8 1	N	9 34	N	1049	...	12 6	1254	..	2 26	N	4 3	...	5 1	N	8 9	9 10		7 1
Wellingt'n	8 10	9 42	9 40	1110	1054	..	1211	1 0	..	2 31	4 234	8	..	6 6	45	8 14	9 15			7 1

Timetable of 1906. Note that the railmotors offered third class accommodation only.

Appendix Twelve

Request for a Station at Lightmoor

(Extract from the Madeley District Committee Minutes of 12th February, 1907.)

The Chairman stated that it was the desire of the householders near Lightmoor to have a railway station placed there, and it was resolved that the Town Clerk be instructed to write to the railway company suggesting the erection of a station at Lightmoor.

(An extract from the *Wellington Journal* of 13th July, 1907.)

Lightmoor New Railway Halt

Efforts have been made by the people in the vicinity of Lightmoor Jn to induce the GWR to re-open a station here. Such a boon will be appreciated by residents of the district who at present are somewhat isolated in the matter of railway facilities. Some of the older residents remember the former station which did good business in its day. From May 1859 it was the terminus of the line from Wellington in the direction of Much Wenlock, being abandoned in November 1864 after the railway had been completed from Lightmoor to Coalbrookdale and Buildwas. The first station master was the late Mr Henry Darral of Dawley, and the last to occupy the post was the late Inspector Sankey of Chester. Mr A.E. Evans manager of the Coalbrookdale Company's Brick and Tile works and a member of Dawley U.D.C. has been mainly instrumental in getting the railway company to accede to the request for a new station or halt. Mr Evans started a petition which was largely signed and presented.

The corrugated booking office and waiting room at Lightmoor Platform which was built in 1908. Note the bracket for the tilley lamp. Neither gas nor electric lighting was provided at Lightmoor.

Author's Collection

Appendix Thirteen

The Last Passenger Train
From Craven Arms to Wenlock

(A report from the *Newport & Market Drayton Advertiser* of 4th January, 1952)

The 5 O'Clock Makes Its Last Trip

Fireman Tony Faulkner, silhouetted against the glow of the boiler fire in the semi-darkness, leaned out from the cab of 4406 to catch the guard's signal. A nod to engine driver Joe Watkins sent steam hissing from the valves.

It was a somewhat sentimental journey last Saturday for the 5 o'clock from Craven Arms to Much Wenlock was beginning its last trip, and from then this stretch of line, which runs through some of the prettiest countryside in Shropshire, would be in limbo reserved for the branch railways which do not pay their way.

I was one of the handful of passengers on the train last Saturday, and it seemed a far cry from the 6th December, 1864, when a train service from Much Wenlock to Presthope was started. A few years later on the 16th December, 1867 the service operated from Presthope to Marsh Farm Junction and was known as the Wenlock Railway. In 1896 it was absorbed into the Great Western Railway.

A steady decline in use over the years with the subsequent loss in revenue has brought about the closure of the line, but its absence will hardly be felt. When the idea was first mooted, complaints from those concerned were negligible.

There was very little ceremony on what was to some a sad occasion and in fact, amounted to nothing but a handshake from Mr J.F. Anstey, the district Commercial Superintendent at Shrewsbury, to each station's chief officer. At Harton Road, the first stop, a woman and two children came aboard, and it was never more than this number which left or got on at Rushbury, Longville, Easthope Halt, Presthope, Westwood Halt - the stations in between.

Working on the Craven Arms-Much Wenlock line were three drivers, three firemen and two guards; for this last journey the guard was Mr R. (Dick) Davies, while for Joe Watkins, the driver, the green fields now sodden by rain and snow and the snow covered hills on either side of the track - as they were that day - will hold memories of his twenty years on the route. Of the drivers, however, Mr Jack Faulkner, father of engine 4406's fireman Tony, holds the record for the longest turn on that particular track. He completed his last run earlier that day.

For five Birmingham youths - all members of the Stephenson Locomotive Society - the event was of sufficient importance if not to local residents. Four of them completed the last return journey while the fifth, who had hoped to join the train at Wenlock for the last stage came by motor cycle from Hagley, but because of floods, he missed the train and had to be content to see it pass for the last time through Wenlock.

Tailpiece

One of the few people who will miss the service is Mrs Childs, of Presthope - not that she is a 'regular' passenger. In future she will have to keep a careful eye on the clock because with no 11.40 am passing through Presthope station she will have nothing to tell her it's time to begin peeling the potatoes.

Significant Dates Relating to
the Wenlock Branch

20th August, 1853	Royal Assent given to the Wgton&SJR Bill.
5th September, 1854	First meeting of the Directors of the Wgton&SJR.
November 1854	S&B branch opened from Madeley Jn to Lightmoor.
21st August, 1855	First sod cut of the Wgton&SJR.
18th February, 1857	Trial run of first train between Ketley and Horsehay.
May 1857	Line between Ketley and Horsehay opened for freight.
March 1858	Line between Horsehay and Lightmoor nearing completion.
1st January, 1859	Meeting held at the Corn Exchange, Much Wenlock to discuss proposed line between Much Wenlock and Buildwas.
2nd May, 1859	Wgton&SJR line opened for passenger traffic between Ketley Jn and Lightmoor and on to Shifnal via the Madeley branch.
21st July, 1859	Royal Assent given to the Wen&SJR Bill for a line between Much Wenlock and Buildwas.
26th March, 1860	First sod of the Wen&SJR cut.
22nd July, 1861	Wenlock to Craven Arms & Coalbrookdale Extension Bill given Royal Assent.
1st August, 1861	GWR Lightmoor & Coalbrookdale Extension Bill given Royal Assent.
23rd October, 1861	First sod cut of the Wenlock to Craven Arms line.
1st February, 1862	Wen&SJR line opened between Much Wenlock and Buildwas.
20th August, 1862	Agreement reached between the Wen&SJR, the WMR and the GWR for working the line.
1st August, 1863	WMR amalgamted with the GWR.
8th January, 1864	Fire destroyed the newly-built goods shed and offices at Much Wenlock.
24th March, 1864	Formal agreements with the GWR for the working and maintenance of the Wenlock Railway by GWR; also for construction of the Coalbrookdale extn, and its working by the GWR.
1st November, 1864	WenRC No. 1 Extension opened between Buildwas and Coalbrookdale.
1st November, 1864	GWR Lightmoor Extension opened between Lightmoor and Coalbrookdale.
5th December, 1864	Line opened between Much Wenlock and Presthope for freight traffic only (to passengers 16th December, 1867).
September 1867	Joint goods shed at Wellington purchased by the GWR for use as an engine shed.
16th December, 1867	Line opened between Presthope and Marsh Farm Jn.
21st July, 1873	Royal Assent given to Wen&SJR (Lightmoor Extensions) Bill.
July 1892	Wgton &SJR absorbed into the GWR.
October 1896	Wenlock Railways absorbed into the GWR.
1st May, 1906	Introduction of railmotors between Wellington, Craven Arms and Shifnal.
12th August, 1907	Lightmoor Platform opened.
22nd March, 1915	Madeley branch - passenger services withdrawn.
13th July, 1925	Madeley branch - passenger services restored.
21st September, 1925	Madeley branch - passenger services finally withdrawn.
13th October, 1932	Ironbridge 'A' Power Station opened.
March 1936	AEC diesel railcar introduced for an experimental period.
31st December, 1951	Line between Much Wenlock and Craven Arms closed to passenger traffic.
21st July, 1962	Line between Much Wenlock and Wellington closed to passenger traffic.
December 1963	Line between Much Wenlock and Longville closed completely.
6th July, 1964	Freight working between Ketley and Lightmoor ceased.
27th February, 1970	Ironbridge 'B' Power Station fully operational.
24th October, 1973	Telford Development Corporation purchased locomotive No. 5619.
1st March, 1976	Telford Horsehay Steam Trust formed.
May 1979	Line between Horsehay and Lightmoor closed completely.

Acknowledgements

I am most grateful for the help I have received from Dr Paul Collins of the Ironbridge Institute, and John Powell, Librarian of the Ironbridge Gorge Museum for reading and checking the manuscript, and for the courteous way in which they have dealt with many questions relating to railway matters that I have posed to them over a considerable period of time. My thanks are also due to Michael Hale for his constructive help. Also to Shelley White for producing the maps and plans, and to Tony Carr of the Shropshire Records and Research Centre and the honorary archivists of Wenlock Town Council Records. I am also grateful to Lord Forester for allowing me access to the Forester papers. The detailed information from the Signalling Record Society is also appreciated.

My thanks are also due to the following for providing me with information and material relating to the Wenlock branch: Jack Beard, Keith Beddoes, Fred Bishop, Landy Edwards, Ken and Margaret Fowler, Donald Houlston, Glynn McDonald, Reg Stanley, John Smout, Mary Tarver, Michael Vanns, Glynn Williams and Bryan Wilson.

Also to the staffs of the following:

Birmingham City Reference Library
Chester Record Office
House of Lords Record Office
Ironbridge Gorge Museum Library
Newspaper Library, Colindale
Public Record Office
Shropshire Records & Research Centre

Finally many thank to my wife Dorinda for her help and forbearance over a long period of time when it would appear that my only topic of conversation has been railways and the Wenlock branch.

Bibliography

Encyclopaedia of the Great Western Railway, Ed. William Adams, PSL, 1993.
History of the Great Western Railway, MacDermot & Nock, Ian Allan, 1989.
GWR and the General Strike, C.R. Potts, Oakwood Press, 1996.
Track Layout Diagrams of the GWR and BR Western Region, Section 32 East Shropshire, R.A. Cooke, 1994.
Locomotives of the GWR, RCTS, 1951-1993.
Railway Ancestors, David Hawkins, Allan Sutton, 1995.
The Railway Workers 1840-1970, Frank McKenna, Faber, 1980.
The Industrial Revolution in Shropshire, Dr Barrie Trinder, Phillimore, 1981.
Victoria County History of Shropshire Vol. XI Telford, Oxford University Press, 1985.
The Canals of the West Midlands, Charles Hadfield, David & Charles, 1969.
Eddoes Journal
Shrewsbury Chronicle
Wellington Journal & Shrewsbury News
GWR Magazine

Index

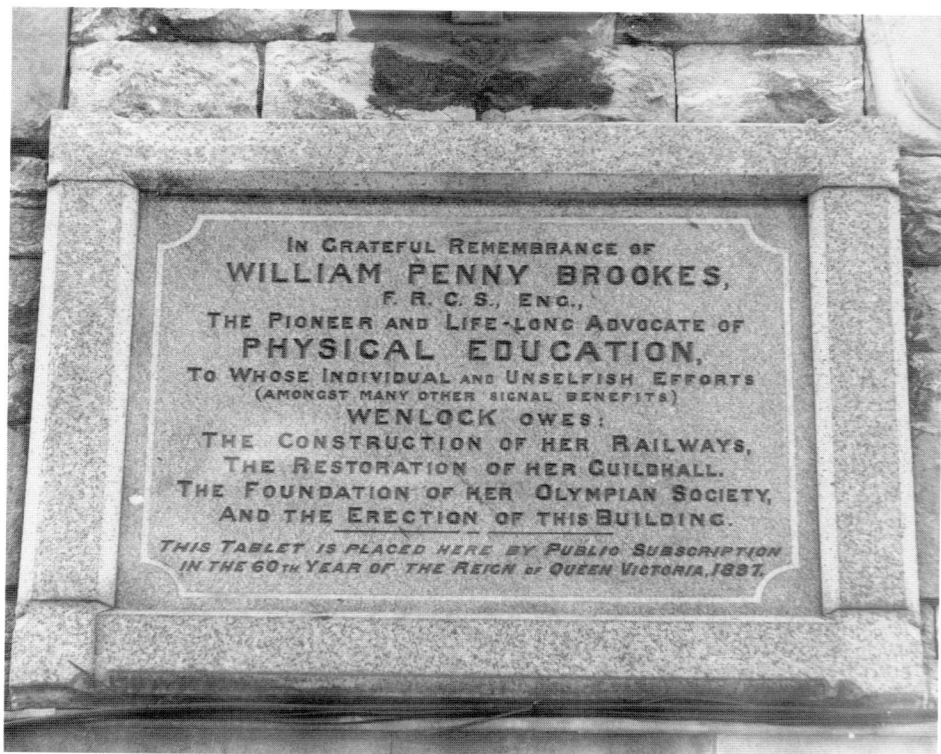

The tablet placed in the wall of the Corn Exchange, Much Wenlock in 1897 by public subscription in the 60th year of the reign of Queen Victoria, to commemorate the work of Dr William Penny Brookes for the town.

Author's Collection